Now You See It, Now You Doughnut

The True, Fictional Biography
of a Larger Than Life Superhero

by Dennis Budka

Illustrated by the Author

DORRANCE PUBLISHING CO., INC.
PITTSBURGH, PENNSYLVANIA 15222

The contents of this work including, but not limited to, the accuracy of events, people, and places depicted; opinions expressed; permission to use previously published materials included; and any advice given or actions advocated are solely the responsibility of the author, who assumes all liability for said work and indemnifies the publisher against any claims stemming from publication of the work.

ISBN-10: 0-8059-7240-4
ISBN-13: 978-0-8059-7240-5
Printed in the United States of America

First Printing

For additional information or to order additional books,
please write:
Dorrance Publishing Co., Inc.
701 Smithfield Street
Third Floor
Pittsburgh, Pennsylvania 15222
U.S.A.
1-800-788-7654
Or visit our website and online catalogue at www.dorrancebookstore.com

To Charlie and Lori Bootz, best friends
To Heidi, Jim, Spencer, Johnny and Max Lindhorst, first readers
And in thanksgiving to Mom and to God
All my love.

Contents

Chapter I

Hard to Swallow

How dark was the night!

Of course it was dark! Nights are expected to be, and almost universally were, dark in these latitudes since the days of Joshua. However, it is important to understand from the beginning just how dark this particular night appeared to be in the eyes of Mister Blob.

Robert Rotundus Maximillion Blob was born fat. One could say that Bob was fat in the same way one could say of the *Mona Lisa*, "that's a nice painting". His obesity seemed vast as the Grand Canyon. No ordinary comparisons need apply. In vistas unplumbed and unimagined he invited second and third looks of awe and disbelief. Tourists could have lined up to take pictures.

For most of his life Bob stood five and a half feet tall. He also happened to stand five feet and six inches wide. You could, I suppose, say that he was classically proportioned.

In short Mr. Blob was a masterpiece of marbleized mass. As he grew, Bob tried to come to an appreciation of his own unique, personal magnificence.

After that he could convince the world.

It was some years prior to the major events of this story, that baby Bob was born to Julio and Tiffany Blob. You may assume that "Blob" was not their real name if Dickens is not your favorite author or you are otherwise numbered among the coincidenciophobic (did I make that word up just now? I certainly hope so!)

At any rate, I will spare you the bouncing baby references. All that comes later. You see Bobby was a most unusual child. It is true that he kept his small family in poverty for years - all unknowing of course. It wasn't his fault that the genetic and evolutionary factors in his makeup happened to go "sprung!" with all the alacrity of a crushed bathroom scale.

Baby Bob was cheerful, intelligent and active. He was also large, a bit weird and always hungry. He would gnaw on things. Things like furniture;

1

plaster, dirt and the occasional chips of reinforced concrete that he worked loose from the foundation of their modest home. That home, by the way, was to become a symbol for the Blobs. The loss of it was to drive a deep wedge between Bob and his parents.

Baby Bob grew up fast. He was getting pretty big for a toddler. The very kindest of visitors, relatives and sitters found it hard not to make unflattering comparisons with the child to medicine balls, the planet Saturn, that sort of thing.

It happened one day that Tiffany was going off to work and was distracted just enough for tragedy to get its big foot in the door. In a moment of unthinking inappropriateness, she had repeated to Bob a phrase she had learned from her mother. She said, "You must not leave the table until you eat everything. I'm going out now and when I get back I want to see everything gone." How could she have foreseen the consequences?

When she returned hours later, there was a smoking crater where the Blob house used to stand. A few pieces of plumbing poked up through the rubble and in the epicenter of that wreck sat a beaming baby boy. It looked as if he had mysteriously expanded and grown in that short a time by at least a factor of two.

Realization of what had happened did not immediately occur for the mother until she heard her son pronounce those awful words that would haunt her nightmares for the rest of her life.

"See, Mama? All gone!"

In his childish innocence, Bob Blob was actually proud that he had literally eaten them out of house and home.

The realization came slowly that Bob was a one-in-a-quadrillion accident; a bit of genetic serendipity had gifted him with super-powers. For sure, this doesn't generally happen to anyone we know personally. That's what makes it so darn unusual.

It seems that since birth, the body of Mr. Blob was only concerned with one thing: getting energy to manufacture more and more of Mr. Blob. This energy came in the form of food. But it was put to use making fat; and the fat had very strange properties. It could jiggle like jelly one moment and grow diamond hard the next. It could expand and contract; squash and stretch; and it could bounce like a Volkswagen in a vacuum on a variegated viaduct.

Now Bob was not made out of dwarf-star material. He couldn't have been. It's unscientific to even think that way. You can ask Stephen Hawking. But Bob did become compact with years of fat under pressure.

This cell compaction even extended to his teeth and brains. Given time Bob could chew through practically anything. Every bit of material Bob ingested was used to build his body and his brain into the densest and most flexible matter possible.

It followed that Bob became a child genius who also ate up every book he could get his hands on (take that either way). At the age of nine he was sent away to super-hero school. They didn't call it that of course. This was the fifties and super-heroes were out of fashion just then. They sent him to Professor Wic's School for Gifted Children (formally known as the Friendly Regimen Extra Ability Kids School).

Wilbur Wie worked as a talent scout for a major motion picture studio that specialized in kiddy movies and animation. After he retired there was finally time enough for him to realize his dream. Wilbur would gather together talented children from every walk of life to form a university and training camp all rolled into one. These few kids would one day save the world, it was hoped. You could say that Bob Blob was his biggest find.

At first the idea was to form a single team out of the twenty-one kids who attended; but everyone knows that twenty one is much too big for a super-hero team. Still, the concept refused to totally die. Even though the official, secret focus of the school was to turn out individual, generic super-heroes, occasionally Professor Wic would try different versions of the team approach.

It was a four-year school and Bob found that he was expected to graduate as a "crime fighter" in the first year. The next two would be spent achieving the status of "side-kick", while an additional year would bring the coveted title of "super-hero". Only the best of the best could possibly hope to scale those heights. Bob hoped to be included in that super-hero graduating class by the time he reached the advanced age of thirteen years old.

The first day of school was a blur to Bob. There were so many new books to get, questions to ask and answer, and people to get to know. The first thing Bob had to do was meet the guidance counselor, Mrs. White.

Mrs. White lived up to her name. She was dressed all in spotless white set off by her knee length cape; pasty looking jump suit; spotless long gloves and a cute little domino mask. Her snow-white hair sat atop her pale complexioned, chiseled features. She had a glance that could frost the insides of an oven roasting chili peppers.

"Mr. Blob, I am sure I want to extend the welcome that Professor Wie offered earlier this morning in the auditorium. We're here to get you straightened out with your name, costume, course assignments and so on."

"But I already have a name." said our Mr. Blob.

"Yes, yes...but what are you going to call yourself professionally?" said Mrs. White.

"I just thought that when people needed my help they could just call for 'Bob'", said Bob.

"Get real, kid!" said Mrs. White, "Who's going to want help from a guy named Bob? You're a super-hero, not a plumber! People don't want 'Bob' to solve the murder, fight the villain or recover the stolen money. They want the Great Bob-O! The magnificent Captain Bob or the mysterious Dr. Bob, that's who they want!"

Bob was impressed with this new idea. "Gee..."

"What'll it be? Doctor, Captain? Is there to be an article before your name? How about a Hyphen? Are you the amazing, great, astounding, or incredible? Will your name end in an 'O'?"

"Now maybe if we start with your powers." she said. "What's your super-power- your gimmick, you know: let me hear your shtick."

A few heartbeats of uncomfortable silence strutted about the room.

"You don't even know what I'm asking you for, do you kiddo?"

Mrs. White sternly suppressed a smile as she tried to put this shy youngster at ease (yet, she couldn't bring herself to think of Bob as a "little kid". Her mind, along with Bob's sagging chair, protested at that idea).

"Okay Bob," she said, "we'll come up with a working concept together. Now let's see. Are you strong?"

"Oh yes," said Bob, "I could easily bash a path through these walls to the outside of the school!" but he swiftly added as he saw White's unmistakable look of reproach and warning, "not that I ever would do that, of course!"

"Um hum," she said darkly and doubtfully, "super-strength to start with. What else you got?"

"Well, let's see now, strength; limited elasticity; I'm pretty good at puzzles and figuring out mysteries."

"Being good at deductions and 'who-done-its' isn't a super-power," she said, "It's a pre-requisite! You'll find you can do away with just about any of the trappings, even a uniform. But from Batman to Tarzan super-heroes are expected to solve the case and make smart choices. More so than ordinary people. This is true even if they can't otherwise communicate very well and lack the social polish our school will provide.

"I'll give you an example." She struck a theatrical pose and said, "Me, Tarzan, catch bad ivory hunters. Footprints go in stream. No come out. Hidden cave behind waterfall lead to lost valley. Tarzan catch."

"There you have it: a solution elegant and simple enough to respect, while still retaining the feeling that the admiring fan is superior to this clod. No," she continued, "we must look further than your powers of deduction."

"I can eat through just about anything..." said Bob.

"Superior appetite and super eating power, eh? That's a new one, anyway!" she said.

"Yeah!" said Bob, "and I bounce."

"You bounce?" her head snapped up, "How high?"

"Oh, ten feet or so. I hope to get into training and better that.

"I think we can help you there Mr. Blob", she said. "Okay, bouncing seems to be your greatest power. Now, you can't be just 'Bob'. It has no showmanship and is impractical in ways you can hardly imagine at this time (remind me to tell you the story of Miss Page Turner sometime). There's a reason for the rules, you know. So until further notice I have designated for your use a professional identity. You will be called the Beneficent Bounce-O! ...with a hyphen, naturally."

"You will have to start work on your costume design. Some good ideas can be found in *Introduction to Graphics*. That's the salmon-pink and lime-green book." She indicated a large book from Bob's stack, which he had placed on the floor.

"And," she said, "You will need to be assigned to one of four teams. There's Red, Green, Blue and Amber. I think we'll put you in the Blue Team to start with."

"Remember," said Mrs. White, "the Golden Age is ended. Soon will come the Silver Age. It will be a new day for the super-hero. In ten years this place will be crawling with would-be heroes of every description. We intend to be ready. The world will have need of us more than ever."

"Yes, but," said Bob, "the world doesn't even know we exist, does it?"

"It is true at the present time that our school's existence is known only to a very few." said she.

"So who does know that we exist?"

"She ticked them off on her fingers. "Ike; J. Edgar; John Wayne; Rockefeller; Jack Kirby (the great comic book artist)...couple others maybe. Only those who need to know."

The education of Bob Blob had formally begun.

That evening, after unpacking, Bob made his way from the dormitory to the building that housed the kitchen. He couldn't wait to get to know the kids, and maybe make some friends. So when he got in line, it was really unfortunate that the very first person he met was destined to become a thorn in his side for a significant portion of his stay at the school.

"Hey, big bottom," several kids in line sniggered. Bob looked up to see who was insulting him.

What he saw was a boy who was maybe ten years old, dressed in a very imposing costume of deep orange, red and black. The design appeared to be based on a triangle motif. Pointy black boots and gloves seemed to draw the eye to the large letters "MB" embroidered on his chest. A large, full-lipped mouth (sneering at the moment) peeped out from a cowl or helmet that shone like burnished, orange chrome. There was a kind of pointy black mask with amber goggles through which intense staring eyes could be glimpsed.

Bob thought that he had never seen anything more impressive than this kid. He felt very self-conscious about the rather plain looking street clothes he was wearing.

"Who me?" said Bob.

"No, Bozo the clown!" There was more laughter. "You're supposed to pick up a tray and keep the line moving. Although I sure hope there's some food left after you get done!"

Oh, this guy had them rolling in the aisles. He was enjoying every joke at Bob's expense.

"What's your name, anyway?" asked the boy.

"When I fail to answer to 'Bozo', most people just call me Bob. Bob Blob, at your service."

"Yeah, and what's your designated pro-name?"

"I'm the Beneficent Bounce-O," said Bob in a voice that trailed off in embarrassment. Coincidentally, it sounded a bit too much like 'Beneficent Bozo' even to Bob's ears.

Several geologic eons passed, it seemed, before the laughter washed over Bob's red, glowing ears.

"Bob Blob is a stupid name!" said the boy with unshakable certainty. "Suppose I call you Blubber-Boy," he said, "then you can answer to 'B.B.' three different ways."

"If my name is so stupid," said Bob, "what's your name?"

"You don't get to know my secret identity, so don't even ask!" said the boy. "Everyone calls me The Mean Blaster."

That explained the 'MB' on his chest. At that point Bob couldn't help reflecting that MB got the best of that round. He even had a cooler name!

Bob learned a lot that evening about his classmates just by keeping his ears open.

The next day was Saturday when most of the students were off campus. Later on in his room, Bob read the class lists. He found a pamphlet with color photos (they spent some money there!) and a description of every student, including himself.

It turned out that MB was on Blue team. It seemed that The Mean Blaster was able to generate "a natural yellow force beam" from his hands and feet. This took great effort and the wider the beam, the more diffuse it became. He had the power of limited flight, too. After groaning about that for a bit, Bob looked at the other members of his team.

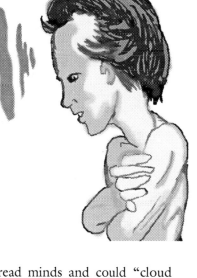

There was The Inexplicable Kid Psyche. The photograph showed a short, skinny kid dressed only in bright green swimming trunks with a wide yellow belt and boots. The boy had a high forehead and no eyebrows!

His powers included something called "telekinetic movement of objects at a distance through mental power alone". Bob grabbed his desk dictionary and looked up the strange new word. It said that "telekinetic" was a term that meant "movement of objects at a distance through mental power alone."

"Oh." said Bob, forgetting himself and saying it aloud for no one to hear.

Kid Psyche could also read minds and could "cloud men's minds", whatever that meant.

Then there was Willow-wand. A weird looking little girl seemed to be looking back at him from the pamphlet. She was even skinnier than that Psyche Kid!

Her costume was tan and forest green with a bizarre mask that wrapped around her head and made her resemble some kind of vegetable stalk. Her powers consisted of bursts of super-speed and strength combined with Olympic style tumbling. Bob hoped she wouldn't be on his team if they were going ever going to play football.

Last on his team (except for Bob himself) was listed The Mighty Vortex Boy. He was a stocky, muscular, older kid with a red and blue colored costume that hurt the eyes to look at. His mask covered his whole head above a v-neck shirt. Two black eye sockets were set above a wide orifice shaped like a big, frozen "O". He had a cape that hung half way down his back and the biggest boots and belt Bob had seen yet. Dazzling silver armbands and leggings completed the outfit.

This kid had lots of gadgets to anchor him when he used his power. From his mouth could issue a vacuum clocked at 800 miles per hour.

And then Bob read what the pamphlet said about him. "Bob Blob, our newest student, is five years old and has the power of mega mastication." (Yes, his dictionary was certainly getting a workout that weekend). "He can bounce more than two meters high and has super-strength." Then there was a little box with the words, "Costume and photograph have not been provided as of publication."

Bob tried and tried but he couldn't escape the horrible suspicion that kept echoing in his brain. "You aren't good enough. You'll never measure up. You are the weakest kid on the team, no! ...in the whole school!"

What Bob never even suspected was that he had just completed two of many happy days to come. Was it possible for him to prosper in this new life? The next four years would tell the tale.

Chapter II

Plumb Fed Up

It was morning and Monday and the first day of classes. Before breakfast Bob was ordered to report to the physician's office for his physical. Doctor Martini was a friendly, old-fashioned kind of doctor complete with suspenders and little black bag. He had been hired especially to do the physicals for all the students before the semester began and Bob found that he was playing catch up in this department also.

After enduring a certain amount of poking about, and the traditional cold stethoscope, Bob was told to get into his new uniform. It was true that someone had based its design on his own notes but he didn't recognize any of it.

The costume consisted of an over-all jumpsuit that emphasized his roundness. There was a simple mask of blue. A wide, indigo collar and belt (with a large silver buckle) circumnavigated an expanse of powder blue; set off with boots and sleeves of deep, dark purple. It looked almost as impressive as Blaster's outfit!

The material from which it was woven felt like nothing Bob had ever encountered before. He found out later that this was a silica-rubber compound in a molecular matrix of steel. It would wear practically forever. At the same time it was both tough as a battleship and flexible as *pasta al dente*. Bob only had time to try out a few bounces before the doctor returned.

"Splendid," he said, "you look -I believe the word is- spiffy! Now we need to talk about your diet." At the sound of that word the color drained out of Bob's face and he began to shake.

Looking alarmed the doctor said, "Sit down my boy! What ever is the matter?"

Bob's head was down and he couldn't look to see the doctor's kindly and concerned expression. Bob mumbled very quietly, "Don't like diets."

"Well", said Martini slowly, "I can understand how you feel."

In his secret heart Bob very much doubted that. He did sense that the physician was only trying to help in what he supposed was a fatherly way.

"Why don't you tell me what it is you are afraid of, son?"

A quick, burning glanced transfixed the doctor as Bob looked up.

"I am not afraid!" It was a low intensity shout. "My weight is something that happened to me," Bob grated, "I didn't ask to be this way!" His teeth and every single part of him were clenched. "I didn't get this way 'cause I wanted it or 'cause I'm lazy or gluttonous or because I didn't listen to the contradictory advice of too many doctors!"

Bob shut up abruptly when he realized that he really was shouting now. He couldn't express all that he was feeling as the smoldering fire in his eyes began to succumb to quenching tears.

"Well, Robert," the doctor cleared his throat, "I'm going to prescribe for you an entire pizza-pie to be eaten every day." Bob shook his head. His ears couldn't be working right, he thought. Why doesn't he check my ears?

"Yes," the doctor went on, "and steak and candy and ice cream too. Every day you will consume about (let me see, an average man of your height requires 2000 calories a day) yes, I think 20,000 a day ought to fit the bill."

"You're serious." It was a prayer instead of a question.

"I'm writing out the prescription now. And if anyone has any questions you can refer them to me," he ended grimly.

"I don't know what to say," Bob none the less managed to say. "How can I ever thank you?"

"Oh, there's a bill to pay, young man," came the surprising answer. "You'll pay through the nose- as I believe the expression goes. I want you to thank me every day of your life by using the gifts your Maker gave you. We don't know the how or why of your physical condition. But we both know that you can choose to use it for doing good things. I believe that's what this school is for, isn't it? I'll be around to monitor your growth next year or sooner if you need me."

"And I will thank you, Doctor Martini, just like you said. You just wait and see."

"I'm betting on you, kid."

Bob ran to the kitchen where breakfast was just ending. He wolfed-down approximately 6000 calories of his allotment in about five minutes. He remembered being told occasionally that breakfast was the most important meal of the day and (even though he felt that way about every meal) he always tried to give special emphasis to it.

"You're Bob Blob," accused a high voice from Bob's left. "My name is Ariel D. Feuce. Pro-named the Wonderful Wisp; I'm in Team Amber."

Ariel had a rather longish face which was crowned with a veritable helmet of auburn hair and completely dominated by large, thick spectacles. She wore pale pink dancing tights (a body stocking really, that did nothing for her match-stick figure). Her boots were aqua; her cape was midnight-navy and she had a rainbow of waves, rippling like a sash across her left shoulder, making a spectrum that ranged from azure through teal, into the lightest of baby blues.

"My power is kind of a gas. What powers do you have?"

Bob was momentarily off balance. Beatnik and jive-talk were only of glancing familiarity to him. Then he caught-on and recovered rather nicely.

"Oh," he said, "you mean you can use gas as your power?" The strangeness of the concept was beginning to hit Bob even as he spoke.

"Not exactly," she said, "I can sometimes sort of turn into a kind of, well, gas, you know?"

"Wow," said Bob.

"That must be..." Bob paused. He really had no idea at all what it must be; but was saved from admitting it by Ariel herself.

11

"Hey! Come on, Bobby! We're going to be late for the first class of the year. That wouldn't be the best way to impress the teacher! Follow me!"

Something happened as the girl got up and moved to the door. Her slender body seemed to have suddenly changed into a steamy cloud of sorts. You couldn't see through her or anything: she just, all at once, became like a mirage on a highway, or a poorly tuned television picture.

"Hurry up, slow poke!" she called behind her.

Bob became aware that she was moving many times faster than anybody had a right to. He found out later that her great speed was due to the fact that she only weighed a few ounces in her gaseous state; yet was able to employ all her inertia and strength.

Bob did the only thing he could think of: he bounced after her. Four strides and a jump he took. As he got moving his speed accelerated also. The first bounce carried him up in an arc; the apogee of which might have been an Olympic record for something or other! At least twenty feet from bounce-to-bounce his flight path measured.

It was amazing and dreamlike. Before this day Bob had always felt inhibited in his powers. For the first time he felt encouraged and free. The bouncing didn't hurt; on the contrary it felt natural. Two, four, ten bounces he jumped before he arrived at the door of the school building. Ariel sprint-ed up just behind him.

"Not bad, Bobby boy, not bad!" was all she had to say.

Another pleasant surprise awaited Bob as he entered the classroom. Someone had constructed a special desk to accommodate his girth. As he moved to his desk (it was obviously intended for him) he noticed that he wasn't the only one for whom accommodations had been made.

Bob knew that his classmates were an unusual assortment of charac-ters, but it was rather staggering to see them all together in one room like that.

Sixteen boys and five girls (including Bob himself) were sitting there in costumes that would be a distraction at a Mardi gras pageant. There were kids with swords and sticks and shields. There were capes; caps; masks and cowls. One guy looked like a boxy robot complete with flashing lights and antennae (he too, had to have a special desk).

Presently, everything became still as a star on Christmas Eve. In walked a most imposing figure of a man. He wore a t-shirt that revealed over-devel-oped biceps the diameter of ash-can lids. A canvas vest of many pockets hung down over a black leather belt holding up old fashioned pantaloons. Black leather boots completed the outfit.

As the teacher walked to the blackboard in silence, Bob noticed that his head and waist looked incongruously small, and that he had a face that looked hard, lined and a bit elderly. "He's seen a thing or two," thought Bob. The man seemed to be peering through tiny reading glasses.

12

He picked out the chalk from the dust and slowly printed the words: DOCTOR UNKNOWN on the blackboard.

He turned, hands on hips, to regard his students. No one even wiggled. Bob thought it possible that no one even breathed.

The teacher opened his mouth and what came out sounded like, "Class, turn to page twenty-eight". But the man was squeaking! He almost quacked the words! The contrast between his tough appearance and his voice was too comic for the general level of maturity in that room. A few students were successful at suppressing their giggles but most didn't even try.

This didn't faze Dr. Unknown (for that indeed was his name) in the least. Perhaps he had grown used to this little ritual by now.

After all, he looked like he might be as old as seventy. It might have been a different century back when he went to school!

"You were already two weeks behind in your reading when you walked into this room. I intend to catch you up." Groans of injustice rose up to heaven.

Dr. Unknown went over some of the material Bob had heard at orientation (but was grateful to hear again). The four year curriculum was divided into three phases. Each year had courses devoted to intellectual development ("Eye-Dee") and physical development ("Pee-Dee").

Some of the course descriptions could have come out of any High School or College course book (such as Philosophy, Equations, Civics or Speech Class). Other courses promised rather more (these included Special Powers, Escapology, and Time Warp and Multi-Dimensional Integrating Seminar).

The whole third year would be done on the "Buddy System". Bob felt that he didn't want to think too far ahead. He would complete this hour of Deduction with Dr. Unknown and after lunch meet up with him again, but this time out on the playing field for Special Powers.

Homework was a nasty surprise. Bob liked to read (he had taught himself to do that). But forty-one pages and an essay on Sherlock Holmes did seem like a little much for a nine year old. Still, Bob was determined to do as well or better than the bigger kids. It was fortunate that he had this attitude as later events would prove.

After lunch he made his way to the athletic field behind the main school building. He was looking forward to Special Powers and briefly wondered when he would get to meet the other teachers.

Mrs. White was his guidance counselor. He had encountered her the afternoon of his arrival (Friday) and liked her. However, it seemed to Bob that she wouldn't let you get away with anything. Professor Wie he had only seen from a distance and he didn't remember much about him.

He had heard that there was a fourth teacher who was very mysterious and strange (and that would have to be pretty strange indeed if the others were any guide). Tomorrow he would have Philosophy with the peculiar Mr. Mann.

That made four teachers in all. Not a large staff, maybe, but then again it wasn't a large school. On second thought there was an excellent student-to-teacher ratio: right around five-to-one. Bob didn't think there were many other schools that could come close to that.

"Alright," shouted Dr. Unknown to the students milling around the field. "Settle down," he said, "If I can have your attention for awhile I promise to give it back to you. Line up in your teams to start with." There was some jostling.

"For those of you who never played 'Hostage" before, the rules are simple. Red and Green will be at one end of the field and Blue and Amber at the other. Since we have twenty one students this year one of you can be the hostage."

"You, Mr. Bounce-O," the Unknown's finger was pointing at Bob. "You're our hostage. Your job is to escape the Bad Guys (if you can) and cooperate with any rescue. You start out at this end of the field in the custody of the Red and Green teams."

"Now you Good Guys, you must use all your super powers to make sure you rescue the hostage within the time limit. Remember, it is considered good form to assure that he survives your attempts."

Bob didn't like the sound of that at all.

"Okay, you have five minutes to huddle and plan your strategy. When I blow the whistle the contest begins."

"Contest!" Bob thought, "And I'm the prize!"

"Come on, kid", said a not unkindly voice, "we have to put you in jail." The voice belonged to the Red team's leader: a boy in a spacesuit who's name was Moe du Jur, Space Cadet.

Bob was surprised by the name (which seemed to be an unusual combination of American and French) but more so by the fellow's skin-tone. Looking through the futuristic helmet, Bob could see that Moe was obviously of African descent.

In that time and place it was culturally popular to refer to people with Moe's skin-color as "colored" (unless *your* culture happened to be the one referred to, of course).

14

Bob had heard this appellation (and others even less savory) before. It seemed to him that super heroes, if anyone, should understand what it's like to be called names and feared merely because you are different. Bob had a strong conviction that all people (inside, where you couldn't see it) were the same. He was determined to be friendly towards Moe.

At that moment the voice of the Mean Blaster cried, "Don't worry 'B.B'; we'll rescue you in time for supper!" That got a lot of laughs. No one but Bob seemed to notice that the Blaster didn't have the courage to call him 'Blubber-Boy' in front of a teacher; even though there could be no doubt among the students what 'B.B.' stood for.

The Red and Green team members surrounded him and escorted him to one end of the field. "At least I'll get to listen in on their plans," Bob thought. Not so! A guard made up of two Greenies and a Red stood next to Bob.

"Don't move and you won't get sliced like bologna," said Swashbuckle, a boy from Red team. He had on a Zorro mask and an Errol Flynn shirt

15

open to the navel. He didn't look nearly as imposing as his long, glistening sword.

"Don't worry, he's not going anywhere," said the Pink Liberator. This girl only came up to Bob's shoulders, but she sounded very aggressive (and she carried a whip)! She wore shocking-pink dancing tights; a ruby mask and a pink rainbow sash with a shield emblem that had the letter "L" emblazoned on it.

"Take it easy, kid, and you'll live to eat supper." This was his other captor who wore a dazzling, bright smile. His name was Nova Rex and he made the remark about supper with a hardy enthusiasm - as if he had thought it up himself.

He had on a body stocking that covered all but the upper left side of his torso. The outfit had a gradation of color ranging from vermillion to fire engine red. A cape like rounded wings stretched behind him in blood-red; matching his domino mask.

"Just relax. It looks like we won't be getting much of a workout today."

In front of him and his three guards, Bob saw that the Red team was deployed an arc around the middle of their side of the field. In front of them were the three remaining Greenies.

On the other side of the fifty-yard line the Blue and Ambers were assembled. They were deployed in a variation of the old "Flying Wedge" football formation. The more powerful kids were in the front of the "V" and the less mighty were relatively protected towards the back in the wings of the wedge.

The Blaster and Willow-wand however, were outside of this protection as they hurried up on opposite sides of the field. They had a style preference for being lone-wolves.

In addition, a character called the Elf (from Amber Team) was ranging on ahead by himself.

The Elf looked like "a lad of nine summers or so". He was dressed all in bright, archaic armor of chain mail and steely scales. In fact, he was on a real quest (and with the characteristic patience of his heritage, he was taking time out for schooling). He wielded what he referred to as a magic spear. His strange looking ears came to sharp points that hung down from under his lobes ("Yeah, they always get that wrong," he was known to complain).

He belonged to another time...another place.

Bob noticed that the arrangement of the teams created a potential problem in chivalry. The uneven number of five girls meant that some boy would have to subdue (or even fight!) a girl. He sure hoped it wouldn't be he who was called upon to do this.

With the suddenness of a scandal at high levels, somebody blew the whistle! The field erupted with 21 screaming kids all running; jumping; dodging and even flying at the same time. Bob made himself stand still for a moment so that he could assess the situation.

Nodding to himself with decision, Bob started to unobtrusively scrunch down low. The Liberator girl was about to ask him something when he sprang straight up into the air. Her whip came back and Swashbuckler's sword got tangled in it. At that same moment, Nova flared up into a figure of dazzling multi-colored light. But his teammates were the ones who were dazzled.

As Bob bounced around them towards the opposite goal, Captain Eugene dived to pursue him like a blue, blurring meteor.

He was one of the older boys (thirteen) and he wore a shirt of blue, spangled with white stars. His red cape flapped in his wake as he rode his

17

Fantastic Jet-Shield. The shield was a small, round turbo-jet disk that could actually skim across the sky. It was powered by something called Radio Utilization of Modulated Power Transmission. RUMPT technology meant that he didn't have to carry his own power source with him but could receive electric power over the airwaves in the form of invisible electromagnetic radiation.

The entire Red and Green squad broke off from their assigned places and came after Bob like iron filings around a magnet. Bob bounced for his life.

After a few bounces carried him half way down the field he stopped with a start. Clammy hands were gripping his left forearm! It was a moment of pure terror until Bob recalled still another student named Morpho Lad.

Now that he knew what to look for, he could see the kid's vague outline. It slowed him down enough for his confrontation with a girl named Bunny Hop.

How, Bob asked himself, was he ever going to keep them all straight in his head! The answer seemed to be that he wouldn't keep track of everybody, at least not yet; not all at once like this.

Gosh, thought Bob, but this girl looks pretty. Then he remembered reading in the brochure about an attribute associated with her name. She was "The Power of Cute."

Her power was to charm her way out of difficulties. She could even use her allure as an offensive weapon. Come to think of it, this is what she was doing to Bob!

But that was too far fetched, thought he. Girls that turned into clouds and boys who shot rays from their fingers he found easier to accept than the concept of a girl who could distract his attention.

Yet, Bob noticed that she did have dimples in her cheeks as well as in her knees. She wore bobby-sox and a very short, pleated blue skirt that looked like a cheerleader's outfit.

The only way to describe her pillbox hat was cute.

Her pageboy hair was soft and shiny like chocolate silk; her button nose, her eyes... "Stop it!" He shouted at the top of his voice. It was too late. The Blue and Amber team had broken through and the confusing chaos crescendoed. Everything seemed to be spinning out of control.

He caught a glimpse of the robot boy (the Crunch) pushing aside people at the head of the pack. Bob himself was pulling behind him a dozen kids. There was a brilliant flash of electric blue light; bright as the center of a lightening bolt.

Bob blinked. Everybody had fallen asleep! He was lying on the grass and kids were sprawled everywhere. Disoriented and confused, Bob wondered how he had got there.

"Rise and shine kids", someone was clapping briskly. "No sleeping in class. It isn't allowed and it didn't happen." It was Doctor Unknown. After blowing his unheeded whistle several times he decided to bring the game to a halt by the expedient of lobbing a few well-placed sleep bombs.

Back in the 1930's, when the mere mention of his name struck terror into the hearts of countless bootleggers, Doctor Unknown was known for his use of all kinds of gadgets and gimcracks in his fight against crime. His most potent and ubiquitous weapon was the little, glass, gas-globe that contained his secret mixture of fast-acting knock out gas.

Having such a resource would certainly help a teacher in the task of class discipline, Bob reflected.

"Nice work, Bobbie," the Wisp called out as they trooped back to the school. He realized with a shock that she was not being sarcastic but really meant to compliment him.

Some others had a good thing or two to say to him as well. Lil' Socko added, "Great battle! You almost got away, Bob." He was using the name Bob with a hint of actual respect in his voice. A short kid with goggles and a beret, Lil' Socko could none the less out-punch Floyd Patterson (it was said).

Socko was the leader of the Ambers, and young Mr. Blob gathered that being complimented by a leader was a big deal.

But if a leader's praise was a good thing, Bob felt it was more than off-set by another leader's scorn. For the sad truth was that the leader of Bob's own Blue team was none other than the Mean Blaster. It seemed he never let an opportunity pass without directing some insult toward Bob. The present instance was no exception.

"Hey Blob, did you ever think to change your name to Super Hostage? How about the Beneficent Victim or – why not make it simple- the Bouncing Flop! No, I got it! The Big, Fat, Flat Tire, ha, ha!"

Some of the other kids laughed and smirked a little, but the general feeling among the rest of Blue team was that this was no way to build *esprit de corps*, to say the least.

That night Bob was pondering recent events in his bunk-bed (he was expected to occupy a lower berth, of course).

In Professor Wie's school, the Girls Dorm was located on the second floor and each of them had a room to herself. But the sixteen boys occupied seven bunk-beds on the first floor with a single bed reserved for the Crunch (who, you may remember, resembled a large, boxy robot). The Cruncher got his own bed because of the nature of his super identity.

Some of the guys felt (as they chattered away in the minutes following lights-out) that maybe you couldn't really trust those students who hid behind a mask all the time.

"I think it's a power thing," said one voice, "if someone's masked, you don't know who's really in there, do you?"

"How do you know if he deserves your respect if you can't see him?"

"Respect should be for what you do; not what you look like," said a voice that sounded like Moe du Jur.

"That's right!" added Bob quickly.

"I think so too," said the Crunch, to nobody's surprise.

"Well, anyway," said Kid Psyche, "it's up to each kid if he or she wants to share his or her secret identity and with whom. Some kids don't want us to know who they are and that's alright. They have as much chance of graduating as any of us."

"Yeah, those who want to keep their identity secret wear their masks to bed," said a voice, "they even shower with them on."

"You get used to it," commented Vortex Boy from behind his fully concealing mask.

At that moment the Mean Blaster walked in from the hall. He had come from the bathrooms and was dressed in a large, blue bathrobe which covered his brown and yellow striped pajamas. He had a bath towel in one hand and nothing on his feet. Yet his chromium mask glistened on his head in all its pointy glory. (The mask was what was pointy, not necessarily the head, Bob reminded himself).

"Anyone seen my shampoo?" he said.

He did indeed look weird.

A chorus of replies broke out.

"No!"

"Yes!"

"Never touch the stuff!"

"I think they served it to us in that soup we had for supper."

"How much is it worth to you?"

"If you seen one shampoo, you've seen 'em all."

"Who cares?"

The topic wound down to a natural death. "We were just talking about who's likely to graduate," said a voice.

"That's easy," said the Blaster, "everyone but the Blubber Boy. He's got to take *remedial thinking* first and that alone will take more than four years."

"Lay off," said Moe, "you been picking on him since he came here; for no good reason."

"I agree," sneered M.B., "that he came here for no good reason."

"That's not what I meant!" objected Moe.

"But, he's so pick-on-able, aren't you Blob-head?" the Blaster taunted. Bob ignored him in what he hoped was dignified silence.

"Anyway," said Mean Blaster, "how come he gets special privileges around here?"

They all knew what he was referring to. Earlier that afternoon someone had delivered a refrigerator-freezer to the dorm and installed it next to Bob's bunk. It had a combination lock that only he could operate.

"He even gets a pizza-pie delivered every night."

"He does?"

"How come!"

Bob felt he had to explain. "It's part of my special powers training. And it wasn't my idea!" Bob said, with stiff truthfulness. "I have a doctor's prescription and everything. It's for my physical development therapy."

"Boy, I wish I was in therapy!" said Captain Eugene.

"Boy, I wish I were in physical development anyway!" said Psyche.

That caused a lot of laughing. A few even laughed without malice; instinctively recognizing the easy, self-deprecating humor of the puny looking Kid Psyche as something that was healthy in his make-up. "Hey, I'll tell you who will never graduate around here," said Swashbuckle, "that Bunny girl."

"The *Endearing Bunny Hop*?"

"The *Power of Cute* herself? "

"What's wrong with her?"

Swashbuckle said, "I tell you she'll be out on her ear within a year...two years at the most."

"How come?"

"What makes you say that?"

"She's real cute!"

"Yeah, the *Power of Cute*!"

"That's right!"

"And she's got all the teachers convinced."

"She gets her way with everyone just by smiling!"

"That's her super-power, dum-dum!"

"Yeah, but what makes you think she won't graduate?"

"She won't," asserted the Swashbuckle boy, "all she has to do is keep growing and she won't be *allowed* anymore. Because," and his voice dropped to a horse whisper, "when she gets a little older, she'll never pass the Comics Code!"

There was some general chuckling at that, but most of the boys just grew very silent and thoughtful.

In the shadows, Bob listened to the snuffling, creaking, mumbling and whispering sounds of his strange new surroundings. "They sure can breathe loud," he thought. He was still young enough to be scared of the dark.

"Listen," he heard again the voice of Doctor Unknown speak in his memory, "the hero who ain't afraid of nothing ain't -I mean isn't- a hero at all! He's a poser with all the imagination of a tree stump. To be heroic means to overcome fear. No fear: no hero. So don't deny you are afraid and never hide from your fears. Face them! Figure out what you're afraid of and go after it. Drag it out in the open and wrestle with it or one day it'll go after you!"

Bob nodded once to himself, turned over and nodded again. Soon he had nodded himself right off to sleep.

The next day found Bob at the breakfast table determined to get to know the rest of the students by the end of the day ("drag those fears out in the open", he reminded himself). There were five he had not yet had a chance to talk to. On his left was an eight year old girl named Goldie. She was enjoying a special milkshake that was supposed to be good for her voice.

Goldie had a super voice- literally. Her singing was a sonic weapon that could shake apart buildings. She had a range from infra sounds, which lay below the frequency anyone could possibly hear (or even detect), to ultra sonic blasts that sent half the dogs in the county chasing their tails.

Dressed in a translucent, golden opera gown and cape, and crowned with a fresh daisy-chain, her diminutive figure gave no hint of the white noise tornado that could burst from her at any time.

"This must be what it feels like to eat breakfast next to a bomb," Bob thought. From three tables away Kid Psyche suddenly laughed very loudly for no apparent reason.

"How long can you hold a note?" Goldie unexpectedly turned to ask Bob.

"Gee, I don't know. I never timed myself."

"Well," said Goldie, "I thought with your lung capacity you might come close to my seven and a half minutes of sustained tone. Then we could sing arias together. One doesn't often get the chance to sing with a challenging partner and one misses the give and take that comes from singing duets," she sighed.

"I'm sure one does," said Bob politely. He thought to himself, "She probably thinks that a fascinating conversationalist is someone who only talks about her."

Out of the corner of his eye he glimpsed the Psyche boy with a wide grin; nodding his head slowly. Bob wasn't sure he liked what he thought was happening. Psyche shrugged.

Bob turned to his right where sat an intense young man with Raymond Burr eyes. His name was True Believer. He wore no mask (maybe because he was reluctant to obscure that penetrating stare in any way). He was about eleven years old and had yellow, swept-back hair which seemed to hang together with an unearthly discipline (except for the comma of a curl in the center of his untroubled brow).

He looked very imposing in his space-black leggings and crisp white jacket and cape. Here was the boy who could move mountains, it was said. His name was Andrew of Chicago.

His super power was officially listed as the power of faith; but there was some

24

disagreement about what constituted his secret identity. Some said his alter ego was his full name: Andrew Anderson. Others maintained that his real secret was his religious denomination. While he spoke in a flowery, biblical sort of way, (and he could even bi-locate!) he preferred to keep his religious affiliation to himself.

"I did once know a man who could sing with a mighty powerful voice," said Andrew, the True Believer. "If you can credit it, all the birds in the trees used to sing harmony when this man lifted up his voice."

Bob was going to once again deploy his politeness when he caught sight of something that disconcerted him. At the other end of the room a boy who looked identical to the True Believer waved a signal.

"I must be away," said Andrew of Chicago, "please excuse me."

It was Nine o'clock. The second hand swept past the mark and all twenty one students sitting in the classroom had the same happy conjecture. Maybe there's no class today. Maybe the teacher's sick. Maybe.

But no, here came Mr. Mann. Bob almost ran from the room. He had heard the teachers referred to by various nicknames: "Uncle Wilbur; The Ice Queen; Dr. Baldy." But when he had heard the name, "Iguana Man," the last thing he expected was a real iguana!

Well, you couldn't rightly say he was a real iguana, really.

Only from the neck up was it truly prominent.

On top of a slightly paunchy, conservative-ly dressed, middle-aged body, the head of an iguana was mounted. It wasn't a mask or Hollywood makeup that Bob was looking at in silent astonishment. The moist, green eyes were able to track you with (Bob was sure) superior intelligence. The pouch at the throat of Mr. Mann began to trill as he addressed his students.

Occasionally, a hiss would escape from his scaled mouth followed by a flash of his fire-red tongue. The students found that they had to pay close attention to make out what the Iguana Man was trying to say to them.

"Philosophy is the study of wisdom. It is the study of study, you may say," he did say. The students were spellbound with the novelty of it all. "This is sort of like snake hypnosis," thought Bob, who was thoroughly captivated by the fas-cinating spectacle.

"Now the word philosophy is taken from the Greek," Mr. Mann continued. "The first part, 'Philo', means love."

Bob was surprised at how much fun it was just to watch this guy talk.

"The second part of philosophy is taken from the word 'sophos', meaning wisdom. Now we are all going to pretend that we are back in the year 400 B.C. I will be the great teacher and your role will be to say to me, 'excellent dear teacher!' Let's practice that for awhile."

And they did.

It happened when Mr. Mann turned his back to write something on the blackboard. A voice said in a loud stage whisper, "Is he for real? It's all Greek to me!" Bob realized that the voice belonged to the kid sitting right behind him, specifically, the Mean Blaster. As Bob looked back to the front he could see what was about to happen. All the kids were suppressing laughter as the Iguana Man whipped around. "That was very amusing Mr. -let me see- Mr. Blob. I think we ought to discuss your humor."

"But I..." Bob started to object.

"After class, if you please."

Bob sank down behind his desk. It wasn't fair! M.B. got away with it because he was effectively concealed behind Bob. Bob made two mental notes for himself. One: he would make sure to explain his side of the story after class. And two: from now on he would ask to have his desk moved to the last row.

At the end of the hour, Bob had fifteen minutes before the start of the next class. It happened that Mr. Mann also taught this class, Sociology. Bob was determined to use every one of the fifteen minutes to explain his innocence.

"Well, Mr. Blob," said the teacher, "out with it."

"I didn't do it, sir. It was another student who said those things, honest!"

"Another student, you say," said Mr. Mann. "But I notice you aren't saying who it is. Well, I can see that you're not going to put the blame directly on another who isn't here to defend himself and I respect that decision."

"Look, Bob," he went on, "Philosophy is a difficult subject; and I need the help of everyone in class to teach it. Therefore, I want you to write a two page paper on what it means to be a teacher's disciple and how that relates to the word discipline."

"You don't believe me," Bob accused.

"What ever I believe isn't the issue here. I have assigned you a punishment, which you will hand in by next class. No excuses, Mr. Blob. That's the issue. It is just barely possible that I am mistaken in my assumptions. (I have been known to make perhaps as many as three mistakes in my entire teaching career)."

"But," protested Bob, "if it's possible that I don't deserve the punishment..."

"...There remains at least as great a possibility that you are guilty," said the Iguana Man.

"But sir, if I really am innocent, to punish me would be unjust."

"That the innocent suffer injustice is one of life's lessons Mr. Blob. Nobody likes it when it happens to him or her. What will you do in the face of injustice, eh, Mr. Blob?"

"Looks like injustice wins this round," thought Bob. But he was determined to find a path in his life where injustice would not prevail. He told himself, "Virtue must win in the end if I remain true to myself."

Bob was learning philosophy.

That morning sped away to where all mornings go. It was lunchtime and Bob was looking forward to his next class with great excitement: Beginners Marksmanship with Professor Wie. The Professor was an ordinary middle-aged man dressed in an ordinary brown suit; he wore a brown mustache (yes, this too, was of the ordinary variety).

They were out on the playing field, standing in front of long tables that had been set up for them. On the tables a number of strange looking guns could be seen. At the other end of the field, paper targets waited for the student's best efforts with a kind of silent arrogance.

Professor Wie lifted his voice above the whispering wind and youngsters. "Two of your classmates have been excused today. Mr. du Jur has already received basic Space Cadet training and therefore will be the beneficiary of private tutoring."

"I will be training you in the safe use of these weapons. No horseplay will be tolerated under any circumstances. This is serious business and I will not hesitate to expel the student who endangers another in any way."

"As your instructor, I am not possessed of any special or super powers. The only power I possess is finding and developing talent. We shall see what I can find in each of you."

"Now, I want you to pair-off and examine the weapons before you. No one is to arm these weapons until I so instruct."

There was some jockeying as a few students tried to team-up with favorite friends (and just as many tried to avoid those they didn't like). A boy who went by the name of The Purple Punisher realized that he was the odd man out and was directed to form a triad with Bob and the Wisp.

The "Purp" (as he was nick named) wore tights of deep purple (what else?) and jet-black. The costume looked very uncomfortable with its wedge shaped visor set into a plastic oval where his face should have been. Apparently his super power involved a lot of jumping and hopping about. He resembled a photographic negative of a tadpole.

Bob didn't intend to eavesdrop, but he couldn't help overhearing the dread "B.B." coming from the next table. Sure enough, the Mean Blaster was saying, "B.B. is the one behind it, I tell you."

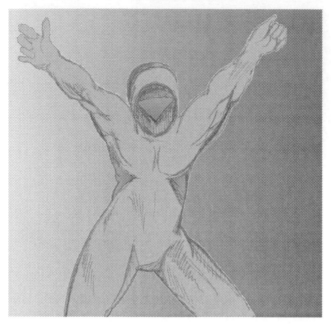

It was at this point that Bob did try to eavesdrop. It seemed that Verity Hammes, otherwise known as The Pink Liberator, was the second student who didn't show up for class. Professor Wie had said nothing by way of explaining her absence. But the Blaster had a theory. He said in a low voice, "I have reason to believe that Blubber Boy *ate* her!"

"He wouldn't do that," said Nova Rex, who was the Blaster's partner that class. "Besides," he went on, "he'd never get away with it."

"Don't be so sure," said Mean Blaster. "All I'm saying is don't ever cross him when he has that hungry look in his eye."

"But he's always got it!" asserted Nova in exasperated tones.

Bob was just about to say something that probably would have gotten him into some kind of trouble or other. He was saved by Professor Wie who said, "Alright class, you have had enough time to look them over. Now listen up. Each of you will get to try three different types of guns. The first is a standard blaster of the kind that technically doesn't exist yet. It has an adjustable barrel that is set by a dial in the handle. The dial goes from 'needle' to 'fan'. There are ten levels of power and the wider your beam, the less range and power you will have. However the needle beam has the least amount of control, as you will see."

"You will each take one blaster and adjust it to level five." He waited for them to comply. "Next, you will pull back the arming lever. All the way back please."

Each gun began to throb and glow with a low humming accompaniment.

"Aim your weapon at the target. When I say the word you will pull the trigger once and only once. Then you will engage the safety by reversing the

28

arming lever and return the gun to the table. Does anyone have any questions? All clear? Then, get ready, aim ...and FIRE!"

Nineteen slices of brilliant sunlight stabbed out from the guns all at once. Since these were trainer guns, they had a "semi-automatic" action. That is, they only fired for an eighth of a second no matter how long you held the trigger contact down. To fire a second time required releasing and depressing the trigger again.

"Good," said Professor Wie. "Solid-state ordinance is not like any other weapon on Earth. Eventually you will be learning how to control continuous-action guns like these. When you graduate from the trainer blaster, the beam will fire for as long as you depress the trigger. You will find that a steady hand is needed."

Bob couldn't believe the feeling of power he got from firing that blaster just once. Even though he hit his target, he was just a little bit scared of the gun. No, that wasn't true, he reflected.

What he was really afraid of was that feeling.

A twelve year old boy named The Silver Baron proved to be so good at shooting that he was asked to help instruct those students having a more difficult time. Bob was frustrated to find that he was included in this group.

"You're supposed to squeeze the trigger gently and not hold your breath," the boy explained to Bob. Whether he was a real, titled Baron was occasionally disputed among the students and something that Bob didn't know. The Baron usually carried a walking stick with a weighty silver handle on it and a lot of tricky gadgets built into it. His costume consisted of tights that looked like they were made of aluminum foil. He had a large letter "S" slashed across his chest and a short cape made of the same shiny material.

His helmet and cowl concealed his entire face. On exceptional occasions, he would cause his visor to become transparent and you could see his freckles and red hair with passable clarity.

As Bob was practicing he reflected that The Silver Baron had perhaps the second strangest costume of all the kids.

The prize for first place would have to go to a boy named The Absolute Locus. When I have described him for you, all twenty-one students will have been introduced.

Locus was nine years old. All of these years had been spent attempting to harness his unbelievable power. This boy had the ability to alter the shape of space-time in a limited area. This aptitude, called temporal stasis, enabled him to slow down his own personal time stream as well.

Games like Ping-Pong were no fun for him. It wasn't much of a contest when he could practically freeze the ball (and the opponent!) while he adjusted the paddle. It goes without saying that this sort of thing was no fun for the opponent either.

Oh yes, about his costume: it was very colorful. A forest green mask, shaped like a shield with a copper vent, was strapped to the front of his cowl.

The vent, through which Locus gazed out at the world, kind of looked like the radiator grill of a 1938 Packard. On the top of this was perched a circular, silver antenna. A kelly-green shirt was covered by a yellow and red scarf which had large glowing orange buttons. The scarf was attached to a chartreuse and lavender cape. Scarlet gloves and leggings held up by a belt of tan completed the outfit.

There had been speculation among the students that the Locus was color blind.

Now you have arrived at the point in the story where you should recognize all the students quite as well as Bob did (which is to say the acquaintances will require some attention as events continue).

As lunch time grew closer, one last category of gun had yet to be introduced to the students. The Repulsion Gun fired jet bullets with explosive tips. The range of these was somewhere on the order of two kilometers.

The paper targets were abandoned.

As in horseshoes and grenades: "almost" was close enough in this instance.

As professor Wie yelled the order to fire, Bob felt the ground shift under his feet. This caused his shot to go very wide of the target.

When the smoke cleared it could be seen that Bob's shot had taken out the exterior wall of half the girl's dorm. Without saying a word Bob replaced his gun on the table and walked back to the school building.

The babble of voices behind him registered in his ears without conveying any meaning or sense. He could only put one foot in front of the other as the numb realization hit him. His career as a super hero was over before it started. "Now you see it, now you doughnut!" he thought hysterically as his eyes glazed over with tears.

"Today is Tuesday," he reflected bitterly, "I never even lasted five days in this place. Now what do I do?"

Bob tried to think of practical things like what he would eat; where he would sleep. Where would he go? What about lunch? What could he do? His thoughts were churning just as much as his stomach!

Bob had no doubt who was responsible for his plight. It was the Mean Blaster. Sure, there were others who could have caused the accident: anyone from Morpho-lad to Vortex Boy. Psyche could have done it and Locus certainly had the power. But he knew who was out to get him.

There was only one student who had hated him and picked on him consistently since the first. That "natural yellow force beam" was the culprit. A quick burst in the right spot under Bob's feet at the right time and Bingo! it would be all over. The Mean Blaster lived up to his name too well.

"The Big, Fat, Flat Tire, ha, ha!" Bob heard that smarmy, piping voice again in his imagination. "It wasn't fair!" he thought, "I never even had a chance! Nobody even cares if live or die, let alone if I get expelled from this stupid school!"

"Well I've had it! I won't wait around for Professor Wie to kick me out. I've had it! They can find someone else to laugh at for a change! I've had it! I'm plumb fed up!"

Bob felt an unbearable wave of emotion swelling inside of him; making him sick with its intensity. "IT'S JUST NOT FAIR!" he screamed.

Then Bob heard another voice say, "What will you do in the face of injustice, eh, Mr. Blob?"

Bob Blob froze to the spot like a rabbit in a gun sight. He realized that he had a choice to make. Maybe he would end up being expelled (and the thought of what might lay beyond that dead end really terrified him). Yet that didn't mean he had to hand injustice an easy victory.

What could he do? He could pack his clothes and slink away. Or, what else? He could stop. "I already did stop," said Bob to himself. Yes, and he could turn around and face the consequences of his actions. "But I'm afraid," he thought.

Still another voice interrupted his reverie, "To be heroic means to overcome fear. No fear: no hero. So don't deny you are afraid and never hide from your fears. Face them! Figure out what you're afraid of and go after it. Drag it out in the open…"

For the space of a dozen heartbeats; for the amount of time it takes to read this sentence, Bob hesitated.

Somewhere a bird chirped twice in a row.

Slowly Bob turned and headed, with ever faster and firmer tread, back to the playing field. The uncertainty of what waited for him there represented everything of which he was afraid. Humiliation, failure, ridicule and shame all lined up to take a poke at his ego.

Bob Blob had decided to fight back.

Chapter III

Rye Humor

Once the decision was made, Bob found it easier going. No matter what was going to happen now, the die was cast. Even though his apprehensions did not completely melt away, he could feel them starting to thaw a bit.

As he approached the field once again, Bob saw that most of the kids had been dismissed in the time that had elapsed since the accidental explosion.

Only four students and Professor Wie were gathered around one of the tables. Purp, Wisp, and Locus were bunched up on one side of the table that held the gun Bob had used. Professor Wie and the Mean Blaster were on the other side.

"Just great!" thought Bob in frustrated exasperation, "he's telling the professor his side of the story. That ought to be good enough to get me expelled for sure."

"Oh great!" groaned the Mean Blaster when he saw Bob coming back, "This ought to be good!"

"Where were you?" called out the Professor.

"Yeah; and why did you just walk away like that?" added the Wisp in a voice that sounded full of concern.

Bob walked up to the table. "I just had to get away to think about what happened for a while."

"That's what we are all going to do," said the professor. "I intend to get at the truth regarding this incident. Tell us about it in your own words, Mr. Blob."

"It all happened very fast," said Bob. "I was shooting the Repulsion Gun..."

"Before or after my command to fire?" interrupted the professor.

"This was right after you said to fire. I felt the ground give way under my feet. It felt like a fast elevator dropping; or as if a half-inch hole had suddenly opened up beneath my heels. I felt my hand jerk up (I suppose I was trying to keep my balance) and my shot went wide."

"That's all you have to say?" asked Professor Wie.

Bob replied, "When I saw what I had done, I made sure the safety was on and put the gun back on the table. I never meant to cause all this trouble," he ended in a quiet voice.

"Well, I still say," said Blaster, "that it looked to me like he was aiming for the girl's dorm."

"And just how would you know that, Mr. Blaster? No, don't answer just now. You'll get your chance to say what ever you like in a moment. Right now I want to hear from Mr. Locus. Tell us what you saw."

The Locus spoke with apparent reluctance. "I saw what looked like a sparkle or flash. It flared up just out of the corner of my eye, you know. It only lasted for a second. I knew it wasn't from any of the guns because it was too low down, almost on the ground."

"Could it have been a reflection?" asked the professor.

"I don't think so," said Locus, "there was nothing but grass there and the flash was the wrong color for a reflection."

"The discharge from a repulsion gun is characteristically blue-white in color. What color was this flash you saw?"

"It was yellow," said Locus.

"It was not!" said Blaster.

"Was too!" said Locus.

"Hold on now boys!" said Professor Wie. "There's a way for us to see for our selves what really happened. If Mr. Locus will be kind enough to accommodate us we can all watch history repeat itself."

"But that's no fair!" shouted the Blaster, "He can show what ever he wants us to see! He's going to show…"

"Yes?" asked the professor, "I would be very interested to know what it is you are afraid we will see."

"I'm not afraid of anything!" said M.B., "it's just that he's gonna take that Bouncer's side!"

"I think," said Wie, "you will find that our Mr. Locus does not have the power of hypnosis. His power has nothing to do with creating images. Believe me, I will see through any deception that can occur here. The Absolute Locus will now show us what is going on in the cross section of space-time that exists five yards and twenty minutes away."

Sure enough, about five yards in front of them they saw a vision. It looked as real as an alarm clock on Monday. The Locus had his hands stretched out in front of him, straining, as if he were trying to push an invisible elephant.

The vision showed all the students firing their guns. There was, however, one bright spark out of place. It was right at the feet of Bob.

And it was yellow.

"That doesn't prove anything," protested the Blaster; with a voice that sounded for the first time less than certain.

Professor Wie turned to the Locus and asked: "Can you just give us the slice that has the flash in it?"

The boy nodded and spread his feet in a wide stance. His antenna started to glow cherry-red and large ripples of heat, maybe, emanated from it. This time the apparition was broken into discrete parts, as if a deck of mirror-surfaced cards were being riffled in front of them in a kind of visual shuffle. The movement froze and resolved into a tableau that told a story.

There was Bob Blob firing his gun. Just behind him the Mean Blaster was doing the same. But his left toes were raised off the ground and they pointed at Bob's right heal. In that stopped second of time, a pin-point star shone through the spark-gap between the two boys. It seemed to both reveal and condemn the motivation of the Mean Blaster.

And it was yellow.

"Well, well," said Professor Wie, "You are the only one who is looking down as the guns are fired. It almost looks as if you are exercising your Blaster power through your foot. We all know the method you use to fly. I'm tempted to say that it looks to me like you were aiming."

"Accidental discharge! It wasn't my fault!" the Blaster's protestations almost tripped over each other in their haste to be expressed. "It could happen to anybody! I'm so powerful that it just leaks out once in a while. The power circuit was accidentally triggered, like a static electricity shock! I didn't even know what was happening."

"You heard me warn the students that horseplay of any kind would not be tolerated?" asked the Professor, "You remember the penalty I prescribed for anyone who endangered another?"

"But I didn't endanger anybody!" said Mean Blaster.

Professor Wie responded, "That is the only reason I can find for using the punishment of suspension rather than expulsion."

"But why?" said the Blaster.

"You will refer to me as Professor Wie!"

It looked like justice was going to win this time. That thought made Bob feel almost as good as his relief at being exonerated. Bob was determined to fix things in his life so that justice could win even more times. He had some thoughts about that. It only took him a few hours to figure out how to do it.

The real start of Bob's big inspiration had been earlier, during lunch hour. It was true that all his inspirations were accompanied by food one way or another; but as food was such a big part of Bob's life anyway, it would be hard to say if there was a causal relationship.

Now it was fortunate that Bob had almost two full hours in which to work undisturbed. Beginners Marksmanship had of course ended early that day; and the next scheduled event was recess and then study hall with Dr. Unknown. Everyone knew that the Doctor didn't mind if you came late for study hall, so most students naturally did.

Bob couldn't wait to be alone. The perfect spot for isolation happened to be the one room that was least likely to see student activity: the library.

Out of his school bag (which was a kind of kiddy brief-case popular with parents at that time) Bob produced a brand new, college ruled 80 page notebook with a shiny red cover.

At first he was going to draw a skull and cross bones with a warning to keep out on the cover. Then he thought of two things that made him change his mind. A warning might backfire and maybe intrigue and invite rather than discourage potential unauthorized readers.

In addition he remembered that his artistic ability might well encourage more laughter than terror. His tongue was spotted with blue ink before he finally wrote: "Homework and Extra Credit Notebook," on the cover.

Leaving the first few pages blank he started to jot down ideas and plans. By the time three whole pages had filled up, he had started making graphs and charts. Soon he was cross-indexing lists and details and breakdowns of ideas. The ideas came faster than he could record them.

Within the joy of his creative fog he started to see a master plan take shape. Even at his tender age he had read enough to realize that he couldn't strike back at the Mean Blaster on the Blaster's terms. It wasn't that Bob was exactly afraid of him, but Bob didn't want to take a chance that he might become like him.

"I don't want to solve all my problems with force and fists," he thought, "I don't need to cheat and be sneaky to get ahead." He was writing all this in his book. "I don't want to feel good by making others feel bad. I may be big and strong, but the last thing I want is for people to be afraid of me."

"Besides," he wrote on, "evil is sticky and hard to get rid of once you start to use it. You can't accomplish good by being bad – not in the long run."

The idea that Bob was trying to tease out of his brain was beginning to crystallize. "I will use humor as my weapon." He circled that sentence and underlined it three times. "I will look for the funny side of situations that I don't like."

"This will be a challenge but I won't ever have to feel bored again because I'll never run out of funny juice. From now on my greatest super power will be my brain!"

He wrote a list that would become something of a creed to guide him through life.

1. No matter how ridiculous some rules may seem I will obey all of them (yes, all of them. Just for practice. I am, after all, a good guy).
2. I will never take myself too seriously.
3. If I laugh at myself first: I win.

That evening Bob ran into Kid Psyche on the way back from supper. "Hey Bob," he said, "We need to talk."

"Sure," responded Bob. They were making their way back to the Dorm, and by mutual agreement started to walk the long way around the campus.

"There's a reason for it," said the Psyche boy.

"What are you talking about?" said Bob.

"You are wondering why I walk around like this with only my swimming trunks on."

"Well, since you brought it up, yes. I mean, don't you ever get chilled?"

"Naah," said the kid, "It's all a state of mind. I can be as snug as I want, even in a winter storm, just by psychic power alone. The reason I dress this way is because I receive psychic emanations through the pores of my skin."

He continued, "That's why I must expose the maximum amount of surface area possible: to facilitate reception. Like a radio antenna: my body is sensitive."

"Wow," said Bob, "how many channels can you get?"

"Huh?" said Kid Psyche.

"Never mind," said Bob, "I was just making a little joke."

"Oh," Psyche replied, in a tone that conveyed some doubt, but then he continued almost without a break, "Hey! You really did mean it as a joke. I mean, you wanted me to laugh, too."

"Sure, what did you think? You must be able to sense that I only want to be friends with people."

"Yeah, I know."

Bob said, "You know something? This is not so easy: with me talking on my end and you mind –reading on yours."

"You don't know the half of it!" said Psyche with sincere assurance. "All I do, all day long, is pick up the crumbs of resentment all around me: the core of your ideas, the spice of your daydreams."

One could have gotten the impression that Psyche was deliberately choosing metaphors Bob could easily relate to.

"Most times it takes all my energy just to make you guys shut up in my mind. But it's easier for you.

Earlier this afternoon, you were able to escape for a while, so that you could think things over. And you did it by just walking away. Or later, when you wanted to be alone to work on your big, secret project..."

"Hey!" said Bob in an injured tone, but Psyche refused to be interrupted. "When you needed privacy to write in your notebook, all you had to do was go to the library. But where do I go to be alone? Did you ever think of that?"

"You're right," admitted Bob, "I never considered what it would be like to be a mind-reader who could never turn off his power. It must be like having to listen to the radio all day while you're trying to do other things."

"You got it! That's just what it's like; only you don't always get to choose the program!"

"But that's what makes it so..."

"Creepy is the word you're looking for," said the kid. "Look, I respect other people's privacy. I really work hard at it." Psyche continued, "I knew you had a big important idea you were working on; you couldn't hide that strong an emotion from my attention. But I never looked at the information you wrote down."

He went on, "When I come across private thoughts I try to look away. And if that doesn't work, if I see something by accident, I never tell anyone else what I see. It's none of anybody's business what you think in private."

"Well," Bob said, "that makes me feel a lot better. Come to think of it, if you wanted to, I suppose you could cause a lot of trouble and gossip and stuff. The fact is, you are a pretty quiet guy and stay mostly in the background. I don't think of you as a trouble maker."

"Not like the Mean Blaster," said Psyche.

"Well, I can't hide what I think about him, not from you. But I'm going to try to stay away from him if I can't win him over."

"Yeah?" said the Psyche boy, "Good luck!"

It was at that moment their full attention was captured by Bunny Hop waving and calling to them. "Boys," she sang, "I wanted to catch you before tomorrow. Did you hear about that Mean Blaster?" She didn't wait to see if they had heard anything but went right on talking very fast.

"Professor Wie suspended him and he's confined to the kitchen building, they have a small apartment there for visiting parents and people, and he's got to stay there and help the kitchen staff and he can't come to class or see the other kids for a week but he has to have all of his homework done on time."

Bob marveled at her ability to say so much in one breath. "I'll bet she could give Goldie a run for her money," he thought, and Psyche suppressed a snicker.

"I just wanted you to know, Bobby," she continued as Bob winced at the name, "that all the girls don't really believe that you meant to blow up our dorm in fact you did us a favor it turns out because they have to fix it up real nice now and in the meantime we get to camp out in sleeping bags and tents in the back yard and it's like a pajama party every night so thank you!"

"You're welcome," Bob managed to get out. As she began to maneuver away toward the backyard, she waved goodbye. Bob and Psyche exhaled together like swimmers who just broke the surface after a long dive. This coincidence of feeling caused them to laugh in concert. The laughs grew into a second-class fit of the giggles, complete with guffaws and snorts.

"Boy!" said Bob, "as Groucho Marx once said, she must have been vaccinated with a phonograph needle!"

"All I can say," laughed Kid Psyche, "is sometimes I'm real glad that nobody can tell what I'm thinking!"

Next day Bob woke up, eager to try out his new ideas. The day would start with Mr. Mann in study hall (this being Wednesday) and continue with Mrs. White the rest of the day. The first class was in General Science, and then came Fencing in the afternoon.

Bob thought he was very lucky to have such interesting subjects. It must be said that he regarded learning as another juicy morsel in the smorgasbord of life. This was probably due to his very dense brain cells: which were just as hungry for fresh thoughts as his stomach was for fresh food. Bob was a high-capacity kind of guy.

When Bob got in line for breakfast he and the Mean Blaster saw each other at the exact same time. M.B. had a bucket and sponge and was wearing a flower-print apron of blue and green. It was, perhaps, a practical thing to wear, but it clashed badly with his uniform.

"Be sure to leave some food for the rest us!" he called out to Bob who responded, "Isn't that joke getting a little old?"

The students all stopped what they were doing. They could sense the battle of the titans that was about to commence. Some of them were frankly hoping for a fight and not just for the excitement of it. Regretfully, the Mean Blaster had never really cultivated a sympathetic following among any of his classmates.

"Better watch your step," said the Blaster, "I won't be stuck in suspension for long and when I get out I'll pay you back good!"

"That's okay, M.B. You don't owe me a thing. Glad to be of service." The laughter that followed this rejoinder was like a landslide that caught the blaster off guard and threatened to bury him alive.

He rallied with: "Think you're funny, eh?"

"It looks like I'm not the only one," said Bob, and indeed everyone was laughing and clapping as if they were at a show. In fact the first act had only begun to warm up.

"Oh yeah?" said the Blaster, "meet me outside after breakfast and then we'll see who's laughing!"

"Good idea," said Bob. We can sit down and I'll start the conversation. We can have a nice heart-to-mouth talk."

"Oh yeah?"

"You said that already."

"I'll teach you to insult the Mean Blaster!"

"Thanks, but I know how already!"

"You're just asking for a fat lip to go with the rest of you," said M.B.

"Wow! Said Bob, "for a moment I had a notion that you made up something intelligent out of your own head; but I know there's nothing in it."

About half the kids laughed at that one.

"I'm going to change the shape of your face!" yelled M.B.

"Since I only believe you about one word out of thirty; I'll come back in a half an hour when you've worked up enough for a whole paragraph." Bob turned to his audience, "Ever notice how some people compensate for a lack of brains by yelling?" That got some more applause.

"You putrid lump of lobotomized lard!"

"I want you to know," said Bob, "that verbal displays like this will not change the level of respect I have for you."

"If it's a battle of wits you're after..."

"No, no, I wouldn't dream of fighting an unarmed man."

"Oh yeah?"

"That again? You just go on and practice talking to yourself until you get the hang of it. We'll all wait."

Even the Mean Blaster could see that he was loosing control of the situation (the horrible suspicion that he had never even been in control in the first place was just beginning to dawn on him). He decided to beat a retreat while he still could.

"Just try to stay out of my way, fat stuff! I'll get you when you least expect it and you'll be sorry then!" He threw down the bucket and fled from the room to thunderous accolades. Bob took a bow in what he hoped was a humble way.

The congratulations that swelled up around him made him feel accepted; and that feeling was even better than the triumphant realization of his plan. He had used his wry sense of humor as a weapon successfully.

"Bobby, you were great! I had no idea you could do like that," said the charming Bunny Hop. "Yeah," added the Pink Liberator (who loved to read history and historical fiction as a hobby), "You were just like Cyrano de Bergerac!" (At this point "Bobby" was hoping that this was a good thing).

"Not bad, Bobby boy, not bad," came from Ariel, the Wonderful Wisp. "I want you to promise me," she said, "that you won't go getting into a fight with him later on. Come on! You gotta promise."

Even though it wasn't quite clear to Bob why he should be the one who's "gotta promise," he found himself doing so with thirty eight ears as witnesses.

The Wisp took him by the arm and escorted him to a seat. "Now you just relax and we'll get a couple of trays for you. I want to see you eat hearty so you can keep up your strength."

This remarkable turn of events was the subject of discussion as soon as Bob could get away from the impromptu breakfast party and talk to Psyche.

"I wanted to talk to you alone and I knew I didn't have to signal or even look at you," Bob said.

"She likes you," said Kid Psyche.

"Talking with you," Bob replied, "is a little like talking to a fortune teller. You know that, don't you?"

"Yeah, and the Mean Blaster is going to do his best to see that you have a lot of fortune: all bad. You know *that*, don't you? I realize you aren't afraid of him, but maybe you should be. He's really almost as smart as you are - and he outweighs you."

"Huh?" said Bob.

"You heard me. He's got about five hundred pounds of hate and spite and meanness on you. He didn't pick his name by accident you know. What ever is bugging him, it's eating him up like acid. It happens that you are number one on his hate parade."

"Don't tell me about how he got that way," said Bob, "I don't want to know."

"Good," came the reply, "because I ain't talking. I don't know the whole thing anyway."

Bob said, "I did figure out that Ariel is nice to me because she thinks I need a mother. That's right, isn't it?"

"Sure hope," Psyche said, "that we have chicken tonight. I can't stand that chipped beef stuff."

"You're a good friend, Psyche," said Bob. He had trouble feeling bad about anything for quite some time after that.

"You must come to think of yourself *as* your persona," the voice of Mrs. White was reverberating from the walls of the practice room. She too, had proven to be a pretty good teacher, reflected Bob. Her explanation of television transmission was the neatest thing that had happened in General Science class. Now Bob and his classmates were lined up for their introduction to the art of fencing.

"Being described as super, is more than just a matter of showmanship for each of you," she was saying, "You don't merely have super powers, you know: you are super. You will be called upon to live up to that."

M.B. was not present at this class, of course. Bob was thankful, because it eliminated the danger that they might end up having to spar together.

He noticed that Moe, the Elf, and Swashbuckle were all missing as well. That made sense, Bob thought. They had been trained as expert swordsmen even before they enrolled in the school. Bob briefly wondered if they got extra free time because of this; but then came to the conclusion that they were probably sweating and stomping away in another room with advanced instruction.

A wave of excitement broke and drenched each student to the bone, when the special, safety-tipped foils were issued.

It was true that no student was allowed to benefit from, or misuse, his or her super power. Each student was closely supervised. Bob could wave his sword around all he liked, just as the other students were doing, but he was forbidden to bounce. The Wisp and Morpho were compelled to remain solid; Nova couldn't glow; Locus, Psyche and True Believer were on their honor not to use their considerable extra abilities; and Vortex and Goldie (respectively) couldn't inhale or exhale too much. After what happened with the Blaster, the teachers were more alert than ever.

Much of the time was spent learning basic positions and postures. There was a correct way to hold the foil (never bend the wrist!) and it was all much harder than it looked. Willow Wand, Lil' Socko, Captain Eugene, the Silver Baron and Goldie were all very good at it right from the start.

Mrs. White had them all rotate sparring partners so that Bob got to try his stance and technique, such as it was, with almost all of them.

The Crunch seemed to be having a particularly difficult time of it. His favorite strategy for most things was the straight ahead, direct approach.

On the plains of equatorial Africa, the gazelle and the rhino both have their own methods of doing business: each has its advantages. One would have to say that the Crunch subscribed to the rhino school.

"Mr. Blob and Mr. Crunch," the crisp, no nonsense voice of Mrs. White broke in, "I would like you to demonstrate what you have learned for the rest of the class." It was obvious, despite the phrasing, that this was not any kind of a request.

"Why is she doing this to me," thought Bob, "I don't need any more attention in class. Doesn't she know that I just blew up half the school yesterday and started a riot for breakfast today? Maybe she figures the day is young, yet."

It had to be admitted that the two opponents were fairly evenly matched. Even Vortex Boy, who appeared to be a little bit muscle bound, wasn't as ungainly as Bob, who had to move a lot more bulk around. Both Bob and the lumbering Crunch had to reach around their own torsos to get their swords properly aligned.

At the signal, the Crunch lurched forward swinging his foil like a sickle. Bob didn't wait for the harvest but blocked left and then right. He tried a feint but the Cruncher was wise to it. Like an elephantine tango, the two worked up and down, up and down the floor. Bob looked for an opening and in one quick move used his wrist (not his arm!) to bat down the Crunch's foil.

"Hold!" Mrs. White called out. "You all saw what happened there. Mr. Blob used his head as much as his energy. You must all stop swatting at each other and start to think. A rapier wit is what's wanted. The object of this class is to train you all to think. Training your hand and eye is a desirable secondary goal."

"Mr. Crunch you also did very well not to loose your cool. If we were awarding points I should give you both full marks. What do you think, class?"

The students didn't have to think. They all broke into applause. A warm thought came to Bob, like a hope that he didn't want to frighten by paying too much attention to it. "Maybe she did know what I've been going through recently. Maybe she called on me for that reason; and because she figured I could do better than even I thought I could."

The Crunch took him aside and told him, "I know who really won that round." In a good natured voice he went on, "If I was a villain, I'd have to say, *foiled again!*"

This left Bob to reflect on the fact that he wasn't the only one with wry humor.

Chapter IV

Gumming Up the Works

Professor Wie's School for Gifted Children
Class Assignments for the Year 1957

First Year Student: Robert R.M. Blob (Beneficent Bounce-O, Team Blue)

MONDAY	TUESDAY	WEDNESDAY	THURSDAY	FRIDAY	PERIOD
		Breakfast 8:00 - 9:00 am			
Deduction	Philosophy	Study Hall	Deterrence	Study Hall	9:00 - 10:00 am
Dr. Unknown	Mr. Mann	Mr. Mann	Prof. Wie	(Teacher Rotation)	(1 Hour)
Study Hall	Sociology	General Science	Logic	General Science	10:15 -11:15 am
Mrs. White	Mr. Mann	Mrs. White	Mr. Mann	Mrs. White	(1 Hour)
		Lunch 11:30 - 12:30 pm			
Special Powers	Beginners	Fencing	Green Belt	Green Belt	12:45 - 2:45 pm
Dr. Unknown	Marksmanship	Mrs. White	Dr. Unknown	Dr. Unknown	(2 Hours)
	Prof. Wie				
		Recess 3:00 - 4:00 pm			
Study Hall	Study Hall	Study Hall	Study Hall	Study Hall	4:15 - 5:15 pm
Mrs. White	Dr. Unknown	Mr. Mann	Prof. Wie	(Teacher Rotation)	(1 Hour)

Dinner 5:30 - 6:30 pm
LIGHTS OUT AT 10:00 PM

Bob was examining his schedule carefully. There was no mistake. There were 17 hours in every week devoted just to class time. He found that he could not include all the time he wanted for developing his special project (which now included a log or journal of important events that happened each day). He simply could not fit in all the homework and practice and ongoing training (not to mention time for play and goofing off). There just were not enough hours in a day.

Later on that week, Bob found himself paired with the Crunch Boy again (and for reasons that seemed familiar) in a class called Greenbelt. There were a number of students who were perhaps strong enough to wrestle with Bob; but the Calamitous Crunch was the only one who could really give him a workout.

At least in this class, Bob was not singled out to demonstrate anything. Dr. Unknown was saying, "You must not come to rely too completely on your super powers."

"Take it from me. For years I used a lot of scientific devices to defeat crime. But the time will come when one of them will fail you. The gun will jam, the thingamajig will misfire, the widget will turn out to be a dud and the gadget will gag in your suddenly sweaty hands."

"What will you do when your jet shield fails, your whip gets tangled, you loose your spear, or some electric-blue ray gun drains your superpower? Then where are you, eh?"

"Never!'

"Can't happen!"

"Unthinkable!"

"That only happens in cartoons!"

"Unrealistic!'

Resounding was the chorus of emphatic, negative responses. Yet, Bob remembered that in the game of Hostage (was it only last Monday?) the Pink Liberator's whip did get tangled long enough for Bob to affect an escape.

"Can't happen, you say? Well I say it will happen. It will happen to you; and not in some comic strip, either. Unrealistic, you cry! I'll tell you what's unrealistic: it's the idea that you can't make a mistake. There's nothing more comic than the guy who knows everything."

"All I'm saying is learn your limits before the bad guys do. Trust to your brains, creativity and experience, because luck and gadgets will let you down. It happened to me often enough."

"Tell us about it, Doctor," said Moe.

"No sir! I ain't falling for that one. You kids just want to get me talking so you can get out of doing work!"

"Oh, no," said the students in unison.

"Oh, yes," thought the students in unison.

"Not today, you rookies," said Dr. Unknown. "Let's see some jumping-jacks!"

"Oh, no," said the students again, this time with much more feeling. The exercise of Jumping-jacks was not a popular one and more than half of the students cheated. The way to cheat at jumping-jacks was to pretend to scissor your feet and hands open and closed; while really just waving your arms in time with the others.

No one hated this exercise more than Bob, who figured that a certain amount of discrete cheating was expected and acceptable, as long as he maintained the spirit of the thing.

After a good deal of this, the students were allowed to play "King of the Mountain" for a few minutes. This, Dr. Unknown felt, was a good technique for letting off steam that may have been pressurizing inside the students; making them susceptible to disruptive hi-jinx.

In this contest, Bob and the Crunch found that they had all the advantage. After the class (and the victorious game) they agreed to spend Saturday together at the Crunch's secret headquarters, where Bob could meet the Cruncher's parents. Bob was assured that Mr. and Mrs. Crunch would love to have him join the Crunch family for dinner.

"And you can play Monopoly with us and visit our secret laboratory and everything," assured the Cruncher.

"Sounds great," said Bob, who never really expected to actually have somewhere to go on a weekend. "How will we get there? I heard you once say that you live up on Windridge. Does the bus go that far?"

"No bus for us, Bobby boy. My dad's picking us up in the Impervo-car. One thing, though. Well, two really. You understand that you must swear to never reveal our location to anybody."

"I solemnly promise, swear and agree," said Bob.

"Good."

"What's the other thing?"

"Oh, yeah. Two other guys are coming with us."

"Who?"

"The Elf, for one."

"Uh huh, go on, who else? Don't tell me it's Mean Blaster!"

"Golly, no! I wouldn't do that to you even if I liked him which I sure don't!"

"Then who else is coming?"

"Well, I'll tell you," the Crunch sounded reluctant to come to the point, "it's Moe du Jur."

"Moe," said Bob, "what's wrong with Moe?"

"Nothing!" the crunch sounded defensive. It's just that I'm not sure how my folks will like me bringing him along to dinner and all."

"Why shouldn't they?"

"Well, they're a little bit old fashioned, you know,"

"So?" said Bob.

"Look, my parents are the greatest, really. It's just that they never learned to like...*space cadets*."

"Oh." Out of a million things Bob could have said in response, this seemed the safest.

Saturday morning arrived in the wake of a furious thunderstorm. Rain sluiced from every sluice; washed through all the washes; and came out in puddles lighted by every lightening. Gravel throated thunder cannonaded over the competing din of wind and beating sheets of rain.

It looked pretty wet to Bob.

Bob had been given the loan of one of the school's patio umbrellas. He had to hold on tight in the blasting wind, as the Crunch accompanied him to the front gate.

The sidewalk from the kitchen (where they had just finished breakfast) led past the school garden plot. Fresh flowers and vegetables were cultivated there, and volunteer students tended it with a great sense of ownership, not to say possessiveness.

They could see two of these "garden angels" out there now, drowning in drizzle and their oversized yellow rain coats.

"They must be nuts!" the crunch shouted his opinion at Bob.

"Everyone ought to have a hobby!" Bob's estimation came right back.

The school grounds now led out to a roadway that must have been a carriage drive when the place was built. Just past the ten foot high main gates, a car was waiting. Bob thought it was a car; but as he got closer he wasn't so sure.

Lester the guard, waved them through from the snug confines of his shed; and the gates opened to reveal the Awesome Impervo-car. It looked like a First World War tank; with a metallic dome covering the top half of it. It had several large fins with rocket tubes and colored lights protruding from these in the back.

The front swept down in a rounded skirt that covered whatever its mode of propulsion was. It seemed to have no doors. However, a galaxy of chromium-blue rivets pocked the exterior in patterns that looked more decorative than structural.

All in all, Bob thought, it was a beautiful car that never the less looked impervious to everything but laughter.

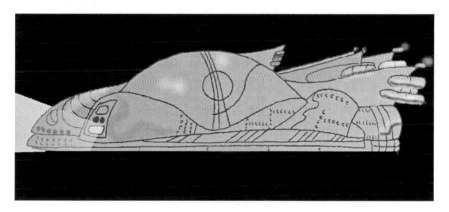

As Bob was looking with admiration at the gleaming thing, the crown dome cracked open and started to fold back like a baby carriage top. The interior was revealed to already contain the two boys, Moe and Elf, scrunched up in the back seat. They were having trouble making room for the Cruncher boy who had to squeeze in without sitting on Elf's magic spear.

Bob got to sit up front with Mr. Crunch, senior. Filbert Ulysses Crunch used to be a millionaire playboy until he settled down to marry his secretary, Ivana.

Raising a family meant that Filbert had to go to work each day in the superhero trade. Bob got the impression that this didn't pay as much as his former occupation (whatever it was that playboys did; it must be lucrative, Bob thought. He had never heard of any playboy who wasn't a millionaire and he made a note to himself to ask Mrs. White, his guidance counselor, all about it.)

"Close the door!"

"We're getting wet!"

"Get in, quick!"

"Hello, Robert," said the Cruncher's dad. He was outfitted as an older version of his son, complete with blinking computer lights and antennae.

47

"We're happy to have you visit with us," he said as he worked the control switch that closed the dome access.

There were a bewildering number of gages, levers, meters and dials all around the dashboard, sides, ceiling and even the floor of the car. There were three working television boxes built into the cab, each one showing a different black and white image of the road outside.

"You took the oath, of course?" asked Mr. Crunch.

"Huh?" said Bob, and then he remembered. "Oh, sure. I will never reveal the location of your secret headquarters; on my honor as a super hero."

"Thank you, Robert. Now you boys better put on your built-in, seat, safety belts."

Bob had never even heard of such a thing. Sure enough, there were wide canvas belts with heavy chrome clasps. These were attached to the back of each seat. The belts were a part of the futuristic look that permeated the whole car. The boys had to put them on before Mr. Crunch was willing to take off.

With the dome closed, a warm green glow illuminated the interior of the vehicle. Some of this was provided by the built-in computer cabinets and mini-vacuum tubes, all of which contributed to a rippling, undulating effect. Bob almost felt as if he was under water and he wondered how the Crunch's avoided getting car sick on long trips.

Bob noticed that he could now see out of the dome in every direction with surprising clarity. It was made out of some kind of weird metal that had all the properties of a two-way mirror.

"Deflection mode is green," said Mr. Crunch joyously and cryptically. "We're off!"

Boy, were they ever! The engines came to life with a rocket roar and the acceleration pushed back at the passengers with a jolt. They all became better acquainted with their spines (and perhaps their favorite prayers, too).

Bob thought that they were easily going twice as fast as he had ever traveled before. They negotiated curves as if they were being pulled at right angles along a pre-set track. In fact, that's a fairly good description of was occurring.

He found out later that "deflection mode" meant they were steering by computer. The calculating hardware took the data from the T.V. cameras and plotted a three dimensional course for the car. Next, a series of invisible electron-beams shot out ahead of the car, much in the same way that their headlights did.

The computer locked on to these guide waves and the rockets provided the propulsion. As the electronic information processor detected changing terrain; cars; or (Lord, help them) pedestrians; it adjusted or deflected the path of travel.

They were deflecting down the road and into the city at somewhere in the neighborhood of a hundred and twenty miles an hour!

Soon – how else at that speed? – they were through the city and snaking up the road that led to Windridge. The mountain road was winding and the grade was steep. Bob would have been afraid of falling off even in a normal car. He thought that Dr. Unknown would have been proud of him because he sure had no problem identifying this particular fear.

They turned off on to an unimproved two lane highway that led through a stand of pine and birch trees. Next came a gravel road that looked more like a path for horses or something. A tall fence opened up to admit them to a field that was marked by a big sign that read:

Government Testing Grounds
Army Corps of Engineers
Atomic Energy Commission and Strategic Air Command
Internal Revenue Service
Keep out!

At first Bob felt okay about entering because he knew that he didn't belong to any of the forbidden agencies on the list. Then it hit him that these agencies were forbidding him. But before he could ask about this, Mr. Crunch addressed the subject.

"Our family is permitted to live in a secret, government testing facility in return for some research I am conducting for Washington. So, when you promised to keep the secret of our location, you were also being patriotic."

"Wow," the guests said. The boys were very impressed and felt important and proud to be trusted in such a way.

The research that was mentioned consisted of investigations into the properties of something called Metal 46. M46 was discovered or invented by Mr. Crunch. The details were a bit obscure. So was the metal.

It could be molded and formed like plastic. It was flexible as cloth; yet it could be finished with a hardness surpassing tempered chrome-steel. Polarization made it transparent as glass. An electronic signal could change its color, texture or reflective index. All of the members of the Crunch household wore costumes of M46.

They had been riding off road for some time when the Junior Crunch announced, "There's our house!"

It looked like a small ranch style home with a long shed attached to the side. All of it was well hidden in the surrounding woods. Bob thought that it would be real hard to see even from an airplane.

As they approached, the door of the shed slid back to reveal a sloping ramp that led down into darkness. They hit that incline at a mere eighty miles per hour.

Bob sensed rather than saw the door close behind them. Along the walls, strips of ultramarine light revealed that the ramp had turned into a descending, spiral road.

It took them only a few seconds to hit the underground lake.

There was a mighty splash. It appeared that the road led right into the water. "That's just our braking system. We're home!" This last was said by Mr. C. into a microphone that had popped out of the dashboard.

The words seemed to trigger a battery of bright lights. They were in a dock surrounded by all sorts of tackle and rigging. Powerful electric cranes stood ready to hoist the Impervo-car to any of several service bays. The boys didn't get a lot of time to see much. As soon as the car hit the side of the dock, a great magnet clamped on, fore and aft, with a lurch.

The car dome opened and the boys were shooed into a passage that led to a corridor that let out into a large kitchen. It was a kitchen bigger than Bob had ever imagined possible. The sides of the room were supported by interlacing struts of arching metal (no doubt made from M46).

There was a cluster of stoves and cooking stuff. Some of the arches opened into other rooms. There was a sizable mahogany dining table and a smaller counter with barstools around it.

Mrs. Crunch looked like a slightly rounded version of her husband; but Bob's eye was immediately caught by the two girls. One was a small girl who was five years old, the other was a teenager.

Pat or Patty Crunch was the older of the two. She wore a metallic jumper of grey. Baby blue arms and feet were trimmed in what looked like bronze. Her shiny helmet of matching blue came down to a point just above her eyes. Three blond pony tails hung from openings in her headdress.

Her face, like that of her little sister's, appeared to be painted on. This, in fact, proved to be the case. Bob watched as they spoke, but he could not see their lips or mouth move behind their fixed smiles.

The younger sister was named Georgette Crunch. She stood all of one meter high. A single pony tail of red hair waved like a centurion's plume from the crest of her helmet. She held on to a doll made of straw which looked like a robot with two red buttons for eyes. This she referred to, with childish formality, as Mr. Blinky.

Mrs. C. was calling out, "Young lady, what did I tell you about jetting indoors?" Patty could be seen, hopping and jumping all around the room, as if she was riding an unseen Pogo Stick.

"She can only go this high," Georgette explained to the boys. She held up her hand to indicate the limit, which was about as high as she could reach on tip-toe.

"That's my big sister, Pat," said the Crunch Boy, "She just passed her *Jumper Jets* and now she wants to show off all the time.

Bob suddenly realized two things. First, his friend didn't have any Jumper Jets of his own. The second thing was that he had known the Cruncher for more than a week now; but he had never even heard what his first name was. He didn't think it would be polite to ask.

However, Mrs. Crunch settled that question right away. "Derick," she said, "maybe your friends would like to see your room and the rest of the house? I know Elf has been here before but I never met these two boys.

"This is Bob Blob," said Derick, "and this is Moe du Jur who's also in our class."

"Thanks for having us over Mrs. Crunch," said Moe.

"We're glad to have you, boys."

Bob couldn't figure out what all the fuss had been about. It looked to him as if Derick's parents really liked Space Cadets just fine.

"Derick will show you where to wash up and you can have some milk and fresh cookies."

"Yea!"

"Wow!"

"Great!"

"Thanks, Mrs. Crunch!"

Mrs. Crunch's cookies enjoyed a very exalted reputation among the students. The Cruncher frequently received "care packages" from home and he was conscientious about sharing.

"Patty Crunch!" Mrs. C. called again. "Don't make me come after you!"

"Aww, Mother!" said Patty.

"Don't 'Aww, Mother' me! When you have your own house you can jet around all you like and bounce off the walls for all I care!"

She stopped herself and turned to the boys. "Oh. No offence, Bob dear."

As they were getting cleaned up Derick said, "I can't wait 'till I'm old enough to get my own Jet Poppers. I'm mostly stuck using training Poppers with lines attached."

"Sometimes they treat me and Georgette as if we were the same age!" he complained, "I can jump just as high as Patty can though. I did twenty feet once and my boot shock absorbers were just as good as hers."

After the cookies (which lived up to their reputation) they took "the fifty cent tour" as Derick called it.

The house was laid out on three levels. Level One had the big kitchen, the living room, den, and guest rooms.

Level Two was located underneath them. It had four bedrooms and an oversized swimming pool.

Level Three was the lowest level. Here was found the secret labs and game rooms. A series of locks gave the Impervo-car access to all levels.

"How far underground are we?" asked Elf.

"Let's put it this way," replied Derick, "if there's an emergency we can use the steps. That takes about an hour."

Bob hoped that if there ever really was an emergency, it would be an awfully slow one."

Despite a nagging sense of envy, Bob found himself impressed with the Crunch family and their home. He wished that one day he could build a secret, underground headquarters like this. It would be fun to design, Bob thought. He also wished that he had his secret notebook with him. There were a lot of observations he wanted to record for later digestion.

Bob had fun the rest of that day playing with the Crunch kids. He learned that Patty was dating a sidekick named Spell-boy, Master of Misdirection.

He also learned that one could hold Georgette's doll for her, but that one was never to call him "Blinky".

"It's *Mister* Blinky!"

They all got to tour the Crunch boy's bedroom and secret lab. The Crunch possessed the unheard of privilege of having his own television set in his bedroom. It was capable of receiving six stations including the new U.H.F. broadcasts. The antenna for this sat atop the T.V. consol and Bob thought it resembled the antenna of the Absolute Locus.

There were banners tacked onto the walls from The Cincinnati Redlegs, The Boston White Sox, The Milwaukee Braves (World Series champions that year) and from every baseball team there was.

The boys were most impressed with the Cruncher's closet where he kept his comic book collection. When you opened the door the first thing you saw was a startling vision of a dagger floating in mid air!

"That's to keep my sisters out," asserted Derick. Closer inspection revealed the knife to be made of soft plastic. It was hanging from a very slender, hard to see wire. "Armature wire," he explained, "When you unwind the wire from a small toy motor you get this thin, copper stuff that's hard to see."

"Boy!"

"Neat!" the Cruncher's guests asserted and they meant it. Derick would have been devastated to learn that both sisters regularly read his comic collection and laughed at his security precautions.

So they never told him.

That afternoon they played in the fantastic game room. (That one room was larger than the whole dorm at school, Bob thought.) They played baseball, statues, tag, and a new fangled game called "Frisbee".

They played Monopoly and Old Maid and Dominoes. They swam in the swimming pool (and they were allowed to swim in their costumes and drip dry while playing Red Rover).

They played with the Chruncher's new Chemistry Set until the sulfur (and other more mysterious fumes) sent them gagging from the room. They had fun with electro-magnets and gyroscopes and oscilloscopes.

Finally Mrs. Chrunch's voice sounded from an overhead horn, "Derick, it's time for supper. You and your friends come to the kitchen and wash up."

"Okay, Mom!"

"We're on our way!"

"She was talking to me, smarty!"

"That's only because you never listen and we do."

"What do girls know about listening, anyway?"

"More than you any day!"

"Yeah!"

Such casual sibling banter enthralled Bob. He was getting a glimpse of family life. It was a new hunger he didn't even know he had.

They were seated at the big mahogany table and the candles were lit with a glow warm enough for family and guests and some left over.

Just before prayers of thanksgiving, the Crunch's removed their head coverings. For the two girls this meant removing their M46 face masks. These simply popped off and were put aside. The faces inside looked much like the painted versions on the masks. But now everyone could see their features change naturally as they talked.

A tousled mop of raven-black hair crowned the slightly chubby face of Derick, the Cruncher, as he discarded the gimmick-laden box that normally concealed his features.

Bob realized that his promise to the Crunch family now took on new significance. He felt proud, affectionate and (most importantly) accepted.

"Hope you boys are hungry," said Mrs. Crunch as she set out the banquette fare and Bob answered in the affirmative (just so there'd be no misunderstanding).

Broasted chicken with crispy skin, surrounded with cranberries and orange slices, took center stage.

Two mountainous bowls of home-made mashed potatoes shared the spotlight with stuffing and dinner rolls.

Buttered beans, peas, mushrooms and corn co-starred with red Jell-O that had real cherries and mandarin oranges inside.

Each place setting had the diner's name along with a clever little drawing of his or her costume or symbol, decorating a Dixie cup full of candy.

Three kinds of pie and cookies (and all the kids) waited for dessert.

"Tell us about your family, Moe," said Mr. Crunch, senior.

"Yeah," said Georgette, "What's it like being a real Space Cadet?"

"Now, Georgette..." said Mrs. Crunch.

"That's okay, Mrs. C." said Moe, "Not much I can tell, really."

"Why, Moe," she replied, "you don't strike me as a shy boy."

"Aww," he was stirring his mashed potatoes and it was hard to tell if he was blushing. "I really do mean I can't tell much. It's my brain block."

"You see, when the Unspeakables sent me back in time to round out my education at Professor Wie's school, they put me under compulsive protection."

"That means that my brain processing has been suspended when it comes to revealing future events. It's illegal to contaminate the time-stream."

"So I can picture my life on the space station as if it were yesterday; but I can't talk about it much. Space Academy can be referred to only in general terms. If I get too specific my voice chokes up and I get a headache."

"Same thing happens to me when I think about my in-laws," said Mr. Crunch. Bob wasn't sure if this was a joke until Mrs. C. scolded him.

"Filbert! The children will think you mean it! Well," she went on, "there's nothing to prevent our friend the Elf from telling us some more about his family, is there? I think you mentioned that they traveled a lot. Isn't that right, dear?"

Bob could see that Derick's parents were just trying to put them at ease with this conversation; but he was real interested to find out this stuff too, if he could.

"Far away the foam-flecked sea meets the land of my kin," began the Elf. "Nestled in the bounteous hills of Havenhold, the flocks and fields, wondrous woods and perilous mountains have nourished my people for time out of mind."

He went on like that a good deal, and though Bob didn't learn very much from Elf's monologue, it was very comfortable to listen to. So much so that the next question caught him daydreaming and off guard.

"That's very interesting, thank you. Now Bob, why don't you tell all about where you come from?"

Bob looked at Mrs. Crunch with his best blank face. His mind was racing. Why couldn't *he* have a brain blocker, so that people wouldn't expect him to explain about the family he mostly didn't have?

"Now, Ivana," said Derick's dad, "I'm sure the children feel that they have been made to wait long enough for their ice cream and pie. I know I have. We can pick up this conversation another time, I think."

"Hurray!" shouted the kids.

As Bob ate his dessert he reflected on the fact that Mr. Crunch seemed to be a most perceptive gentleman.

All through the long ride back they sang songs and laughed as if they had been doing it together for years. From that time on the four boys grew in friendship.

In the weeks to come Bob would remember how much fun they had experienced that day; and the warm, family feeling, deep inside, that accompanied these memories.

The next day the same quartet joined up with Psyche and the True Believer to go to church. The boys all dressed up in their best secret identities.

Bob speculated on what would happen if the Crunch had not adopted an ordinary disguise but instead walked into church in all his blinking glory.

"Who knows," said True Believer, "you ought to try it someday, Cruncher. It might get some backsliders to really start praying with a will!"

In the Sundays to follow, these five students were generally the ones who went to church together.

You may find it hard to believe, but the television and radio programs of that time used to actually encourage people to go to church on Sunday.

They did this as a public service.

In the weeks and months to follow, they got to go to a Synagogue, a Mosque, a cathedral and a Baptist church where the singers could put Goldie to shame.

Bob enjoyed something different about each one of the experiences. In one house of God you were encouraged to clap hands, in another you didn't dare; but were instead bathed in polychromatic shafts of stained-glass light.

In one place they would tell great stories and in another they would sing them.

Bob figured that, while he may not have a home like the Crunch family, if God let him visit all of his houses, then that was kind of like having a home anyway. A family is that place where they always have to take you in.

Church made Bob very thoughtful. Bob knew that he could always look in a mirror to see if he was growing thinner or taller. But how does one discern spiritual growth? How does one put honesty up on the scale? How could Bob measure his capacity for compassion? Where was the next notch in his belt of justice and mercy? Was there more this week than last?

Church helped with these questions and gave Bob a sense of perspective. He was going need that and all of the positive feelings he could muster. This was because the Mean Blaster got out of his suspension the very next Monday morning - one day early.

"For good behavior..." said some, although no one could really believe it. There was a lot of speculation about what sort of revenge the Blaster would cook up for Bob, and how Bob would strike back. Bob couldn't help overhearing and in fact he found it hard to get away from.

Nova was telling Captain Eugene, "There's this cool looking metal-flake blue I'm using for my bicycle. You could spray some of it on your Jet Shield if you want."

"It's a Jet Shield, not a hot rod! Besides, where are you going to get the money for this paint job? Aren't you broke?"

"Sure," responded Nova Rex, "but I'll soon be rolling in it! The kids are all betting on the fight between the Blaster and Bounce-O. When M.B. meets B.B. I bet there won't be any fat left in the poor kid. He'll have shaken it all out in fear!"

"That's silly!" said the Captain, "Bob Blob has no fear, take it from me. Besides, he out weighs the blaster by – what - a half zillion pounds?"

"So what? How's he going to stand up to those mean, yellow blaster rays? Man, I wouldn't want to be on the receiving end of that!"

Just then all the girls walked by creating a sort of mid-day rush hour in the halls. Bunny Hop was talking and that meant lesser sounds had to wait their turn.

"Of course it's stupid I said but Bobbie can bounce just as high as Blaster can blast so they're really very evenly matched and the only question is when and where the fight will take place not if because things have gone too far between those two and one will just have to put the other in his place as I have been saying all along since the first day of school..."

She and her crowd were already fading away into the general bustle of changing classes. Bob had heard it all trailing along some distance behind.

"How come," he thought to himself, "girls always clique together?"

"Because they prefer their own company," said Psyche from right behind Bob with a suddenness that startled him.

"You gotta work harder on your cerebral etiquette! You enjoy making people jump a little too much."

"Yeah, yeah. You're absolutely right as rain. Did you notice how they all can't stand Bunny except when they're with her? Then, despite prior determination, they all fall in line and she's the leader."

"Psyche, what am I going to do? They all want me to fight Mean Blaster."

"Have you seen him yet since he finished suspension?"

"No," said Bob.

"Well buddy, looks like you'll have to fight him sooner or later."

"But I promised in front of the whole school that I wouldn't."

"Not the whole school," reminded Kid Psyche, "remember that the teachers and the Blaster weren't there. They don't know about that promise– I hope!"

"I suppose just this once you couldn't..."

"Now Bob! What happened to cerebral etiquette! Morality and rules don't count for much if you can turn them on when you like and off when it's inconvenient. You don't want me reading your secret mind so why would you want me to get into a tempting habit with Mean Blaster's secrets?"

"Yeah, yeah. You're absolutely right as rain."

"Ha!"

"But," said Bob, "what if you came across a thought of his that was just lying there kind of. Not a real secret, secret; just a hint of how I can get thru to him."

He continued, "I would like nothing better than to smoke the peace-pipe with Blaster. I'll never get anywhere making friends and becoming a super hero with him gumming up the works every time I turn around."

"Look," said the Kid, "I can read minds, right?"

"Right!"

"Wrong, Bob-O. Wrong, wrong, wrong!"

"But I thought..."

"It's always a question of interpretation. People don't think in whole sentences, you know. Or even in whole thoughts, sometimes."

"Huh."

"You make my point for me. Here's an example: can you tell me what you had for breakfast?"

"Sure."

"Don't bother," said Psyche. "I know what you had and how much and how much you enjoyed it. But do you remember the taste of the milk? Its coolness and texture? The way it felt coming off the aluminum glass when it gave you a temporary mustache? Can you picture its color, somewhere between that of paper and fresh snow? No! What you *do* remember is only a memory of a memory."

"We all do that," he went on, "It's because of capacity. We can only carry around just so much experience. No one can use it all. I'm not a real mind reader 'cause I don't want all that stuff in my head. Thank you, no!"

"Well," said Bob, "I've got to try to talk some sense into him. If that doesn't work…"

"I know what you are planning," said Psyche, "Most guys would just say, it's either him or me! Get him before he gets you! But you're going to try…" began Psyche.

"I'm going to surprise everybody, I think," said Bob.

"You're a good friend, Bob Blob," responded Kid Psyche.

Chapter V

Piece of Cake

"Please compose your features Mr. Blaster. We are talking about the administration of an ordinary homework assignment; not castor oil or capital punishment."

It was Wednesday afternoon and for almost three whole days the Mean Blaster had been avoiding any contact with Bob.

"He's scared," was the most popular explanation. But there was a difference of opinion regarding this question.

Was Bob avoiding the Blaster or was it the other way around? The truth was they were probably avoiding each other. But everyone knew that couldn't last. A showdown was coming.

Everyone was quite right for a change.

Mrs. White had just assigned the class the most amount of homework ever, and M.B. wasn't the only one who failed to hide his distaste.

"It merely feels like capital punishment!" thought Bob. The next moment he realized, to his horror, that he had said it out loud, and a little too loud.

The surrounding students caused a ripple of giggles to swell, from the last row all the way up front, there to lap and splash around the desk of Mrs. White.

"Don't worry, B.B." said the Blaster in unmistakably hostile tones, "if they ever do execute you no one will know the difference. You've been brain-dead for years!"

Bob's answer crashed back at once, "And if anyone ever did capital punishment on you, it would be a service to the rest of us!"

"He just threatened to kill me! You all heard it!" cried the Blaster in his most dramatic tones.

"Boys, Boys! I cannot believe what I'm hearing! Is this any way for students to behave? And you want to be super heroes! Howdy Doody and Clarabelle clown would make better heroes than you!"

"Please, Mrs. White," said Bob, "I never meant..."

"Don't listen to him Mrs. White! He got me in trouble once before when he went crying to a teacher! Now he's pulling the same stunt in front of the whole class!" he turned to face Bob. "You really are a big cry-baby, a regular Blubber-Boy!"

"Silence!" Mrs. White swept the room with a glare that could have glanced off a polar ice-cap. "Never have I heard of such a sorry display in a classroom!"

"In all my years of teaching..." she seemed to think better of that one and started again. "Has it ever occurred to either of you to try to settle your differences like gentlemen?"

"Oh, I'll settle him!" said the Blaster boy caressing his knuckles ominously.

Bob shrugged and gestured his mute helplessness.

"Very well, so be it. Class, the homework assignment must still be completed by all of you. But next week this class will be canceled."

There was something about the way she said that. No one felt it was safe to voice any approval of this turn of events. They all waited with a kind of dreadful curiosity for the inevitable explanation.

"Instead of class next week we will all assemble here. Mr. Blob and Mr. Blaster will settle their grudge in a fencing contest. The looser will make a full apology to the winner and both students will promise to put all differences aside."

"You are not required to like each other but I will have civility and respect from all my students. My decision as judge will be final. Is that understood?"

"Yes, Mrs. White," they all said.

"I want you students to learn that there is more to fencing than waving around sharp sticks. Fencing is a way of life with its own code. It is, or should be, an honorable way to settle differences."

"Yes, Mrs. White," they all said.

"Don't do that," she replied in a distracted way.

"Mr. Blaster, would you please tell the students the name of the class that Professor Wie teaches?"

"Deterrence," said the Blaster in a puzzled voice.

"No, the other class, please."

"Oh, it's called Beginners Marksmanship."

"Very good. Now can you tell us why our class is not called Beginners Fencing?"

"I don't know, Mrs. White."

"Ah, that's very, very good Mr. Blaster. I prefer the sound of truth in my class. Please remember that."

"The reason that this is not Beginners Fencing is because when you have studied for a half of a lifetime and trained until you have become the greatest swordsman in the world, only then will you have earned the right to call yourself a beginner."

She turned to Bob, "Mr. Blob, do you know who the greatest swordsman in France fears the most?"

"I suppose," answered Bob, "he fears the second greatest swordsman."

"Wrong! He fears the amateur, the man who has never touched a sword before. The second greatest swordsman can be counted on for certain moves and responses. But the novice does the unexpected. This is what makes him most feared."

She drilled a look at him, "do the unexpected, Mr. Blob. Surprise your opponent and you will put him out of reckoning. Practice the unexpected, Mr. Blob."

As the bell rang Bob thought to himself, "What in the world is she trying to tell me?"

At supper that night, only Psyche, Elf, Moe, True Believer and The Crunch sat anywhere near Bob's table.

"Don't you get it?" asked Moe, "You have the pox, the plague, the curse of the mummy. Nobody wants the Blaster to think they're helping you."

"I'm not so sure," said Psyche. Sure enough, the Wisp and Bunny came over to sit next to Bob. "Bobby," said Ariel, "You promised you wouldn't fight with Blaster. I'm disappointed in you Bobby boy."

Before Bob could respond to that, however, Bunny Hop voiced her opinion and they all had to wait for the charm to wind down before the conversation could continue.

"It's not really a fight," she said, "it's more like a contest or game where the teacher keeps score and sees that certain people don't get a chance to cheat or anything not that he could get away with it with all of us watching as witnesses and I told the Absolute Locus he had to stay especially on his guard because he might have to settle things with a photo finish like he did when you-know-who got suspended and one can always hope it will be for good this time."

"Wisp," said Bob, (because he liked her, he didn't dare call her Ariel) "don't be disappointed in me, because it wasn't my idea. How could I tell Mrs. White that I didn't think fencing was a good way to solve arguments after all she said?"

"Just tell her you promised."

"He can't do that!" said Moe du Jur, "it's against the code to back out now. A Space Cadet never backs out. He goes in no matter what the odds!"

"I'm sorry Ariel," said Bob, forgetting himself and using her name instead of her title, "my hands are tied."

"Most people," said Ariel, "are bound by their word; not tied up with some silly code!"

"Aww," the Crunch broke in, "why don't you go sit by the Blaster's table and cheer-lead for him."

"Maybe we will! Come on, Bunny. Let's go before they decide to pick a fight with us. I'm sure there's something about *that* in the code, too!"

"Bye, bye, boys," said Bunny Hop.

"Bye, bye!" they found themselves answering much to their chagrin.

Bob had a whole week to get ready but he also knew that he had a tendency to put things off when they were distasteful to him. "Where is the humor in this situation?" he wrote in his secret book. No answer seemed forthcoming.

He needed to get away and think. But even in the library he found that he couldn't completely escape to find that isolation inspiration required, and to which genius generally gravitated.

"I wish my skin looked as fair and radiant as the Elf's," Bob heard the voice of Verity, the Pink Liberator. A whole gaggle of girls (all five) were whispering and giggling at the next table.

Bob considered moving but he found himself drawn to listening with a feeling of disinterested fascination.

"I asked him and he told me you have to change your diet. How, I said, and he said that he eats these elf biscuits." The girls chuckled.

"No!"

"Yes! And these are enchanted biscuits made with real magic."

"Enchanted biscuits!" the girls tittered while Bob fumed. Why couldn't they go exchange recipes somewhere else?

"You can eat all you want and there's always some left over."

"That's weird!"

"Yes, the only problem is: now he's addicted to the stuff and has to eat some with every meal."

Bob had forgotten that when the Elf had visited with him at the Chrunch's house, he saw the Elf munching something taken from a leather purse attached to his belt. He never gave it a second thought at the time.

"How awful, being addicted to food."

"Yeah, just like Blubber-Boy."

"Bobby's not addicted any more than you are or anyone else," said a voice that sounded like Ariel's.

"He just has a large capacity. And his name is Bounce-O, not Blubber-Boy. How would you like to be called a name like that?"

"Oh ho! Getting all 'wispfull' for the big guy now, are we?"

"Not necessarily..." there were more giggles. "It's just that everyone's taking sides and I'm getting sick of it."

Bob tried to scrunch down behind his book (which was a little like hiding a locomotive behind a hand-car) as Ariel walked away from the chortles and cackles that pursued her.

"Bobby," she said with some surprise, "I didn't know you were hiding back there listening."

"I didn't mean to eavesdrop," said Bob.

"That's your trouble, Bobby boy. You never mean to anything."

She poked a finger at him, "I thought you were a good guy until this fight or contest or what ever it's supposed to be. It doesn't matter what you mean by things! You are going ahead to fight him anyway just to get even. Don't you know that revenge is for the bad guys, you big lug?"

"I am not a bad guy!" protested Bob.

"That's what Lex Luther said just before he pulled out the Kryptonite. All the bad guys are heroes to themselves. Genghis Kahn was just trying to make a living."

"Who you think you are," she concluded, "isn't necessarily who you really are."

As she walked away Bob found himself writing this down in his notebook. He also wrote the one about how revenge is for bad guys.

The days went by quickly now. The two contestants made a point of not noticing one another. The code indicated that this, while not strictly obligatory, was good form.

And Bob was having trouble practicing his swordplay. The best swordsman among the students by far was the Swashbuckle boy. But he had gone over wholly into the Mean Blaster camp.

Elf and Moe were taking turns coaching Bob but it seemed like a hopeless cause.

"You are forbidden to bounce and the Blaster is faster," said the Elf. "You may be stronger than he, but that will only aid your defense.

Eventually he must get through your guard. Your only hope lies in his mind. You must become master of his thoughts."

"What do you mean?" said Bob.

"Fear, distraction, yes and humiliation; these are the arrows in your quiver."

"You mean if I can't scare him, I have to distract him or make everybody laugh at him again. Won't that just get him angrier?"

"You must fan the flames of his fury. Answer each blow with a jest. When he gives way, press him the more!"

"But it might be hard thinking and talking and fighting all at the same time."

"Thus is the battle ever won. Brain and sinew are brothers who fight better together."

"What you say makes sense, Elf, my friend. I will follow your advice."

"Then victory is ours!" said the Elf.

"Victory!" cried Bob. But he thought privately, "I'm going to loose."

With all the speed of an approaching dental appointment Wednesday arrived. Although Bob had decided on his strategy a week before, he was far from sure about the outcome. Even with all the teachers there, anything could happen.

Everything that day conspired to increase Bob's sense of choking anticipation. He wasn't exactly afraid, he thought, but he was very nervous. The kids didn't help matters with half of them giving encouraging advice (go for the knee-caps!) and half of them describing with relish his impending doom.

Twelve-noon arrived and Bob found he had no appetite. He merely ate the same portion of food everyone else was eating, promising himself that he would make up for it at supper.

At twelve-thirty he made his way over to the practice room where the students were already assembling. There was a kind of roped off platform with chairs on either side, reminding Bob of the boxing matches he had seen on television.

Lester, the Gatekeeper and Janitor for the school, was in the back, fiddling with the lights and pretending to work.

The teachers all sat up front behind a table that had been set up for the occasion. Dr. Unknown was swinging a sword that wasn't there, to illustrate some fine point or other, for Mr. Mann.

Mrs. White had put on a referee's shirt and was inspecting the swords and equipment to be used.

The Mean Blaster was sitting in his corner with Morpho-Lad and Swashbuckle on stools next to him. They were laughing and didn't seem to have a care in the world. Bob, of course, didn't feel nearly so confident.

Morpho kept flickering in and out of sight and was told, "Keep your insignia turned on when you do that! We keep bumping into you!" This was a reference to the large letter "M" which just about constituted his entire costume when he was visible.

Morpho wasn't the only one who was excited. Nova Rex was flickering like a neon light in the last stages of serviceability.

Lil' Socko and the Purp were hopping around each other in a playful dance, and Goldie was singing excerpts from *Der Fliegende Holländer* as a kind of warm up act.

Bob knew that there would be a point system for keeping score and a time limit but he had decided not to worry about all that. He was not yet good enough to be concerned with these finer details. He had decided to leave them out of his strategy as much as he could.

Professor Wie signaled for quiet and came forward to speak. You could have heard the third echo of a pin drop.

"You all know why we are here. Mr. Blaster and Mr. Blob have had a disagreement which could grow into something very nasty if left unaddressed."

Bob wondered briefly if the Professor had really meant to say their names in alphabetical order, or if it was just a coincidence.

"The outcome of this contest will put all hostilities to rest. These two students are encouraged to become friends. After all, they both aspire to the common goal of our school: heroism. More specifically, super heroism. They are, and we all are, called to a higher expectation of goodness."

"If close friendship proves impractical for the two of them, and I say impractical; for such friendship can never be impossible, then they both agree by these proceedings to abide by the decision of the judge in mutual tolerance and forbearance."

"From this day on, they will be called upon to exercise a formal politeness that will permit of no recrimination, expression of hostility or desire for revenge. The desire for revenge is the surest sign of villainy."

Bob wondered if Professor Wie had been talking to Ariel. Suddenly, there was no time for any more wondering. He had been given his foil and Mrs. White indicated that Bob should proceed to the corner on stage right.

"Both of the contestants have promised not to use their super powers until the concluding whistle blows. Should either of the contestants fail to comply with this restriction, Doctor Unknown assures me that he has the means to end the contest immediately." That elicited a knowing laugh from the spectators. At her signal the two boys walked to the center to shake hands. The whistle sounded in Bob's ears along with the excited gabble of the students.

"Here goes," he thought. Bob came out swinging frantically. He was a mad Dervish, and a blurring propeller. He was Zorro swatting flies. He was the pendulum come unhitched from the pit. Curlicues crafted cursive correspondence unreadable in the air before the Blaster.

His opponent was easily keeping out of the way. Bob panted and sweated. His efforts distilled and condensed and flew dripping off his nose. His teeth were locked and his eyes looked twice their normal size. Now he was stamping and lunging and starting to gasp for air.

The actual contact of blades was infrequent. Bob was swinging far too furiously for very much to happen that might be called authentic fencing.

"Ha! Arrrg! Ooft! Ugh!" Bob was shouting as he slashed. He was doing appalling hurts to a dread army of ghostly frustrations and misunderstandings. "Take that!" he shouted to his secret fear. "Ah, you would, would you? Bologna!"

Now it was the Blaster's turn for his eyes to get big. Was his foe going nuts? Did the big boy finally slip a gear in his brain box? Icy fear began to nibble at the Blaster's heart. He really didn't know what wild move Bob was going to make next.

M.B. could hear his own voice in his memory, "Don't ever cross him when he has that hungry look in his eye." Bob's eyes were looking positively manic by this time.

Suddenly Bob ran at the Blaster with his sword upraised as if it were an ax!

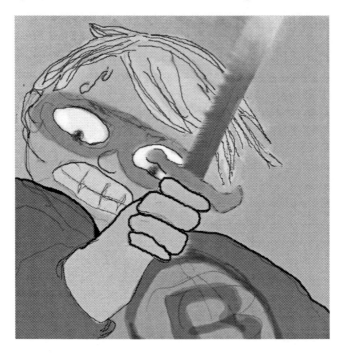

"Yi, Yi, Yi, Yaaaaaaa!" Bob was screaming as if all his emotions were being torn from him. It was worse than a war cry and it made the Blaster want to stop his ears. But before anything else could happen, the foil flew from the grasp of the Beneficent Bounce-O. They all watched as the weapon slid across the floor and skidded to a stop at the Blaster's feet. The world paused one quarter second for profound silence.

"I surrender, I yield," Bob gasped. There was clapping and shouts of, "Hurray for the Blaster! Hip! Hip! Hurray!" Mrs. White was blowing her whistle. The students quieted down again with some effort.

"The contest," she said, "is over. By my decision I declare that the winner is the Mean Blaster." There was more clapping. "The two contestants will shake hands."

Bob moved to the front. He felt that he was called upon to say something.

"The competition between the Blaster and me is over. And I mean that it's over for good. Some day I hope to be as good a swordsman as he is. But he is a better man than I am. It is my firm intention to never say anything against him again. The Mean Blaster has nothing to fear from me. Our fight is done."

He turned to face the Blaster boy and said, "I regret the friendship we never enjoyed and I apologize to you, humbly, and ask for your handshake in token of forgiveness, for all the bad things I said about you."

Bob held out his hand. The Blaster approached him and said, "I'll say this for you, Bounce-O, when it comes to having to do something you don't like, you sure do it up right. Let no one ever say that the Mean Blaster was an ungracious winner. Shake hands, kid."

It was a solemn moment when these two shook hands. Then the Blaster turned to the students, "...and let it never be said that Mr. Blob is a poor looser!"

"Yaaaay!" The students cheered wildly and stamped their feet with happy abandon as the Blaster held up Bob's hand over his head. As Bob broke into a wide grin, and saw that it was answered by the Blaster's smile, he felt like anything but a looser.

It was pretty much taken for granted that study hall would be canceled that afternoon and within a few minutes Professor Wie made it official. Bob made his way through the crowd to the exit.

He could already see Psyche rounding up Elf, Moe and the Crunch. He followed them out to the deserted stands by the playing field.

Soon Bob saw that the Cruncher had brought along his school bag, and from it he produced five bottles of pop and a big bag of potato chips.

"The runner-up consolation banquet will now commence," he announced.

"Yeah, this was going to be a victory party," said Psyche, but we can celebrate your brave effort instead."

"Aye," said Elf, "Never did I see sword or blade wielded with a better will! But will you not tell us how it happened that you did not tease and jest with the enemy, as we all expected you to do?"

"Sure," said Bob, "Now that it's all over with, I can talk about it. But you must all keep what I am about to tell you a secret, okay?"

"Okay."

"Psyche, you knew some of what I had in mind, but I didn't even dare to whisper it out loud to anyone. Because if the Blaster ever found out; then it wouldn't work and my plan would be spoiled."

"When Mrs. White set up this contest a week ago, I didn't have a clue what I was going to do. All my thoughts were bent on somehow defeating Blaster. But how? Could I get good enough in time? Now, M.B. isn't as good a swordsman as Swashbuckle; but he is pretty good. And he had Swashbuckle helping to train him."

"If only I could think of some strategy or trick that would insure victory. I had all of you to help me, but back then, last Wednesday, I was very anxious."

"So that night I had a dream. I dreamed that I was the owner of a hotel. Outside my hotel there was a billboard. LOWEST RATES IN TOWN, it said. I was admiring it, but then I saw that the Mean Blaster had snuck in and changed it to read, LOWEST RATED IN TOWN. But after he did this he went away. That's just like him I thought: very clever and very efficient. He changed the 'S' to a 'D'. All you have to do is change one little thing."

"I woke up with that thought echoing over and over. 'Change one little thing.' I remember thinking how profound it was. Then my memory of the dream changed and I heard the phrase: 'Change one little thing and *he'll go* away.' What did that mean?"

"And I woke up thinking, 'that's the key! If I'm not a threat there's no contest!' You see, I thought that maybe if I stopped being a threat to him, a constant target for him to shoot at, maybe he would stop bothering me."

"I was determined to do the unexpected, as Mrs. White suggested. I figured out how to end the contest so that the Blaster wouldn't think of me as a threat anymore. And in my little speech at the end I made sure to tell him: 'No contest. I'm not competing anymore. I won't hurt you.' I even said it more than once so there'd be no mistake."

"I never wanted to even have to deal with him at all. But my dream helped me to realize that *he* didn't know how I felt. It took his victory in this big contest to drive home the message."

Psyche said, "So that was your plan! Loose on purpose! Brilliant! Boy, you ought to become a psychologist!"

"Not me," said Bob, "that sounds more like something you would do."

The Elf raised his bottle as if in salute and said:

Oft it is said round the campfire red
As the bard invokes the Muse,
The victory today may hasten away

But sometimes to win is to loose

Nobody knew if he had made that up on the spot, but it was felt that to ask him would spoil it somehow.

It was at about this time that the others started to show up. First came Ariel, congratulating her "Bobby boy" for good sportsmanship, as if she had never been mad at him.

Next came those students who had at least been neutral when everyone was taking sides. These included Bunny, Silver Baron, True Believer, Willow-wand, Captain Eugene, Locus and Lil' Socko.

It seemed to be the case that everybody knew of the party and had raided their hoards of goodies and care packages.

Last of all the Mean Blaster himself showed up with the rest of the students in his wake.

"So you guys are having a party, too?" he asked, "We had the same idea. Then someone figured out where everybody else had to be, so we decided to merge our merrymaking."

"Great!" Bob waved, "Come on in, the water's fine!"

The Pink Liberator had even baked a victory cake and it was big enough for everyone (Bob had long ago learned how to keep his serious meals separate from social occasions. His real feasting would take place after everyone else had gone to bed. In the meantime, he ate what the others did, just to keep them company).

As they munched on their cake, someone asked the Blaster if he had been worried, before or during the match, about how the fight was likely to turn out.

"Nope. It turned out pretty much the way I expected."

Then he took a huge bite.

"Piece of cake!" he said.

Chapter VI

Crumbs of Comfort

As the weeks processed down the aisle that was Bob's life, he felt things were finally coming to a point where he could feel good about it all. His problem with the Mean Blaster seemed solved and although they never became close friends, there was now a mutual understanding.

The topic of how to spend summer vacation came up more frequently now that the month of May was approaching. There were several possibilities open to Bob.

"Why don't you come over and spend some time with our family?" said the Cruncher, "I could talk my folks into it easily because they really like you."

"And besides, my uncle Speedball is coming for a visit. My parents say that he's eccentric but we all know he's really crazy. You haven't lived, Bobby boy, until you've gone fishing with my crazy uncle. Even if we don't catch anything (and we usually do) we don't care 'cause it's so much fun."

"Sounds great!' said Bob.

"So I can tell them you're coming?"

"I still have to find out if I can," said Bob.

This was true enough. Professor Wie was acting *in loco parentis* as long as Bob was in school. Bob knew why he had been sent to super hero school and it wasn't just because of his abilities. He could tell from little hints and snatches of overheard conversation: his parents didn't want him around.

Bob tried not to think about this most times; but he knew. There was not much he could do about it. He realized that Tiffany and Julio no longer wanted to be his parents (if they ever really did in the first place). They had enrolled him with the thought that after graduation, young Bob could make his own way in the world.

Mrs. White had talked about the subject with him one day after General Science. "Mr. Blob, you will meet me in the Guidance Office after

70

class," she said. "Now what did I do?" Bob asked himself. But it wasn't like that at all.

"Please sit down, Robert," she said, and then she handed him a super-large bowl of ice cream! "I trust that chocolate mint is satisfactory?"

"Huh? Sure! I mean, gee, thanks, Mrs. White!"

"Bob, I asked you to come here because we need to talk about your plans for the following year. Normally, when I meet with a student we talk about the courses and electives needed for graduation. Then we set up a schedule. This includes reading and any remedial work that may be needed over the summer."

"I must say I am pleased with your work and your conduct in general this past year."

"Thank you, Mrs. White."

"I am especially gratified to see that you have successfully buried the hatchet with Mr. Blaster. Both of you have demonstrated a valuable lesson to the whole school. It can not have been easy for either of you and I want you to know that I am grateful."

Bob didn't know what to say to that; so he offered what so often turns out to be the best thing to say in situations like that. A simple "Thank you," was all he said.

"Robert, you know that most of the students are going to stay with their families for summer vacation." She looked at Bob with an understanding smile and said very gently, "And you know that you will not."

"I know," Bob was looking into the depths of his ice cream.

His mind he seemed to wander back several months in time. He could hear snatches of conversation through his bedroom door as if he was still living with Julio and Tiffany.

"He eats enough for ten people. That can't be right."

"Well, don't expect me to take him to see the doctor again because he'll only try another diet that won't work."

"Diets aren't the only thing that don't work around here!"

"He needs new clothes again."

"What does he do, eat them?"

"No, I put a stop to that. I'm teaching him to sew but it's hard to find clothes that fit. He keeps ripping his pants. I told him he must never bend or sit down again."

"I caught him bouncing the other day. The neighbors are starting to talk."

"Where are we going to get the money to feed him?"

"We can't put him to work; he's too young and they have laws against child labor."

"We tried paper delivery; mowing lawns; lemonade stands and professional wrestling."

"Yeah, I'll admit that was a good idea until he got unmasked."

"He still eats more than he can earn."

"Well, one of the doctors gave me a brochure. It's a school for special children. You pay a flat fee and they take him off your hands for four years."

"A lot can happen in four years. Maybe he'll be self sufficient by that time."

"It says here he gets an education and *they* get to feed him!"

"Let me see that..."

"You do have several possibilities open to you." The voice of Mrs. White was speaking again and it brought Bob back to the present with a start.

"We keep the school functioning with a limited staff in the summer, for the benefit of the teachers who tend to come and go, on and off campus, all summer long; and for the occasional situation like yours."

"If you wish, we could have you help Mr. Lester keep the grounds during the week, and you would occasionally be asked to help out in the kitchen."

She paused for a moment, "There is another option open to you. A scholarship grant has become available and you could join Professor Wie and me, along with two other students, for a trip to Europe. We will visit England, France and Germany on a recruiting tour for the school."

"Gosh," said Bob.

"Yes, the talents this school is devoted to cultivating are rare, and the Professor tries to find new student candidates each year."

"You don't have to decide right now, Mr. Blob. Think about it and we can meet next week at this time."

"I will," said Bob.

"Bob, why don't you come and visit with me?" said Moe du Jur when Bob told him about his impending decision. "We have room on the station and we can visit the Academy and you can learn all about the future."

"But won't that mean I'd have to get a Brain Blocker like yours to keep from spilling the beans?"

"Sure, but it doesn't hurt; and you would have the experience to keep in your memory."

Privately, Bob wasn't so sure about the painlessness of it all. He trusted Moe but he thought it would be real hard to keep a whole summer as classified material that he couldn't share with anyone else.

"I don't know how I'd feel: not being able to talk about my vacation with anyone for the rest of my life."

"It wouldn't be like that," said Moe. "You could always talk about it with me."

"Oh, yeah," said Bob. Well, can I have a week to sleep on it?"

"Oh, sure. Take two weeks if you want. These arrangements can be made at the last minute, believe me."

There was something about the way he said that.

"I'll get back to you," said Bob.

"Hark!" it was a few days later and the Elf had cornered Bob after supper. "Can you not hear it?"

"What are you going on about now?" said Bob with mock impatience.

"The birds, the trees and the majestic mountains of Havenhold are calling to me. Their voices wax louder as the spring matures into summer. Can you not hear them? The laughter and the songs beckon. The sound of children dancing in the streets bids all nature to join in the eternal celebration of renewal."

"All I can hear is my stomach burping."

"It is no jest, my friend," said Elf, "come away with me and we shall have wondrous fun before the autumn leaves blush and we must return to lessons and books."

"How would we get to Elf country," asked Bob.

"Oh, there is a magic that can carry us hence in the flicker of a thought. I have been given an incantation that has strong roots in the stuff of existence. Ancient is that lore."

"Uh, huh," interrupted Bob, "let me think it over and I'll let you know by Thursday.

"Thursday shall be the day that decides our course, then. I will await your decision."

Bob realized that he could not do everything he wanted to that summer. Some of his friends would be inevitably disappointed with his choice. As he wrote in his secret book, he thought of a way to let the others down easy. He would not say "no" to anyone. Instead he would postpone.

"Next year I can visit with Moe and his family. The year after, 1959 will be the year of the Elf, and we can quest together for a whole summer. The year after that, he would graduate class of 1960. In the summer, Psyche can take me to the Inexplicable Bros. Circus. His dad is part owner and I can work the carnie as the Fat Boy who guesses your weight."

1961 (that year had a real futuristic sound to it) would be his debut as a fully graduated super hero. Maybe he would take that summer off and go to Europe with Professor Wie.

By process of elimination Bob made his decision and when it came time to tell Mrs. White he had no doubts. "I am thankful for all the opportunities that the school offers me. I don't think I am ready to travel overseas, and I don't feel cut out to be a gardener or landscaper. I'm pretty sure Mr. Lester would find that I was more work for him instead of more help."

"So with the school's permission I would like to accept the invitation to stay with the Crunch family this summer."

"That will be fine, Robert. You have both the sanction and the encouragement of the school. I've known Filbert and Ivana for a long time, and you will not find a better family than the Crunch's. I know they will take good care of you."

"But," she said, "you may find yourself in the position of venturing out into society with the children. You may even chance to find yourself unsupervised and alone on occasion. Please remember that more than your personal honor, or even the honor of the school, is at stake in such a case."

"I will, Mrs. White."

"No, now Bob, I want you to think about this. Do you know why we keep the school's existence a secret?"

"Sure! It's because ordinary people would freak-out if they suspected super heroes were for real."

"Purged of your appalling use of slang, your statement is essentially correct," she said, "people would indeed *freak-out* as you say."

She went on, "Super hero activity is kept very secret, so much so that most everyone thinks it's purely fictional, the stuff of comic books."

"This is intended for the good of all involved. The super heroes are not to be tempted to pride; or the idea that they can just take over."

"It's also a good idea for those who have no super powers, for they would be subject to a far greater temptation."

"I can't imagine what that could be," said Bob.

"In a word, it is dependence, Mr. Blob. Dependence would be the great temptation for the non-empowered. Can you imagine what it would be like if we were revealed to the world?"

"Baseball, football season, and the Olympics are all canceled, for starters. Why bother to compete when the Wonderful Wisp can run faster and the Beneficent Bounce-O can bounce higher?"

"No one will try to climb mountains. Forget about Sputnik and Outer Space. Moe's already been there. IBM will close its doors when they get a load of the Crunch's computer."

"No one will bother to fight fires and the police will all find other jobs. Who needs it? Vortex is on the job, and the Mean Blaster can catch more crooks in one day than J. Edgar Hoover could in ten years."

"Politicians stop making speeches and Congress adjourns for the last time. Some would call this desirable. But think: people will loose all initiative to fight for what is right. They will instead call upon Locus to freeze world events so that just laws can be enforced."

"Can he do that?" asked Bob, somewhat taken aback.

"No. But they won't believe it. They will come after you with demands for a perfect world. And when you can't deliver, there will be war."

"Why strive for excellence when super heroes have achieved it already? Why worry about getting yourself out of trouble, when someone will do it for you; better than you could ever hope to do it yourself?"

Why try to improve and work for justice and be good when "gods" already walk the earth? It will mean the end of civilization when people believe that all their goals and dreams have been accomplished."

"But," said Bob in a frightened voice, "but super heroes aren't gods. I mean we believe in God, too. We strive to get better and obey a higher good."

"True," said Mrs. White, "but do you think that will keep the strong from crumbling under the weight of our achievements? Will it keep the average man from realizing he can never be average again, only pitiably sub-average? And I tell you, the weak will worship us and the weak of our number will become false gods. It must never happen!"

"It won't Mrs. White! We won't let it!"

"Good boy, Robert. That's what I wanted to hear.

"Well, that's settled," thought Bob as he made his way from the Guidance Office. The first thing he did was to look up everyone who had invited him (except the Crunch); to tell them he wouldn't be coming that year. Only after he explained each postponement did he seek out the Cruncher.

"Hey, Crunch! I can come!"

"Hot zig-a-dee! Boy are we ever going to have a time!"

"You bet! A super-duper time!" said Bob, who thought that sometimes a fellow needs to talk in slang, because ordinary words just don't have enough juice in them.

The final tests were all given; the final projects and assignments were completed. The academic year was rapidly becoming, as far as the students were concerned, academic. The last day of school was really only a half-day. The teachers insisted on this tradition because keeping the vacation intoxicated students in line for a full day was unthinkable.

Classroom discipline had deteriorated in proportion to the approach of summer. Doctor Unknown had run out of his sleep gas some few days ago and was hoping that the kids wouldn't notice.

They were all assembled in the hall where everyone had been orientated almost nine months ago. Professor Wie was making a "Be Safe This Summer" speech that even he knew wouldn't be heeded. Suddenly it was over and the irrepressible, would-be super heroes stampeded from the school building into the great outdoors of summer.

Captain Eugene and Blaster were neck and neck with the Wisp a close third. "He always looks like he's going to fall off of that thing," said Psyche. He was referring to the receding jet shield and its pilot who, indeed, was pumping his arms as if he had just completed a year of hummingbird flight academy instead of super hero school.

"Well, we may as well get this over with," said Bob, and he opened the ocher colored envelope and extracted the dread, blue card.

Professor Wie's School for Gifted Children
REPORT CARD for the Year 1957
First Year Student: Robert R.M. Blob (Beneficent Bounce-O, Team Blue)

SUBJECT	GRADE	TEACHER	COMMENTS
DEDUCTION	A	DR. UNKNOWN	EXCELLENT
SPECIAL POWERS	B	DR. UNKNOWN	GOOD WORK
PHILOSOPHY	B	MR. MANN	COULD BE BETTER
SOCIOLOGY	B	MR. MANN	MORE READING NEEDED
BEGINNERS			
MARKSMANSHIP	B	PROF. WIE	STUDENT IMPROVED
GENERAL SCIENCE	A	MRS. WHITE	KEEP UP THE GOOD WORK
FENCING	C	MRS. WHITE	PRACTICE BASICS!
DETERRENCE	A	PROF. WIE	STUDENT HAS A NATURAL APTITUDE
LOGIC	B+	MR. MANN	A BIT MORE STUDY EARNS AN "A"
GREENBELT	A	DR. UNKNOWN	AN ADEQUATE ACHIEVMENT
DEPORTMENT	C+	STAFF	NICE RECOVERY

STUDENT IS READY FOR YEAR II

"It could be worse," said Psyche who was taking turns peeking over Bob's shoulder along with Elf, Moe and Crunch.

"Yeah," said Moe, "I got a 'C' in Deterrence and I had to work like a Martian to do it!"

"Okay," said Psyche, "I guess this is it. I won't be seeing you guys for three months but I have a way we can keep in touch." He handed each of them a small, smooth marble. Each stone was perfectly spherical, highly polished and beautiful to look at; with swirling colors of umber and caramel, or cinnamon and crimson, or violet and heliotrope, or blue and chartreuse.

"This," he said, "is a reflection marble. Each one has been imprinted with psychic vibrations. Keep it with you all the time and at 10:00 each night I'll send out a thought blanket. I can only do it for about 30 seconds but if there's a real need, concentrate on your mental image of me and I can make full contact."

"Gee wiz!"

"Psyche, Oh boy!"

"Golly!"

"Swell!" came the awed responses.

Psyche explained that it was a good idea to have a set time for contact. While he had the ability to send a thought burst to any of them when he felt like it, he believed it was better not to risk a distracting call while the receiver was perhaps fielding a baseball!

It is possible that Moe's idea was a bit more practical. "Let's exchange phone numbers," he suggested. No one commented on the fact that a telephone line wasn't likely to extend through the future all the way up to Moe's space station. It was enough for them to realize that he had some advanced technological means to tap into their phones when needed. The details would be top-secret (and probably incomprehensible) anyway. May as well take the Elf's attitude Bob thought: "I'll think of it as magic and let it go at that."

"Good by!"

"Fare you well!"

"Stay out of trouble!"

"Look who's talking!"

"Take care of yourselves!"

Bob and the Cruncher got into the Impervo-car. Bob only took along one large suitcase of a week's worth of clothing and snacks. The only book he intended to open was his secret journal.

The whole Crunch family was packed into the car. "We're going to pick up Uncle Speedball from the airport," explained Mrs. Crunch. Bob had never seen the family in their secret identity disguises before (although he did see them all unmasked at that dinner a few months ago).

They looked like a typical family (except for Derick who would wait with Bob in the car since both boys still wore their super uniforms). To be sure, the car itself elicited more than a few glances, but it was easy to dismiss it as a new kind of armored car for delivering payrolls or something.

Soon Mr. Speedball took his place in the back seat. It was fortunate that the car's interior was much larger than it looked. Even so, everyone was a bit crowded. Georgette was scrunched between her dad and Bob in the front seat. Mrs. Crunch, Patty, Derick and Mr. Speedball were packed into the back.

Uncle Speedball looked like a trim, athletic man in his thirties. His short "flat-top" haircut (the popular style was named after a comic strip villain, Bob remembered) crowned a lean, tan face with prominent cheekbones and deep blue eyes. Bob was waiting to see him show any signs of being crazy. He didn't have to wait long.

"Violins are my favorite color," he said.

"Filbert, dear," said Mrs. Crunch, "turn on the radio for uncle Speedball."

"Yep," Speedball continued, "the woodwinds can articulate delicate shades and the brass and percussion can rock you out of your seat, but only the strings can pizzicato. Violins can do the work of percussion and melody at the same time. They do it all. That's why they're my favorite tonal color in the whole orchestra."

When he heard that explanation, Bob thought Mr. Speedball's initial statement made sense. Maybe his craziness had to do with his automatic assumption that everyone would know what he was talking about. He could be crazy like Einstein: brilliant but misunderstood so often that it seemed like absentmindedness; or just weirdness. That's why such people are called "peerless", Bob reflected, because genius gets awfully lonely at the top.

Bob learned that Captain Speedball (to give him his pro-name) was Filbert's brother. Years ago Mr. Crunch had changed his last name as a business move. But Mr. Speedball kept his family name as his secret identity. His full name was William David Shoemacher or Bill D. as he was more often called.

"It will be a pleasure to unpack and change," he said. And then he addressed Bob, "You might just serve if you live up to what Derick has told me."

Bob briefly wondered if Mr. S. wanted him to help with the luggage.

"Uncle Speedball is always looking out for a side-kick to help him," Mr. Crunch explained, "I told him you had a year to go before the position could even be considered."

When they arrived at the Crunch family secret headquarters, Captain Speedball got into his super hero uniform right away. "Ah, it's great to be back in harness again," he said, and Bob was startled to realize that he wasn't speaking figuratively.

The Captain was indeed wearing an elaborate harness. Two large, bronze plates were attached, one on each side, to his legs, ankles and hips (Bob would have bet that these disks were made out of the mysterious metal, M46; since they seemed very light yet strong and since Mr. S. was, after all, a family member).

His colors were rust, burnt orange and the kind of green one finds on an old penny. Many straps or belts circled his torso and they seemed to be the connecting points for the two wheels. On his back was fastened a rounded canister with many vents and controls. This was his power source.

The wheels were not designed to spin in contact with the ground as Bob half expected. Instead they drove Speedball's legs like mechanical pistons at ever faster speeds. He could outrun most cars, turn on a dime and still climb steps.

"The chase after crime has commenced!" he announced, "The pursuit of perfidy will progress and the race for the right is ratified by CAPTAIN SPEEDBALL!"

Everyone who heard those stirring sentiments broke into applause. Bob couldn't wait to see his new hero in action.

Bob learned that the Captain had hip gyros and a knee axis and ankle grooves that revolved in an interlocking complex pattern to make his feet go fast.

"Why don't you just let the wheels spin on the ground at high speed?" Bob asked.

"Because then I would be reduced to a mere Bicycle Boy. I can go faster and turn more accurately with this rig. I'd like to explain the science behind the wondrous workings of my costume but even the kids who like to read about me in the comics skip that part. So if you ever need help falling asleep at night give me a call and I'll tell you all about my origin story."

"That'd be swell," said Bob.

"Hey, I was just kidding you kid," Speedball said in an alarmed voice. "If I ever had to actually explain myself I'd probably wake up sane and that would drive me nuts. Look, I'll see you get the comic book, okay?"

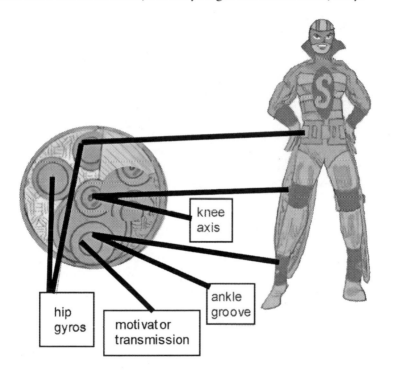

knee
axis

hip
gyros

motivator
transmission

ankle
groove

It was okay with Bob as was almost everything that he experienced that summer.

That night, Bob remembered what Psyche told him and at five minutes to ten he cleared his mind of as many thoughts as he could. They were in Derick's bedroom. Bob sat back to back with his host. It was felt that there would be less chance of distraction or psychic interference if the boys didn't look at each other.

They both held their reflection marbles in their right fists. Bob's thoughts began to go all dreamy and it was a surprise to him when he began to sense the presence of others in the room. He didn't hear voices or words, but afterwards recalled the conversation as if he had.

"Hey! This thing is really working!"

"Not so hard, we can hear you."

"This is a surpassing enchantment, my friends. Never did I understand until today that my friend, Psyche, is a wizard to equal any mage of
legend."

"I can sense what you're thinking and feeling!"

"Me too! And I know we're really alone and it's all quiet but it's like
we're all back in the dorm after lights out; and we're having a conversation
without words."

"This is very, very weird!"

"Yeah? Well, it's a psychic accomplishment not a telephone party line.
We can't keep this up for more than a few more seconds."

"Wow."

"Sorry, Psyche."

"That's okay. You guys doin' alright?"

"Sure!"

"Swell!"

"Aye!"

"You bet!"

"Well, take it easy until tomorrow. We'll do this again at the same time."

"Okay!

"Bye!"

"We'll be thinking of you!"

"Obviously," Psyche's droll reply died away and the psychic connection broke contact as if hanging up on a wrong number.

The experience gave Derick and Bob something to talk about long into the night.

A few days later they did go fishing with Uncle Speedball and Mr. Crunch. Mrs. Crunch preferred to stay home that day so as not to miss her radio soap opera.

They all went in secret identities and Bob and Derick got to row their own boat. The two girls also came along and they were in another boat with their father and Uncle Speedball.

"Fishing is like kite flying," declared Speedball. "Put a line out there and see what happens. Maybe there's a tangle or a bad break and you get all frustrated. Maybe you get a tug and something fun will happen. And once in a blue moon, bright colors and splashes in the sun; and jumps and excitement, will make your eyes water and your heart pound, and you'll end up proud and happy."

"Hey, Uncle, can we fly a kite tomorrow?"

"If it don't rain, we'll build the best dang kite that never passed a flight inspection!"

"Hurray!"

It was a wonderful day but there was a fly in the ointment, or more precisely, a worm. Bob didn't like putting the worms on the hook. This wasn't just squeamishness (he told himself); he could do it (although it was a yucky, slimy prospect). What got to him, was taking the life of a helpless worm that hadn't done any harm to him. Bob felt silly for feeling guilt about this and would have been embarrassed to admit any such thing.

He realized that it was best to express feelings like these somehow; to get them out in the open and try to understand them.

So that night he wrote a poem, just for himself, in his secret book.

I'm sorry
For every squirm
Of every worm
I ever took
Upon my hook
But, O Lord
Look!
Here I go again
Fishing

The next day they did fly homemade kites (which are always the best kind). In the days to follow they tramped in the woods and got all scratchy. They went to see a baseball game (Derick, you will remember, was a big

81

fan). They visited the zoo and the museum and once, the symphony. (Goldie would have really liked it: they played Wagner).

They went on a car trip in the Impervo-car (and nobody got sick!) They went on little jaunts and picnics just to see what was over the next hill or in the next town.

They drank a lake of lemonade and consumed a crate of candy while reading comic books. They ran and jumped and wrestled and played.

They shot each other dead with cap guns.

The other boys had nothing other than good stuff to report in their nightly psychic pow-wows.

The days wound down. There was some excitement in getting new school supplies (Bob got a fresh, new, red notebook so he could start volume two of his journal when the time came). He didn't get to do everything he wanted to do that summer but he got to do a lot.

On the last day he gave his best, most sincere thank you to the whole Crunch family for making him feel like one of them for a whole summer.

"We feel that you *are* one of the family, Bob dear," said Mrs. Crunch, "you are welcome in our home always."

"Yeah, come over and play anytime!" piped in Georgette.

"That's right," said Mr. Crunch, "and if you ever need a new costume, I can whip you up a batch of M46."

"Filbert!"

All summer long, Bob had secretly wanted to go out on superhero patrol with Captain Speedball even though he was considered to be too inexperienced (his mind shied away from the words "too young").

That didn't happen.

For the immediate future Bob had to settle for the meager diet of adventure that could be sampled in his classes and training at school.

But, he told himself, he could look back on all the adventures he did have that summer as some crumbs of comfort.

Chapter VII

What's Cooking

"This year will be devoted to finishing your phase I work." It was Monday morning in a class called Detective Science and Doctor Unknown was declaiming in his best serious (but peeping) voice."

"As you know, the improbable task of getting you ready to be scientific crime fighters has fallen to me. I like improbable tasks."

"In the spring you will graduate to the status of 'crime fighter'. That is, those of you who don't 'wash-out'. No foolin', you guys, I think some of you won't make it unless you apply yourselves more than last year."

"As Sophomores, you are to be prepared for next year's focus when you will complete 'sidekick' training. Thereafter, you will spend all of year three on the 'buddy system'. Your buddy will share your projects and training assignments. He or she will also share your grade."

There was a buzz of whispered commentary at this news. A hand shot up.

"Yes, Mr. Punisher."

"Please sir, do we get to pick our own buddy?"

"Nope."

(More buzz).

Bunny waved her hand and the students held their collective breath. There was no telling where or when the cuteness would strike and how it would affect their lot.

"Please, Doctor Unknown, can't some of us students help pick the partners – maybe just a little bit?"

"What do you think? This is not a game of tag football we're talking about. I know you guys. You'd all want to team with the strongest and the best."

"I happen to think you people don't have a planted clue about who among you is really best. Be that as it maybe, no student will be left on the sidelines because of popularity or prejudice. When the time comes we will have a random drawing. Picking names out of a hat is the only fair way to do this."

(Buzz, buzz).

"Unless, of course," he continued, "any of you has a better suggestion?"

If Doctor Unknown wasn't expecting an answer to that one, he was surprised when the Blaster called out, "I'm thinking of a number from one to twenty-one."

Everyone laughed, including (fortunately for M.B.) Doctor Unknown.

"Mr. Blaster, anytime a statement from you starts with the words, 'I'm thinking,' I have learned to approach what follows with great skepticism."

Everyone laughed again (except the Blaster boy who could only muster a wry smile).

"But just so no one says that I don't encourage class participation in the decision making, Mr. Blaster can pick out the names from a hat next semester. I'm sure I can count on you to remind me when the time arrives."

Doctor U. added, "This way, all of you students will know the picking process was absolutely fair," (the Blaster smiled at that.)

The Doctor continued, "And those who don't trust the process can always blame Mr. Blaster," (the smile was gone.)

It was a few months into the semester when the Great Rumor first started to surface in the school. Everyone began talking about it at once one day and no one could pinpoint who started it. There was nothing anyone said that actually had any authority or proof behind it. On the contrary: it was as if a plague of pure conjecture had infected them all simultaneously.

"Did you hear? A super villain has threatened to destroy the whole school."

"I heard he left a ransom note."

"Boy, I hope he doesn't attack 'till after movie night."

"What's the name of this villain?

"Yeah, what kind of powers does he have?"

"When will he strike?"

"No one knows. He's some kind of gangster."

"His real identity is hidden but he goes by the name of The Big Cheese."

"How corny!"

"You mean, how cheesy!"

"Well, I'm not worried. It's nothing we can't handle!"

"That's right, and if we get stuck the teachers have lots of experience fighting bad guys."

"Yeah, mostly you and your jokes in class."

"But this is no joke, it's for real. I heard Mrs. White sounding actually worried talking about it."

"Why didn't you ask her what it was about?"

"She kind-of didn't know I was listening."

"Well, I think the teachers are the ones behind it all."

"What do you mean?"

"There's no real information, right? I think they started the rumor of the Big Cheese to see how we'd react. There is no Big Cheese."

"Why do you say that?"

"It makes sense, doesn't it? It's all going to turn out to be a big test, you wait."

"But why?"

"That's the answer to your question! Wie! He wants to weed out the scaredy-cats and the weaklings and this is a good way to do it. He's been itching to put together an elite superhero team. And you just can't have more than five or six on a real good team; it would be too unwieldy."

"Well, something's cooking; that's for sure," said Bob.

"Yeah," said the Crunch, "and I hope it's Big Cheese soufflé!"

It turned out that something indeed was cooking. Soon, even the teachers started to admit the existence of the rumor. One day in Black Belt Class (designed to build on the lessons of the first year's Green Belt Class) Dr. Unknown spoke of the rumor directly.

"I hear some of you students are worried about the Big Cheese. Maybe he's hiding in the laundry room or Mr. Lester's gatehouse. Did you look under the carpet? You're behaving like a bunch of kids, not heroes. There's nothing to this stuff. Next you'll be worried about the Boogie Man."

"Now I recall a time where the need to hide was all that stood between me and death."

"Tell us about it, Doctor Unknown," the students said in unison.

"Well, there I was on the eighty-sixth floor of the Empire State Building, clinging to the ledge outside a window. Suddenly a true auto-gyro came at me (that's a kind of hybrid helicopter and airplane combination together)."

"My line had been cut. The ledge was too narrow to get a running start and I couldn't jump to the next one. The gyro was also too far to jump for it. I had nowhere to go but down. But I didn't like that option so I created a new one. I got down on my hands and knees and edged into the deep shadow cast by the Chrysler Building next door. There I hung by my fingers until they gave up looking for me."

"Remember that! When you get into a spot where you have no power or advantage, emulate the humble chameleon, who survives by being overlooked."

The students clapped at that point and Dr. Unknown made an effort not to look pleased.

"What happened next, sir?" said Moe.

"Well, my sidekick was back at the...Hey! No you don't! You guys just want to get me talking. Time for some jumping-jacks, I guess!"

As the class continued, Bob was startled to find himself almost nodding and falling asleep. Not that this was an unheard of thing in the Doctor's class, but it came on very suddenly. As he jolted awake, Bob thought he could hear a voice shouting from the edge of his dream: "Don't do it!"

Bob looked over at where Kid Psyche was sitting; but the kid was deep in note-taking and seemed totally unaware of Bob. "I wonder what it is that I shouldn't do," Bob thought. Then he put his hand into his back pocket (his uniform had several unobtrusive pockets hidden in its design. This was mainly for snacks and other things he might have to carry during the day).

He removed the object from his pocket. It was his reflection marble. Bob gazed into its glossy, swirling depths. It looked like the image of some strange planet from outer space reflected in the eye of a cat.

He thought he heard the echo of a warning thought: "Don't!"

Psyche still looked absorbed in his own thoughts. Could someone else have the power to send thoughts through his stone? As the bell rang his concentration was broken and later, he forgot to ask Psyche about it.

That evening at supper, Bob got another big inspiration. But for some reason he didn't tell Psyche about it. Instead he sought out the Cruncher.

The cool autumn air seemed to discourage after dinner walks so Bob felt confident their conference would not be interrupted. "Derick, I got a great idea but I need your help."

"Well," said the Crunch, "out with it! Don't be so dramatic!"

"This is real important and nobody must know because they wouldn't let us do it if they did."

"What wouldn't they let us do?"

"Capture the Big Cheese."

"Paging Doctor Killdare," Derick cupped his hands and made his voice go all metallic and hollow sounding, "Doctor, we have a super nutty patient for you, please book a room in the funny farm..."

"Aw, come on, Cruncher! We can do this."

"Oh yeah? How are you going to find this Big Cheese guy? No one knows where he hangs out. No one even knows what he looks like."

"We could find out! We could go out on patrol tonight!"

"On patrol? We can't go out on patrol! We haven't even had sidekick training yet."

"The main purpose of a side kick is to help the hero get out of a jam, right?"

"Sure, everyone knows that, I read the comics too!"

"Okay, so we just take along our little psychic reflection marbles and call Psyche to send help if we get into a tight spot. He'd have half the school and all the teachers show up before you could say, 'twenty-four pages for only a dime!'"

"I don't know, Bob. You still haven't said how we're going to find him."

"Standard procedure," said Bob, "patrol the city until he robs a bank or something. Follow the squad cars and 'Zap!' I'll bounce him and you crunch him and the good guys win."

"You make it sound easy."

"It will be!"

"What if we don't find him right away?"

"Then we go out on patrol every night until we do. What do you say?"

"I say you flipped your lid. You know this is going to cut into our study time. Not that I mind that so much, but I need my beauty sleep."

"We'll meet out here right after lights out," said Bob, "If we don't find any clues by midnight we can come right back and we're in bed by 1:00. That's still six hours of sleep and plenty of time for breakfast."

"You say that as if missing breakfast was more important than missing a good night's sleep!"

Bob rolled his eyes and sent him an exasperated look.

"Okay," Derick sighed profoundly, "I guess I'm as loony as you are. Count me in. But now, tell me why you didn't ask Moe or any of the others to come along."

"We can always do that if we decide we need more help. You never take a large force out on scouting patrol. I figured we'll need the psychic boy back here to sound the alarm if needed. And I didn't think this was the kind of job most suited to a spear or a ray gun. You and I can cover more ground in a search than they can. Besides, the fewer who know about this the better."

"Brother, you can say that again! If any of the teachers find out they'll have us doing more than extra dishes!"

A smoky, dusky, mysterious pink-orange moon crawled out like a fat beetle up from the lake's horizon; reflecting then projecting its fevered glow to break apart dappled shadows; tinge the pale remnant of color - or the memory of colors - that held the evening at bay; finally to glint in splintered shards off lake, and lawn, and the lenses of Bob Blob's wondering eyes.

It was 10:15 in the evening and the hunt had begun. Bob loved the quixotic romance of venturing out into the night. He was hungry for adventure in a way that surpassed any hunger for food he could remember. He met the Crunch boy in the agreed upon spot. A certain amount of hoisting and bouncing later and the boys were up and over the fence.

They went along for a few hundred yards before Derick undimmed his computer lights and calculated the shortest route into the heart of the city.

"There seem to be unusual radio transmissions coming from the warehouses on Third Street," said the Crunch.

"Let's check it out," said Bob.

Dim yellow light spilled out from a door as it opened to admit a man in a costume. The man had a visor and goggles and the letter "J" printed on his chest. He looked like a super hero. He also, it occurred to the boys, looked like a potential super villain. Was this man their quarry, the Big Cheese?

Bob didn't think they'd be that lucky the first night. Yet the Crunch did have those strange radio waves as a clue and it led them right to this spot. Somehow they had to get a better look at the man in the costume.

Between the dark sides of the buildings there was a fire escape. The two adventurous boys now climbed this to the second story. There the Crunch carefully and quietly pushed at the lock on a door until the steel bar bent right out of the striker plate. They went in and followed the voices coming from the floor below.

"We only have to wait for National Hank and we're all here," said a voice like oiled gravel. Bob signaled Derick to follow quietly. They would try to get a look at the speaker. This involved quietly propping open a fire door on its inclined tracks and then descending a flight of creaky wooden stairs.

"The Wheelmen are all here, boss," said another voice as Bob slowly inched the last door open. He saw a room full of large and small crates

and boxes all stacked on pallets and looking like a miniature city skyline lit by dim overhead lamps. Some of the crates had been arranged into an informal conference space with the boxes serving for chairs and table. Bob had the impression he was spying on a meeting of gangsters all dressed up in colorful costumes.

There were four of them with a fifth man hidden in the shadows near the back of the truck loading dock. The first man was the one with the letter "J" on his chest. His costume was a symphony of greens that was topped with a helm and visor not unlike the Mean Blaster's. Bob later learned that his name was First Impression Joey. He probably had the best costume and wore a set of brass knuckles, but he had no super powers to speak of.

Ostensibly, he got his nickname from his skill as a counterfeiter. But it was also appropriate because it seemed he never stuck with his first opinion but kept changing his mind.

Then there was National Hank. He had lost his right arm in a safe-cracking accident years ago and had replaced it with a massive cylindrical prosthetic. This artificial limb ended in a steel hand. The arm was almost as thick as its owner's waist at its widest point and could telescope a good many feet, the better to grab you.

Henry Baker, alias *Henry the Hand*, got his nickname a few years back. At that time a large photograph on the front page of the local paper featured his leering face. It was captured by a new-fangled device in the fight against crime: the surveillance camera.

In the picture Hank was holding up his prominent bag of loot and posing as the outrageous bank robber. Stenciled on the bag could be read this partial identification:

"ATIONAL
ANK"

Then and there he became National Hank and he was never allowed to be called anything else after that.

The third member of the Big Wheel Gang was a very short man who looked extremely young for this sort of thing. His name was the Material Delinquent.

Below his flaxen hair he wore a simple mask of purple which covered part of his baby face. He could actually float in the air and bob like a cork on invisible air currents. But he could only float as high as he could jump (about two feet) or as high a person could throw him. Here, at last, was a crook that you really *could* trust (to be crooked) as far as you could throw him.

His costume was a vivid blue-green with a purple padded vest.

He also wore a cartridge studded belt and holster for a very peculiar gun. This gun fired jet bullets and with these the Material Delinquent could tow himself thru the air with his steely line. The gun also shot puffs of carbon dioxide gas to aid in the task of propulsion.

When the last member of the gang came into the light (he had been leaning against one of the forest of support beams that propped up the floor) Bob gave a tiny, involuntary gasp. What he had mistaken for a shadow-shrouded piece of machinery (perhaps a boiler) turned out to be hideously alive.

This was a man called the Thug. He was bullet-headed, cigar-smoking, ill-proportioned and evil tempered – and these just about summed up his good qualities. I refuse to write about some of the bad things I have heard about him, not because I fear they may not be true but because I fear they may well be possible.

The Thug was not a pleasant man to know. He also wore loud colored shirts. As he once reported to a fellow gang member, "I get the shirts made special for me. No store has my size. I got this tailor friend I let live. Hee, hee."

90

Soon the mysterious, oily voice spoke again from the cover of the shadows, "My plans are in that folder on the table in front of you. I want you to study them. We are going to pull the most daring heist ever. We are going to hold the entire city of Chicago hostage. They will have to pay for their safety and they will make their payment to me: the Big Cheese!"

And he gave out a manic laugh that sounded something like, "Moo, Ha, Ha! Moo, Ha, Ha, Ha, Ha!" The laughing continued and built while the Wheelmen clapped and joined in.

Bob's heart was racing. This was it! The Big Cheese himself! He was hoping that the gang boss would step out of the shadows so he could get a good look at him.

Now, Bob knew that, in most comic book stories, it would be at this point that someone could be counted upon to sneeze and give away their position.

As if on cue, a sneeze exploded like a shot!

"Gesundheit," said National Hank automatically.

"Who sneezed?" demanded the Big Cheese.

"It was me; boss," said the Thug in an apologetic voice, "All this dumb dust gets into my sinuses…"

"Shut up!" said the Cheese, "I thought I heard something. For a second I thought someone else sneezed. You guys assured me that we'd be safe to meet here!"

"We are, boss," said Joey. "I mean, I think we are. I'm absolutely positive that no copper can trace the 2-way radio signals we used to set-up this meeting. I mean, it's not likely they could do it. Nope."

There was a pause and he went on, "I wonder if the prison food has gotten any better?"

"Alright!" said the Big Cheese, "Search the joint! Turn everything upside down. Look into every open or suspicious box! Make sure we're alone! I will not tolerate being spied on!"

At that moment, all the crooks froze. From some indefinable point an eerie sound surrounded them with tendrils of vibrations that made the Goosebumps come out.

It sounded like the whine of a lost puppy.

It sounded like artic wind.

It was mysterious and remote like a ghost's song or a fragment of half-remembered dream music.

It was Goldie! She stepped out of a doorway on the opposite side from where Bob and Derick were watching. Her diminutive figure seemed to glow in the dim light. Her opera cape billowed dramatically behind her.

As the crooks started to move in her direction, her song changed. It grew in power until it became a force that held the gang at bay; as if it were an army of windy banshees.

Goldie was a little nervous, so she didn't give them any opera songs. Instead she sang:

"John Brown's baby had a cold upon his chest
So they rubbed it with camphorated oil!"

"The bear went over the mountain
The bear went over the mountain
The bear went over the mountain
To see what it could see
To see what it could see!"

"I got two pence to spend and
Two pence to lend and
Two pence to send home to my wife!"

"Hey! I know that one!" said the Thug.

"Shut up, you dummy!" said the Big Cheese.

Goldie was actually using songs she had learned as a Campfire Girl as a weapon to defeat the Super villains.

An ugly yellow claw of a hand came out of the shadows to reach for the folder containing the plans that were left on the improvised conference table.

Bob was on top of things in two and a half bounces. He snatched up the folder as the shadowy figure ran away. Just before Bob could bounce after him he heard the Crunch yell, "Help!"

The Thug had pinned him against the wall with a massive metal pipe while the Material Delinquent was wrapping his steely line around and around the Cruncher.

It was at this point Captain Speedball showed up. The first thing he did was leap between the Crunch and his attackers. Bob couldn't believe what happened next. It looked like Speedball took a disastrous slip and fell on his back. But then his metal disks began to revolve at a fantastic rate.

With eye-blurring speed his leg disks were pumping like locomotive wheels. And each oscillation caused a kick. The Speedball's kicks connected with the legs of the Thug making him drop the pipe that was imprisoning the Crunch. Next, in a move so fast Bob would have missed it had he blinked, Speedball pivoted on his backside and brought his pounding legs into contact with the Material Delinquent.

At the first touch of those whirling feet, the Delinquent flew backwards like a toy balloon escaping the fingers of a child.

Then, just as National Hank had started to grab Bob with his telescoping arm, the Material Delinquent came flying like a guided missal into

Hank's chest. Both Wheelmen went down in a tangle, slid across the floor and tumbled into a heap. Fortunately their heads struck a cast iron radiator and they were out of the fight.

The Thug was clutching his calves and moaning in pain. And Joey had suddenly remembered another appointment.

The battle was over.

Now Bob was surprised to see that Ariel, Willow-wand, the Liberator and Bunny had arrived on the scene. They were accompanied by six police officers who handcuffed the remaining gang members and took them away in squad cars and motorcycles.

So five girls, two boys and Captain Speedball had come real close to capturing the Big Cheese all by themselves.

After the police left, they held an informal pow-wow just outside the warehouse.

"Quiet down," said Speedball, "I know you're excited, but the last thing we need is neighbors phoning the police and reporting a disturbance."

That settled them down alright. Then Goldie told the story of how she happened to be on the scene that night.

"I saw Bobbie and Cruncher climb the school gate after curfew."

The Crunch quickly broke in, "You see, I picked-up these weird radio signals and we tracked the crooks here."

"What were you doing out after curfew?" asked Speedball.

"Well..." said Crunch.

"...It was my fault," said Bob, "I talked him into trying to catch the Big Cheese."

Speedball turned to Goldie, "And what's your excuse?"

"I was riding my Atomic Rocket Bike. I never really have time to ride it during the day. So I often take a little ride at night. Mr. Lester always let me in and out."

It seems Goldie had learned to telephone the Girl's Dorm from the phone booth just outside the school grounds. Within a few minutes of calling, Bunny Hop would appear at the gate with a very understanding Mr. Lester.

That night, after Goldie saw the boys climb the fence, she followed them. Putting her bike in "stealth mode" she extinguished her rockets and pedaled her bike in a normal fashion. It was in this way she was able to follow the two boys silently to the warehouse.

When Goldie saw what was happening there (she was standing on a box near an open window) she jumped down and ran to the nearest gas station and phoned the Girl's Dorm.

You can picture the four giggling girls listening in on one phone receiver.

Slowly they realized that the boys might be in for serious trouble. Ariel phoned a taxi and Willow-wand had just enough money for the cab (of course, Bunny helped negotiate the fare).

The girls arrived just in time to pursue the fleeing gang boss.

"But the Big Stinker Cheese got away," said Willow-wand.

"We'll get him next time, kids," said the Pink Liberator.

"I'm not so sure there's going to be a next time," said Captain Speedball.

"Aw, gee!"

"Mr. Speedball!"

"Gosh, uncle!"

Bunny held up her hand in a gesture that seemed to say to the kids, "Let me handle this."

"Captain Speedball, sir," said Bunny Hop, "you never mentioned how you happened to come in the nick of time to rescue all of us."

"Got a call," he said, "from a kid at your school; someone named the Inexplicable Kid something."

"Psyche!" they all said.

"Yeah, Kid Psyche, that's it. He told me something about mind reading marbles and I thought, yeah, he lost his marbles all right. But I had to check it out, especially when he said the Crunch was involved."

Then Captain Speedball made the kids promise to never do anything so stupid again without permission and they all agreed.

"Now, let's have those plans you grabbed Bob," he said.

Bob handed over the folder.

Later that night, as the two boys crept back into the Boy's Dorm, just outside the bedroom door they had a little conference of their own.

"Boy, that was scary but worth it!"

"Did you see my uncle kick them bad guys?"

"Yeah," said Bob, but his voice sounded sad.

"What's the matter?"

"We almost got the Big Cheese but he escaped. I had his plans right here in my hand and now Speedball's got them and we'll never get a look at what may be our best clue to catch the Cheese. And worst of all, we can't go after him again without breaking our solemn word!"

"Well, there's a way around that you know!"

"Huh? What is it?"

We'll just have to get permission," said the Crunch

Chapter VIII

Fat Chance

"**F**at Chance!" said Bob. "We'll never get permission to risk our necks and go hunting the Big Cheese."

It was a rainy Tuesday and Mr. Lester didn't mind a few of the students hanging out in the boiler room while he attended to other duties. Psyche, Moe, Elf and the Crunch were all listening to Bob try to talk them out of getting into trouble again.

"Your parents won't let you and even if they did you could never talk the teachers into it; especially Professor Wie."

"Well," said Moe du Jur, "if we had been with you the last time, we'd have caught the Cheese by now."

"I know," said the Crunch, "and I'll say it again: we're sorry! If we could go back in time and do it over again I would. But even the Absolute Locus can't do that. What's done is done."

"He's right," said Psyche, "let's forget what should have happened and focus on what we're going to do next."

"It looks like we won't be doing anything next," said Bob.

The Elf spoke up, "Perhaps there is a way to accomplish the task, my friends. One does not consult a cook to build bridges or a warrior to bake cakes. If the task is to climb a mountain you need to call one experienced in mountain climbing."

"What are you getting at?" asked Psyche a split second before Bob was going to do the same.

"We have no mountain climbers in the school that I am aware of," said Elf, "but if the task is to convince the reluctant you may need to call…"

"Bunny!"

"Of course!"

"Why didn't I think of that!"

Within five minutes they had tracked her down in the library. She did not seem at all displeased with the unexpected attention.

"We want you to help us convince the teachers to let us finish catching the Big Cheese!"

"Please!"

"Come on, Bunny! Say you'll help us!"

"We need you!"

Bunny's response will have to remain a mystery because at that moment the school's public address system announced a mandatory assembly in the school auditorium. They all filed out into the halls and joined the other students.

The buzz of excitement only increased when the students arrived and saw the teachers seated at a table on the stage and with them was Captain Speedball.

"Holy Cow!" said Moe turning to the Crunch, "There's your uncle! He wouldn't have snitched on you guys to the teachers, would he?"

"Not in a ka-zillion years!" said the Cruncher with some heat.

"Yeah," Bob was stoutly supporting his friend, "the Captain would never do like that!" But secretly, Bob didn't feel so sure.

Doctor Unknown began to speak to them. "Yesterday, you students heard me say that there was nothing to this rumor going around about the Big Cheese. Well, today I found out I was wrong. There is a super criminal called the Big Cheese and several of our students had a run-in with him last night."

Bob could hear the Crunch groaning next to him.

Then Professor Wie took the microphone. "This morning we received a police report that a number of our students were found in the company of the Big Cheese and his gang."

"Captain Speedball (whom many of you know from his adventures in the comic book of the same name) was also on the scene. When I called him today, he graciously and immediately agreed to meet with me. The Captain related to me the story of what had happened. He did not tell me the names of the seven students who had broken curfew but I was able to deduce quite a bit from the police report."

"The student who breaks curfew is subject to suspension. However there were some extenuating circumstances. A rescue was organized in time and Captain Speedball has assured me that the students subsequently behaved in a brave and honorable fashion."

"That is just as well. It would be awkward to have to suspend one third of the whole school."

The student body chuckled at this and one third of them really put their hearts into it.

"Please understand I am determined that the safety of the students must come first. We are training you for just this type of adventure but you are not yet ready. There can be no more unauthorized escapades. I have consulted with the staff and your parents. As a safety measure, I am initiating a new school project: the capture and defeat of the Big Cheese and his gang!"

The cheering and stomping that resulted from this announcement turned the assembly into a pep-rally.

Yes, it was all very exciting for the students but there was another side to it.

The teachers enforced curfew more strictly than ever. Mrs. White was the official second floor adviser and lived in her own apartment there. Now, Professor Wie took up residence on the first floor. Mr. Lester found additional aid from Captain Speedball who began to help in night patrol duties and guarding the school grounds.

The class schedule was changed; Civics and Equations with Mr. Mann were the only courses done totally in a classroom. The courses named *Detective* and *Forensics* were merged in order to use scientific devises for clue analysis. But first there had to be found some clues to analyze. Since Dr. Unknown's class, *Training and Control,* could easily have been renamed, *Advanced Jumping Jacks,* almost all of it was now devoted to brainstorming clues.

The students and teachers had at their disposal a large analog computer that took up most of the basement of the school building. It worked with a complex punch-card system and the Crunch boy proved most adept in operating it.

"You can be our *numbers cruncher,*" Mrs. White said one day, and the new nickname stuck with him. While the Crunch took on the task of coordinating raw data and detecting strange radio signals, other students went out on scouting expeditions or supervised patrol.

The scouts consisted of those students most able to cover a lot of ground in a short time. There were students like the Wisp, who could propel herself at a prodigious speed while in her gaseous state; Captain Eugene with his Jet Shield; the Blaster; and Bob himself, who could bounce for hours without getting tired (although not always without getting hungry).

The mysterious Goldie was another scout. She was delighted with the opportunity to ride her Atomic Rocket Bike all over the city.

When she felt that she was drawing too much attention to herself she would simply slow down to a more sedate coaster-brake speed and become just another little kid on a bicycle.

If that didn't work, an attentive observer was likely to see only a bright flash of red and orange light with brilliant silver-blue sparks; a blur of yellow and chrome; and a rapidly dwindling speck accompanied by what could only be a sonic boom.

The students allowed to go on patrol were primarily Morpho, who could blend in anywhere; Psyche and true Believer. All of these students scored

extremely high on intuition. The rest of the students would take a turn on Patrol under the supervision of one of the teachers.

All of the students coordinated the gathered information at home base (as the school was now called). They also had a contest to see who could think up the best name for the new super group that consisted of all four teams of students.

Here are just some of the ideas suggested: The Wie-unit; Super school; Star Kids; Wonder kids; Babes-in-Arms (that one was suggested by Dr. Unknown with a straight face); Thunderstrike (the boys favored this name); The peace Corps (a favorite of the girls); the Knights of Now; The Modern Squad; The Supremes; The Unofficials; Team of Teams; and many more names like that.

"You ought to call yourselves the Optimist Club," said Mrs. White.

Captain Speedball donated to the effort a copy of the plans that Bob had snatched from the Big Cheese. The folder consisted of notes and drawings that were photographed and enlarged by the students (using their own darkroom) and hung on the bulletin board of the classroom that had become their center of operations.

It turned out that blowing up the city of Chicago didn't quite mean what everyone thought. The Cheese claimed to have invented an enlarging ray. If this were to be unleashed upon the city, the average man would suddenly find that he was nine feet tall. It was even considered possible that the artificially extended molecules would not be compatible with ordinary matter.

Of course it was also possible that the project was all a big bluff to get ransom money. Nobody really wanted to take that chance, however.

Their best hope was to find him before he could act.

One day not long after (it really seemed like no time at all) Bob found himself writing in his journal, "Since I have organized my homework time and school assignments, my grades have improved a lot. Even Mr. Mann has complimented me on it."

"Time is flying (maybe because I'm having so much fun) and summer vacation is only a few weeks away. Mrs. White said it would be okay for me to stay with the du Jur family this summer. I can't wait to see the future — although it is a little scary and Moe can't tell me very much about it."

At last the day came for report cards and the end of the school year. Professor Wie told them all to keep a sharp eye out for clues during their time away. "Even on vacation," he said, "I want you to notify me immediately if you come up with any new information about the Big Cheese.

Mrs. White and I will be in Europe with Nova Rex, the Purple Punisher and Miss Bunny Hop, who has been given special permission to receive her second scholarship."

At this point the Wisp leaned over and whispered to Bob, "What do you bet she goes all four years?"

"No bet," said Bob.

Then, after telling them to be careful (for the zillionth time, thought Bob) he passed out the report cards and dismissed — or more accurately unleashed — the students upon the unsuspecting summer.

Psyche had to leave in a hurry because of his circus schedule, so he said a quick goodbye to Bob, Moe, Elf and Crunch reminding them to use their reflection marbles to stay in touch each night.

"We will," they said, "just like last summer."

"Maybe a little bit better than last summer," said the Psyche boy. "I'm improving with practice, you know," he explained.

It was five AM. Bob blinked blurry-eyed as the Impervo Car pulled away. Mr. Crunch and Derick had given Bob and Moe a lift. The Cruncher had expressed regret that the boys couldn't spend the summer with his family (although the boys did promise to visit the Crunches for a few days before school started again). Bob yawned as he remembered the strange ride through the silent early morning streets with their blinking stoplights.

There they were, two oddly attired kids, waiting all alone on a deserted dock near the shores of Lake Michigan. The haggard grey waters lapped and gurgled around the stones and corrugated pilings.

At length Bob became aware of a disturbance in the water. It looked like the wake of a ghost ship escorted by massive bubbles and a sapphire glow that grew in power. Soon a shimmering, opalescent sphere, about the size of a small duplex house, broke the surface.

"Wait for it now, just hold still," said Moe, and a bright searchlight exploded in Bob's eyes. The air was filled with a strong scent reminiscent of roses.

Suddenly Bob felt as if he was underwater and he involuntarily held his breath and closed his eyes.

Vivid impressions came to him like scenes in a poorly edited movie. Lambent diamonds were pulsing with life on an infinite velvet black backdrop. There were stars wheeling and waltzing above (no, in front!) of his head. Broad tubes stretched bewilderingly ahead like neon spaghetti. There was a tunnel like a playground slide.

Bob remembered swimming without any water. He ate a wonderful meal supplemented with nourishing rays of polychromatic light. There was moving, talking wallpaper. With the visions came snatches of dialogue.

"Tag, you're it!" said the voice of Moe, and Bob laughed to see himself turn blue. He thought about the surprising size of something he couldn't quite picture.

"What do you know," he said out loud, "these guys look just like Mr. Blinky."

The voices came faster.

"Grab a spray can and we'll go for a walk."

"We have to do this: it's a cultural imperative."

"We use Ultra-nan technology when ever we can afford it."

"Our number one concern is computerlock addiction."

"Please don't make me watch my television just yet."

Bob was about to apologize for the loud snort that escaped from his nose when he opened his eyes in wonder.

"Aaarrg!" Bob shouted, "I missed it! I can't believe it! Moe! Where's Moe?"

Bob was looking around frantically. Instead of that giant egg (or whatever it was that blinded him) Bob saw that he was in his own bed back in the dorm!

"What happened!" he cried, "Moe!"

Moe was already running to Bob's side. Sleepy voices all around them were calling out.

"Shut *up*, already!"

"Go back to sleep!"

"Quiet!"

"We're trying to get some sleep here!"

"Too much pizza-pie causes nightmares, I told you so!"

"Hold it down, you guys!"

Moe was hustling the bewildered Bob out of the dorm and into the hall.

"Don't panic Bob, hey, listen to me! Remember I told you this would happen!"

"Moe! I missed it! Don't you understand? I missed out on the whole summer!" Bob was a study in misery. "I can't remember anything!"

101

"Sure you will," said Moe, "just let ol' Doctor Moe get in a word edge-wise," he held Bob by the shoulders and stared intently at him, "listen closely!"

Then Moe pronounced the word that unlocked Bob's memory. Bob couldn't remember or repeat that word. It was beyond his capacity; it was literally unspeakable. But after Moe said it, the whole summer came rushing back into Bob's memory as if there had never been a break in his recollection chain.

In fact Bob was sure that there was no break. He now remembered going to sleep that night and the ride back from the lake and...

What Bob remembered next was a summer spent in the future.

He remembered the moment back on the pier when the light emanating from the undersea shuttle transport had blinded him. Bob had opened his eyes in wonder. Somehow he had gone into the waiting vessel (or perhaps it was the vessel that had mysteriously enveloped him).

He found himself sitting on a weird looking bench with Moe next to him apparently driving or controlling the transport.

"The stringer ship is only a few minutes away, I can't wait to get back," said Moe as he sank his hands into the display control in front of him. In response, the interior lights dimmed to near extinction and a musical hum began to throb as the transport (and Bob!) began to descend and speed through the water.

"When we get to the stringer ship we'll really start to travel." Since Bob looked particularly blank Moe went on, "Getting to the future involves going *slow* enough. We must coax the local universe to speed past us."

As Moe went on about mapping continuums and expanding optional-reality bubbles, Bob kept nodding wisely. He started to imagine how his friend the Elf would respond to such an explanation. He was sure Elf would dismiss it all as magic. It was, Bob thought, just a natural part of life that some things could be experienced but not necessarily understood.

Soon they arrived at the end of the energy channel and started their approach to the stringer ship. If the transport they were riding was as big as a house, the stringer ship was like a whole city, Bob thought.

It floated a few feet above the bottom of the lake as if it weighed nothing at all. Glowing with the same strange light as their transport, it was hard to see very many details. There were fins prominent above all the vents, pods, projections and depressions that festooned the exterior of the space liner.

It turned out that the stringer ship was actually a space station with hundreds of people living and working on board as they traveled through space-time. No windows could be seen but a large oval appeared on one side. Its iris door retracted to admit them. By the time the doors closed again they were very far away from the lake indeed. They were also far away from the Earth and from the year 1958.

Bob gazed in wonder at a vista of the future. It did not look like the neon-lit depictions of metropolis he had seen in science fiction movies. Rather it all looked very organic and peaceful. There seemed to be a blue and white mottled sky above the spot where the transport came to rest. The floor was a checkerboard of textured greens and earth tones.

As they exited Bob pointed overhead and asked, "What are all those hanging sky-boxes for? Is it some modern art decoration?" It did indeed look as if a network of connected planes and cubes were arcing a few hundred feet above in the sky.

"Those aren't *sky-boxes*," said Moe, "see that green section over there? That's number four olive street. I live at the intersection of forest and olive. Patrol headquarters is way off there almost forty-five degrees right. Its address is Purple Prime. We use colors to find our way on the station."

"The station!" said Bob, "You mean this…"

"Yeah," said Moe. "I know it takes a little getting used to. Those buildings aren't hanging overhead. There is no overhead. Nor is there any up or down. We just say ahead or behind instead of up or down."

Bob began to see the miniature city through new eyes. The "sky" of blue and white formed a sphere that measured a little less than a mile in diameter. (It was actually 1.5 kilometers, to be exact. They liked to use the decimal system in the future).

Just under the "sky" was an interlocking network of streets. Bob realized that they were standing on one of them and that they themselves would appear to be hanging upside down from the opposite side of the sphere.

Moe was now leading them to one of the giant pipes or struts that seemed to support the streets. Already Bob could see no sign of the iris door thru which they had entered the station.

"Aren't we still under the lake?" asked Bob. "I thought this was a space ship or is it a space station?"

"Oh, it is alright," said Moe.

"It is what?" said Bob with some exasperation. "How can it be both in outer space and under the ocean at the same time?"

"You must learn to think in terms of space-time. You can't have one without the other (as one of your popular songs puts it). But I didn't mean to sound so pedantic. Don't worry; it just takes a little time to get acclimated."

Bob felt grateful to Moe for being patient with him even as he felt a tinge of regret that he didn't bring his dictionary along. He promised himself he would ask Moe to borrow one as soon as a convenient chance came along.

A door opened in one of the neutral colored struts that connected the many different platforms of housing units and streets. Bob had encountered automatic doors before, but he couldn't see the mechanism that triggered this one. "I suppose I'll just have to get used to all this automation

103

or my whole summer will be spent asking endless questions," he thought to himself.

Through the door was a richly appointed car that traveled through a pneumatic tube connecting to any spot in the station. Bob tried not to even think about the fact that there was no driver. In the three minutes it took him to do this they arrived at the home of the du Jur family.

It was located on a block that really was a block; a cube with a number of houses sticking to it at all angles. The law of gravity seemed to be poorly enforced on the whole station but Bob noticed that nobody was flying around, either in vehicles or using jet packs, because the areas between all the struts and pipes were clear in every direction.

Moe's house looked like a hard boiled-egg stuck half way through a slice of toast. But it was big and roomy enough and had a real lawn and a garden surrounding it. There were hedges and bushes and even trees in the yard (one of which bore an old tire hanging from a rope).

Chapter IX

Chicken

The first thing Bob heard when he entered Moe's house was a pleasant soprano voice half humming and half singing a Gospel song about a Lamb and streams of water. Bob couldn't recall the exact words, but later he remembered a warm, safe feeling –as if he was in church.

"Mom, we're home," Moe announced.

"And this must be Robert," said Mrs. du Jur as she bustled into the room. She wore a bright, expansive smile that stood out from a beautiful dark chocolate complexion. Her kindly eyes were set deep, like two almonds, above her high cheekbones. Her crisp, white apron had a design that looked like a child had painted it with houses and trees and a yellow sun casting its rays upon smiling stick people.

Mrs. du Jur was not tall; she was heavy though not ponderous. Bob felt that she would be a commanding presence in any company.

Very soon the rest of the family appeared in a sort of casual rush. Introductions were made by Moe, "This is my mom, Aura Mercedes du Jur, but everyone just calls her mom."

"And this is my dad. On the Patrol Council he's known as Stewart. Sometimes they call him by his code name which is Umbra (that's Latin for shadow)!" Moe was caught up in enthusiastic pride for his family. "Next is my big brother Mort. He's studying to be a Cadet like me but he's already a Guardian."

"And this little fellow is my other brother whom I love dearly (and I always add that part because I need to be reminded of it so often). Say hello to Buster."

Buster greeted Bob with, "I'm five years old already and I've never seen a kid as big as you!"

"Buster!" said Mom du Jur, "That's not very polite!"

"Aww! I didn't say 'fat' like I was gonna." He turned to Bob, "No hard feelings Bob. I'm going to be a villain when I grow up!"

"If you grow up!" said Mr. du Jur ominously.

"Now, Stu," said mom du Jur, "It's just a phase our Buster is going thru. Robert, you just pay him no mind."

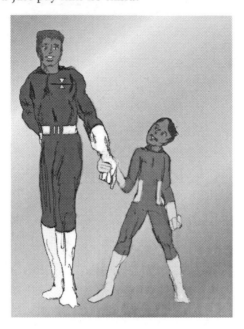

Bob had countless questions to ask but before he knew it they all sat down to supper and he had to pay attention to eating (first things first). Due to the strange time displacement on the stringer ship it was already supper time even though Bob had not yet had his breakfast.

There was a wide variety of dishes; some were totally new to Bob. Gas-charged fruit and plasma coffee accompanied good old corn on the cob and pork chops. Desert came with "foodshine" which was regarded as a particular delicacy.

As the quite ordinary carrot cake was served by Mort (who was something of a cook) a bundle of shiny cylinders sprouted from the center of the dinner table from an inset design Bob had thought was purely decorative. From the recesses of these gleaming tubes a mysterious light welled up. First it was red and then it flowed through the spectrum; orange into yellow and green through deepest indigo. A halo, like the Aura Borealis, shimmered before Bob's ever widening eyes.

Then suddenly webs of light, shafts and beams of color, snapped into existence. The rays, like rainbow ropes, touched everyone at the table; and where they touched was the sensation of food.

Bob felt some sort of fruit on his cheek. That is, where the shaft of color intersected his cheek, he had the sensation of eating the juice and pulp of a fresh, tasty peach. He noticed that this light was peach colored too. On his left hand (where a purple light beamed) was the feeling of plum. Shining on his right arm a brownish-yellow nimbus conveyed the sensation of buttered rolls.

Peas and carrots, ham and eggs, custard and strawberry- the colors and flavors danced for Bob's delight. When it was over and the lighting returned to normal Bob sighed with repletion. Buster was at one end of the table burping up what looked like multi-colored fireflies.

Presently Mr. du Jur said, "Okay, men, it's time for the good stuff!" To his surprise Moe and Mort groaned loudly and Buster cried dramatically, "Oh no! Come on Mom! Dad! Please don't make me watch my television just yet!"

"Moe, you and your friend can work on your Patrol homework together," said mom du Jur. "Moe will appreciate your help tonight Robert, and don't look so worried!' she laughed, "It won't be like the kind of television you remember. This TV is good for you!"

"That means it's deadly boring," explained Moe. Yet Bob found it very interesting. Three dimensional tele-view turned out to have very little in common with the TV with which Bob was familiar. There was an image, but instead of a flat, flickering monochrome (subject to ghosts, and snow and various other ills) Bob saw a credible illusion of reality. In addition, you could talk to it and it would respond ("That's called being interactive," said Moe). That night the two boys interacted with animated objects and people that taught them about grammar, math, biology, and music history.

Some of the subjects seemed a little advanced to Bob and at the end of eighty minutes or so he said to Moe, "I like this guy's music but how much more do we have to do yet?" Moe responded, "Tchaikovsky here is the last for tonight, then we get some free time."

"Hey!" said Bob, "What would happen if I pulled his beard?"

"Are you kidding?" said Moe, "The computer would have a fit! It's only letting us have this discussion because it knows you are new to our culture. We have the cultural imperatives to guide us. Adults can tell the computer what to do, but it's strictly controlled for us kids."

At the end of the lesson the two boys went to what Moe called the outside. "Actually, it's just the outside of our living unit. The real outside is space and tomorrow we'll take a walk out there."

"Really?" Bob responded with the excitement of someone who is going to get to do what was thought impossible, "What will we walk on?"

"Ha!" said Moe, "You'll see!"

Just then a car arrived and Moe grabbed Bob by the arm. "That's Jordan Shipman, boss of the whole Patrol! He's come to talk to dad about important secret stuff! Come on!"

The boys ran to the front yard to intercept the Patrol chief. "Commander Shipman, sir!" Moe called.

"It's Buster, isn't it?" said Shipman.

"No sir! That's my younger brother whom I love dearly. I'm Moe and this is Bob Blob."

"Mister Blob, I heard you were coming to visit us. Welcome to the station. I hope your visit with us is a pleasant and instructive one."

"Thank you, sir!" Since Bob didn't really know what he should say he felt that a simple answer was the best.

"I'll let dad know you're here," said Moe.

"That will be fine, Moe. But keep your voice down; we don't want the whole station to know I'm visiting!"

As Mr. du Jur and the rest of the family greeted the Commander and offered him a cup of plasma coffee, Moe pulled Bob back into a corner away from the others. "This is important stuff," Moe whispered, "This has to do with the security of the whole colony and the Council of the Unspeakables."

"The who and the what?" said Bob.

"Just trust me. There isn't time to explain. Shipman wouldn't be here now, like this, unless things were getting critical. We've got to listen in when they start talking business."

"We're going to get into trouble," suggested Bob.

Moe gave him one ironic, quizzical glance as if to say, "So, what else is new?" Then the two boys crept into the dinning room while the adults finished their coffee.

Moe gestured to Bob to follow him and they crawled under a side table that happened to have a long table cloth. "Doctor Unknown always said to be like a chameleon," whispered Moe. Indeed, as they scrunched way back in the dark corner they knew they could not be seen from any point of the room- even the low sofas. Unless someone were to actually bend down and peer underneath, they were safe from detection.

Voices from the other room grew closer. "I'll close the slider and see that no one disturbs you old space hounds," said mom du Jur as she rolled a partition across the room.

"No one must get word of what we are about to discuss," said Jordan Shipman.

"In that case I will seal the room," said Moe's dad as he took out what looked like a cigarette case from his pocket. He tapped it several times in a certain pattern and the device seemed to grow foggy and dim. "Now not even an electron can get into this room," he said.

"Stu, I'll come right to the point. In less than two months I expect this station to be under siege."

"Frankly sir, that's very hard to believe," said Mr. du Jur.

"I know," replied the Patrol leader, "Everybody's on the alert. The other colony ships are split. Half want to run away and the other half want to unite the stringers and fight. Our friend the Destructor has issued an ultimatum and the Council is taking it very seriously. The integrity of the time stream is in danger."

"Just what did he do this time?" asked Mr. du Jur.

"That, old friend, is where you come in I'm afraid. Get ready for a surprise. He went back in time. We think he's after Wie."

The hidden boys stiffened at those words.

"You mean Wilbur Wie who runs the school for gifted kids? My boy Moe is studying there."

"One and the same," said Shipman. "We have our agents working to keep things safe in 1958 and you needn't worry about the school. In fact we hope to catch the Destructor and stop him here in this time stream before your boy has to go back."

"You must have met his friend Robert? He's from that time period, you know."

"Yes, I know. I was the one who authorized his brain block. Stu, those two boys may prove to be our only direct link with the Destructor. We will use all of the station's resources to protect them of course. I put the entire patrol on alert without leave."

"So you think he will attack here?" asked Mr. du Jur.

"There can be little doubt I'm afraid. He's working without authorization in both time periods and he has issued an ultimatum. We don't have much time before his transports start landing." He let out a sigh that sounded a little like a groan. "We should have seen it coming."

"Well, I suppose I'll have to get back into harness again."

"I'm sorry, Stu."

Mr. du Jur asked, "Still no clue as to the identity of the genius behind the Destructor?"

"No clue at all," came the reluctant admission. "She keeps a low profile."

Approximately an hour later the two eavesdroppers were in Moe's bedroom. Buster was "camping out" in Mort's bedroom for the duration of Bob's visit. Moe was explaining, "My family were all born on Earth but then we joined the colony. There are four stringer ship stations like ours. We're the oldest and so we have patrol headquarters. We named ourselves 'Primus.' The other stringer ships say that we have too many rules, and sometimes it feels like that, but we think it's for the best."

"The colony ship that's going to be fighting on our side is named 'Technopolis'. They were almost taken over by the Destructor (who's a real bad guy- even the bad guys think so)! They have a different cultural imperative: no limits on technology."

"So they have better inventions and stuff?" asked Bob.

"Maybe, but it also means that they let technology rule them. No limits means technology has to come first, last and always with no exceptions."

"There's also a colony of people who put no limits on what can be bought or sold. They call themselves 'Cap city.' You live there and you can buy people, justice, or anything. They put no limit on it; so that's what runs their government."

"There's even a stringer that calls itself 'Freedom.' No limits on anything, so they are ruled by anything. (The rest of us think they're nuts)."

"Anyway," Moe went on, "the colony is going to unite and make one large string. This happens only rarely these days, like when there's some emergency."

Bob asked, "Can't Earth send some ships to help?"

"Not likely," said Moe. "They're too far away. That's why we call ourselves the colony; we're on our own, see? Besides they have troubles enough of their own."

"What do you mean?"

"Well, they have the superscrapers. These are like skyscrapers but bigger; maybe a hundred times bigger and taller all in one skin. The same building techniques made construction of this station possible. But after awhile people break up into their own mini-cities right inside the buildings. Living like that can do weird things to folks."

"What I don't understand," said Bob, "Is how you can bring me to this station all the way from Earth in 1958 but you can't visit Earth in...say, what year is it anyway?"

"Three eighty six, if that's any help," said Moe, "Look, we can spend the rest of the vacation catching up on physics, history, science and politics, or we can just take my word for it and have fun instead."

"Let's have fun, Moe. I'm going to stop asking so many questions and if I forget, you just punch me in the arm to remind me, okay?"

"You bet! Hey!" Moe sat up straight as if he just remembered something of import. "What time is it?"

"Don't ask me! I don't even know the year!"

"No," said Moe, "Look at your watch, you're still on Earth Central time. It's almost 10:00!"

"And what happens at..." Bob's eyes got big. He looked at Moe and they said it together.

"Psyche!"

Frantically they fished in their pockets and took out their reflection marbles. Bob's was of a silky amber hue while Moe's looked like a view from the bottom of a swimming pool in the moonlight.

As they held them in their hands they felt the sensation of heaviness in their limbs and eyes. Suddenly Kid Psyche was with them in some ineffable way. They couldn't see him but they didn't have to.

"Moe and Bob, are you there? Your clairvoyant emanations are weak and vague," the voice of Psyche seemed to be saying.

"Maybe that's because our understanding of clairvoyant stuff in general is weak and vague," said Moe with a laugh.

"Okay, now get this, I think our telepathic communications are being interfered with," said Psyche.

"Then listen," said Moe, "We found out that a villain named the Destructor is working in your time zone."

Psyche responded, "Who's going to restructure our time zone?"

"No! Look out for the Destructor! All of history is at risk!"

"I didn't get that last," said Psyche, "Something about your history instructor...?"

Bob said, "Let me try. Psyche: try to be on guard for any bad guy; any villain, okay?"

"Rodger, dodger," responded the Psyche boy, "I'll talk to you again tomorrow. It shouldn't be so hard..."

The psychic connection was severed and suddenly it was as if the marbles had become cold, lifeless stones in their hands.

"Well, that was weird," said Moe, "I mean it's always weird talking to Psyche, with or without the marbles, but this was like weird beyond weird. What were you trying to get across to him at the end there?"

"I guessed," said Bob, "I played a hunch. It seemed to me that the communications difficulty revolved around the word Destructor. He kept misunderstanding that word. I thought that maybe it had something to do with the brain block."

"That's it!" cried Moe, "I really think you got something there! Our subconscious brain blocks wouldn't let us think certain thoughts clearly and Psyche couldn't pick them up! He can't think past the brain block! We'll have to think up some round-about ways of telling him this tomorrow."

"Yeah, I bet he'll be relieved that the problem isn't on his end; his super power is still working strong as ever."

"Listen, Bob, if your theory is true it means I should fill you in on some other stuff. You asked me why we can't just go back to Earth for help. The answer is we can only go back to Earth as far as 1958."

"Huh?" said Bob.

"That's right. Remember space-time? We are so far away from Earth that going back there means time travel. It only takes the blink of an eye but we can't arrive any later than 1958. To go back to Earth as it is now would be, for us, like traveling to the future- and that is forbidden. We have a Council that watches over the time laws. They are called the Unspeakables. It's their job to see that we don't mess up history or pollute the time stream. Only problem is, once you start controlling time it's like driving a car: you don't dare let go of the wheel. Make the first tiny change in history and you are forever stuck in the driver's seat."

Needless to say, Bob had a lot to think about that night. But it was still vacation and the boys got up early so that they could fit more fun into the day. They went for the promised space walk. The pressurized pajamas they called space suits were flexible enough to fit even Bob.

111

Bob learned to "walk" with the help of a spray can of compressed gas. Mort and Buster tagged along- literally. They were playing a game of space-tag which was kind of like conducting a squirt gun fight while floating in space.

Instead of water pistols they used *vibertoys*. To Bob, these looked like the kind of makeup compacts ladies carried back home. Depressing the side with a thumb (they were magnetic and stuck to your glove) produced a thin string of light. What ever that light hit, turned into the color of the light for a minute or so.

Buster and Mort "stood" Bob and Moe. And Buster kept sneaking up on Bob. He was using the lights of the station's exterior to dazzle and confuse his opponents. Bob spent a lot of time tagged with Buster's blue beam.

"Hey Bob!" Buster called over the radio, "Are you feeling alright? You look a little *blue* today!"

"Ha!" Bob's reply sounded, "When I tag you, we'll see your true color!" The color of Bob's beam happened to be yellow.

"Gotta catch me first!"

So it continued. For several weeks the boys played tag every day and Bob was getting real good at it. Each night they were able to reestablish contact with Psyche and now that they avoided topics that would trigger the brain block they were able to talk longer.

The Crunch Boy and the Elf were also able to join in these conversations. Derick was absorbed with a new game that helped him keep track of his beloved baseball scores. In fact he was building a computer that could predict the whole season (he said). Elf was all excited about horse riding and Psyche was having fun performing as a magician's assistant at the circus.

One day, they toured patrol headquarters and Mr. Shipman gave them the red carpet treatment. The spectacle of the entire Patrol all lined up on parade, clinging with adhesive boots to the exterior of the stringer ship, was one Bob would never forget.

And so an incredible summer full of things Bob had never dreamed of doing was drawing to a close when the Destructor finally struck.

It happened one day while they were playing tag. The station alarm sounded and in five minutes everyone in the stringer ship was encased in a space suit. The Destructor was leading the attack (from quit a ways behind!) with a phalanx of rocket fighters. These were jockeying into attack position.

Bob was being herded with the rest of the boys into position. They were being formed up as the third line of defense. Real Patrol Cadets were checking that all was ready for the attack. (You will remember that Moe and Mort were studying to be Cadets but they were regarded as junior members).

An officer was passing out weapons of a strange design. They were shaped like beer kegs that fit over the arms of the defenders.

"One shot from this baby and it's bye-bye rocket car," said Moe as he fitted the strange appliance over his glove.

When they came to Bob he spoke over his radio for all to hear: "I can't do it. You are all going to think I'm chicken, but I can't fight beside you."

"Bob, what's wrong?" asked Moe.

"I'm sorry, but this isn't a game of tag. We are not practicing hitting targets back at school. I will not take a life and that's final. You can call me chicken if you want to." Bob was embarrassed to see that even little Buster had a gun.

"Bob, it's not like that," said Moe, "We wouldn't ask you to go against your beliefs. It's to your credit. But these cars have nobody in them; they are all robot cars!"

"Robots!" said Bob, "In that case give me one of those cap pistols!"

The little rocket cars were like glowing, bullet-nosed mosquitoes. They were coming in waves, row by row, twenty ships to a file. Movable force fences were slowing up the attack but some heavy radiation was getting thru in places.

They seemed to have the defenders out numbered and it appeared to be only a matter of time before they broke through and conquered or destroyed the station.

The ships were hard to hit. It wasn't like tag where a glancing contact would score. Instead, one had to sustain a hit for a few seconds (which is a very long time in a space battle).

Bob noticed something when he tried to help Moe bring down the ship at which he was aiming (he had never really mastered the idea that there is no up or down in space). He noticed that the beam from his gun didn't seem to help reinforce Moe's ray.

"Can't we gang up on them?" he asked Moe.

"Doesn't work," Moe replied, "Everyone knows you have to go after them one by one. Two beams just get absorbed by their energy intakes. Believe me, feeding them twice as much power will only make them stronger."

Now, it was a fact that even in the heat of battle, Bob's mind was never far away from his next meal. Something in what Moe said triggered his thought process and gave him an idea.

"Why don't we give them indigestion!" Bob said, "If two beams only make them stronger, what would ten do- or fifty?"

It happened that Bob was using an open circuit and Jordan Shipman was listening to the conversation. The Patrol boss quickly consulted with an engineer and then addressed all the defenders through their radios.

"Attention: lines two and three will continue the engagement but those in line one will concentrate all their fire power on a single ship. On my command, line one will take out the first enemy ship on the right."

Since the attackers were lined up in rows it was easy for all to locate the target.

"Fire!" said Jordan Shipman, and nearly one hundred shafts of brilliant energy highlighted the designated target ship.

"Ka-boom!" cried Moe, who knew that sound could not travel in the vacuum of space. The exploding ship flared into extinction without the benefit of a sound effect, so Moe happily provided one.

"Smartly now," said Shipman, "Line one, shift over to the next target. Line two will begin to take out ships on the left side of the attackers. Line three will continue to fire at will. One ship at a time does it people!"

The improvised strategy worked. After loosing a few dozen ships, the Destructor decided to lead a retreat (remember, he was in a very convenient spot from which to do this; namely, quite a way behind the battle lines).

That night they had a big victory celebration for the whole station and Bob was guest of honor. Patrol Chief Jordan Shipman made a speech and then he asked Bob to come forward.

"Sometimes," he said, "it takes more courage not to fight. Robert Blob came among us as a friend from another time. Tonight we honor his respect for human life."

"Because he had the courage to question; because he refused to merely react to what he thought was expected of him; he was able to show us how to defeat our enemy."

The entire station was clapping and cheering every time Jordan Shipman paused. Bob was blushing a deep magenta that rather clashed with his costume.

"Robert Rotundus Maximillion Blob, I hereby confer on you the honorary title of Space Cadet of the Cosmic Patrol. From this day forward, if ever you are in dire need, know that the full force of the Patrol will back you up."

"And now receive this, our highest military award: the Valor."

He paused a moment, "You are the first to receive it for refusing to fight."

There was more applause and some chuckling at the irony of the situation.

Then Jordan Shipman opened a polished mahogany case and removed from it a beautiful chain of silver on which hung the Valor. It was about twenty centimeters long and sculpted in the form of a stylized space ship. On the gleaming award was an inscription that glowed in the dark: TO ROBERT BLOB, PATROL CADET (and then in smaller letters was written the quote) *"You can call me 'chicken' if you want to."*

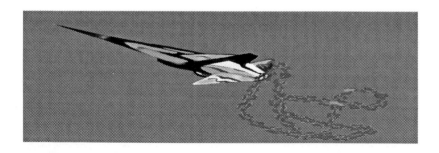

Chapter X

The Big Cheese

Bob and Moe's trip back to the 20th century was just like their first journey through time together, except of course it was in reverse. Moe was very proud of Bob, and he said so. It was hard for him not to reveal the fact that he was becoming a bit envious of his friend and the new prerogatives Bob had won.

"I still can't believe they gave you full Cadet status. They even modified your brain block!"

"Well, I'm very happy about that part," said Bob, "I want to enjoy your gift and that would be hard to do if I couldn't even remember what it was!"

Before they left, Mr. du Jur had given Bob a gift from the whole family. It was a special book signed by each of them (Buster had decorated his signature with tiny drawings of space ships). The book was a comprehensive dictionary in compressed form. "It's a quantum book," he was told. Bob got the impression that it was very expensive. The book consisted of a few sheets of paper bound with a plastic cover. The special pages looked like ordinary paper. However, just by touching them Bob could make it display illustrations and definitions for over *ten million* words (in any language)!

"It will really come in handy for school," Bob said.

"Don't remind me," said Moe, "I had so much fun this summer that the last thing I want is to get up for school tomorrow!"

It turned out that Moe had to wake up far earlier than he counted on. About an hour after lights out, a heart stopping cry pierced the quiet of the boy's dorm. It was coming from Bob's bed: "Aaarrg!" Bob shouted, "I missed it! I can't believe it!"

But since you already read that part of the story, let's skip over to breakfast, the next morning.

Bob, Moe, Crunch, Psyche and Elf were all making their way to a table when their attention was caught by the Mean Blaster. It seemed his summer vacation experience hadn't been as positive as the others.

"All summer I was looking forward to getting back here for some real food. No fooling' kids," said the Blaster boy, "I could eat an elephant, toe-nails and all! I'm starving! From now on I'm going to stuff myself with food 'till I look like a produce truck! I have a hunger big as all…"

He broke off as he saw Bob and the others walk in.

"Whoops! I didn't see you back there, Bounce-O! Now, don't go thinking I was breaking our gentleman's agreement! I wasn't referring to you. All that talk about hunger…"

His voice sounded unsure (and maybe just a bit guilty?) when he said, "Far be it from me to make fun of overeating -or anyone with a weight problem- or anything like that!" He was getting in deeper the more he tried to explain. The rest of the kids watched with some anticipation to see how Bob would take it.

"That's right, citizens!" Bob announced in his best public service radio announcer's voice, as he bounced over to the Blaster's side in a single bound.

"Overeating is unhealthy and may even be not good for you! Everyone whose super power doesn't rely upon eating ought to remember that there are limits! Too much of a good thing can be bad! Just take it from me, Blubber Boy!"

At this point Bob put his hand on the Blaster's shoulder and laughed. Some of the students started laughing too. It was obvious that Bob was in a clowning mood. What was less than obvious was the question of the Blaster's mood. How would he react?

"Now this young man," Bob continued while patting the Blaster on the back, "he's keeping fit and trim by eating in moderation and with regular exercise. So be like our Blaster buddy and practice responsible eating! And remember, unless your body bounces, keep track of those pounds and ounces! Healthy eating is your best ploy, a public service message from Blubber Boy!"

The students all laughed and applauded this performance, and somewhat to their surprise, the Blaster laughed longest and loudest of any of them.

"Man, you should be on television," said the Blaster who was still chuckling to himself, "But I thought you couldn't stand being called…um, that name."

"Oh, that's ancient history," said Bob, "at least I don't mind when I do it."

"Well, let's pull our tables together and get caught up on our vaca-tions," suggested MB.

Despite his protestations of starvation during the summer months, the Blaster seemed to be in a jovial mood. Bob noticed that he didn't actually say very much about what he did on vacation.

"The less said about the last few months; the better," said MB, "but I can tell you that my super powers are growing more in intensity. I find I can float on my power beams longer than ever. And now that they're getting stronger, there's a distinct greenish tinge to the ol' natural yellow power beam. I don't know why but they seem to turn more green every day. Yeah," he looked at Bob with a wry grin on his face, "I'm not getting any meaner but I'm sure getting greener."

In many ways Bob would find this, his third academic year at the school, the most challenging one of all. For one thing he was expected to graduate from "crime fighter" to a fully trained "side-kick". That meant he had to spend the year on the buddy system with Locus.

It also meant his courses were getting more difficult with classes such as *Theory of Leadership; Advanced Weapons* and *Tactics* by Professor Wie.

Mrs. White would be teaching a strange, exhausting course called *Rappel and Skyscraping.* She also gave courses in *Speech; Media; Propaganda;* and one called *Flying and Speed.*

Doctor Unknown would weigh in with *Vehicle Emersion* and something with the ominous title: *Obedience School.*

That left Mr. Iguana Man to teach *Computer Science; Super Science* and *E.S.P.*

After all that Bob wondered if he would have any free time at all, and if he did where would he find the energy to enjoy it?

After breakfast the first order of business was a welcome back talk by professor Wie.

"You will find some changes this year," he said. We have received word that the Big Cheese is on the move again and I believe it is not a coincidence that he chose this particular time to strike."

"Towards the end of the last academic year the Cheese narrowly escaped defeat. It was during this confrontation that we captured his plans along with three of his gang members. But last night he broke into state prison and rescued his henchmen."

The professor waited for the excited whispering to die down.

"We believe that remaining under the protection of the school is the best way to insure your safety; and your parents all concur with that assessment. However, some of your parents will be visiting us this year, from time to time, as an added protective measure."

"At this time I must announce that one of our students will not be returning this year. The Absolute Locus has decided to pursue independent study. I am authorized to say that his choice had to do with the nature of his super power development. I hasten to add that this decision was not made for reasons of security. He will have a better opportunity to advance as a superhero in another environment."

"In addition I regret to announce that our European recruitment effort once again failed to produce any qualified new student candidates. We now

117

number twenty students. This underscores how rare and valuable your super talents are."

"Since this is the year we start on the buddy system, Doctor Unknown will now conduct the lottery that you have been waiting for. Every student will have an equal chance at working with a favorite buddy for side-kick training this year."

At this point about a dozen hands went up in the student body.

"Yes," said Dr. Unknown, "I remember my promise that I promised last year; the Mean Blaster will please come up here and help select the names."

Doctor Unknown nodded and MB began drawing names from an old pith helmet. On the third drawing something happened that Bob wouldn't have dreamed of in a million years.

"Our third team-up will be Mean Blaster and Beneficent Bounce-O."

An electric shock seemed to go thru the room and then all the students began to talk at the same time. Bob noticed that all the teachers were talking too. He wondered in a distracted daze how anyone could communicate that way: if everyone was talking, no one could be listening.

The Blaster leaned over and whispered to Bob, "This is all a set-up, you know. Somebody wants to see if we loose our cool working together. But we're too smart for them, eh?"

"I think you're right," said Bob.

Sometime later the students met at the front gate for their first lesson in Vehicle Emersion with Doctor Unknown.

"Here comes a school bus," someone said.

"I wonder where we're going."

"I wonder if we start our class by learning how to drive a school bus."

"And I," said Doctor Unknown as he jogged to the front of the class, "wonder who's going to be the first to earn extra homework this year."

This statement helped to subdue the excited students as they all piled into the bus and scrambled for their favorite seats. A short time later they arrived at an old warehouse that sprawled along the shore of Lake Michigan. Doctor Unknown had the key to the massive double doors which opened outwards only to reveal another set of doors a dozen feet inside. The students gathered inside and the outer doors closed with a rackety thud.

Next, the doctor manipulated many tiny buttons on a control panel. This time the inner doors (these were made of corrugated steel) sank into the floor as a battery of brilliant lights illuminated the space beyond.

Nobody talked or shoved or even whispered. They were looking at the largest indoor hanger in the world.

Lined up in rows were small monoplanes and jets. There were helicopters and streamlined cars. Special docks contained submarines and speedboats of various sizes. There were at least two dozen of every kind of vehicle under that one roof; nearly 250 of the most amazing ground, water and air craft.

"What country does this navy belong to?"

"When I get old enough, I'm going to buy stock in petroleum."

"I'd hate to have to wax all of these!"

"I hope professor Wie got these at a discount."

"Do we get to actually drive any of these?"

"Okay you rookies," said Doctor Unknown, "let's start at the bottom and work our way up."

They formed a circle around one of the smaller two-man submarines. The shape of this craft was vaguely reminiscent of a paper airplane with a transparent dome on the top. The top opened to admit two voyagers, one seated behind the other. Controls and gages rimed the inside (these were duplicated for each operator) and a number of hatches were evident outboard.

"Port side (that's left to you landlubbers) monitors speed, tachometer, oil pressure, battery..." The teacher continued to describe the mechanical and electronic readouts and controls. When armed each sub carried a jet harpoon; mines, a variety of torpedoes, smoke ejectors and the like. They all had to learn about the radio; radar, sonar, ballistics calculator, robot navigation and the little facial tissue dispenser which Bob thought was the neatest gadget of all.

"Each team will now enter one of the subs," said the teacher, "and we will communicate by radio. Your weapons are armed with harmless dyes for this trip out. Any team that has difficulty obeying orders will find that their controls have locked and I will bring them back by auto-pilot."

The new buddy teams entered the subs two by two.

Elf and Willow
Morpho and Purp
Bounce-O and Blaster
Swashbuckle and Wisp
Moe and Bunny
Vortex and Goldie
Socko and Nova
Silver Baron and Captain Eugene
Psyche and Crunch
True Believer and Pink Liberator

If there had been an observer on that deserted shoreline he or she would have seen the wake of eleven submarines streaming out from under the empty docks in parallel lines. Doctor Unknown was in the slightly larger command ship.

"Student pilots," the voice of the Doctor squeaked over the radio, "your mission today will start with getting to know your vehicle. Also, we want to see additionally how you work together as a team collectively."

Bob had time to reflect that Doctor Unknown, even though he was a great hero and all that, had a tendency to redundant expression.

"So now hear this and listen up," the Doctor said as if confirming Bob's reflection, "you are to stay within a kilometer of this spot. I don't want you to surface. Each student will take a turn trying out the sub's controls. I want you to practice diving and navigation. I'll give you ten minutes and then be ready to choose a pilot and gunner for each boat. We will hunt our target in ten minutes. First team back wins a prize."

"You go first," said the Blaster a half second before Bob could open his mouth. Bob wanted to keep the polite tone that MB was setting. But no, he thought, it's not "MB" that I'm working with now, it's my partner.

"Okay partner," said Bob, "I'll keep time and get to know the other controls."

It turned out that, while the Blaster boy had slightly faster reflexes, Bob could steer better. This might have been due to his recent outer space experiences as much as native ability. In any case, the Mean Blaster recognized it.

"Okay Mister Blob, you seem to have the hang of this thing, for the good of the team you get to be pilot."

"If we're going to be partners, call me Bob."

"Okay Bob," the Blaster laughed, "and you can call me Admiral."

"Aye, Aye sir!" replied Bob with a chuckle, getting into the spirit of the thing. It was wonderful, this feeling Bob had, of at last getting a good rapport with the Blaster. However, he couldn't help wondering how well it would hold up over time or under pressure.

"That's enough time," reported the voice of the Unknown over the radio, "Your target is a wooden piano box painted yellow. It may be tethered anywhere between the very bottom of the lake and the surface. Hit it with a torpedo or a harpoon and report back to the dock first, before anyone else, and you will be the winner. Stay within three kilometers. Get going and good luck."

"Right," said Bob, "I suggest going one point five kilometers out in a straight line. That puts us at the center of an imaginary circle three kilometers wide. We can spiral out from there half way between the surface and the bottom. We ought to be able to spot it that way."

"Cool!" said the Blaster, "That's a plan, man! Let's go!"

Bob drove the sub out at a speed that was near top speed but a little bit under. Blaster called out tachometer numbers and other data that helped Bob navigate without putting too much of a strain on their ship. It didn't take them long to get to the half way point.

"No sign of that box," said MB, "but one of the subs is following us."

"Let them follow!"

Now they began their spiral maneuver. This seemed to confuse the sub that was trailing them. Both boys spotted the target at the same time. "There, on the starboard side!" said Bob. "Two o'clock!" cried Blaster.

The other sub was right behind them and closing! "Hang on!" said Bob as he flipped the boat upside down giving the Blaster a shot at the target.

"Harpoon away," shouted MB, and then, "It's a hit!" he said.

"Congratulations..." Bob started to say.

"Never mind that," Blaster cut him off, "we've got to get back to the dock first or that other sub will win the contest!"

Now it became a race between two evenly matched craft. The boys tried every trick they could think of to keep their course absolutely straight. The Blaster made sure the needles on the gauges stayed just out of the red zone.

Just as it looked like the other sub was pulling ahead, M.B. shouted, "I'm going to try to juice-up the turbines to give them more power."

"Okay," Bob called back, "watch out you don't overload them." Bob saw flashes of strange, greenish light reflecting off the cabin interior. MB was having some effect back there, but whenever the sub surged forward it would inevitably react by slowing down alarmingly.

"No good!" exclaimed the Blaster; I don't dare try anything more powerful." Bob saw that the rival sub was starting to pull ahead. "Check the sonar," he said, "Are any of the kids behind us?"

"No one behind!" answered Blaster.

"Then load up the aft tubes and get ready to shoot off all our torpedoes at once. They weigh almost a hundred pounds each," Bob explained, "That should lighten us up about a quarter ton and give us some thrust as well."

"I get you!" said the Blaster, "Just like a rocket: 'for every action there is an equal and opposite reaction.'"

"Right!" said Bob, "Newton's law! Now we've got to time this right. Ready?"

"All tubes ready, Bob!"

"Okay...FIRE!"

Five torpedoes spread out behind as if they were one. Freed from the additional weight the motors sang a warbling song of power as they shot ahead and entered the docking area. Bob and Blaster had won the contest. And they did it as a team.

The prize turned out to be a special certificate for teamwork and the privilege of selecting the films to be shown at the semi-monthly movie night. "I can see we're going to be subjected to a lot of cartoons," said Doctor Unknown, but the students could tell he was really pleased and proud.

The sub that had been trailing them came in second place. It was the team of Swashbuckle and Wisp. "I told my partner," said the Wisp, "I said:

'Bobby's the cleverest boy in the school and Blaster is the craftiest. Our best chance is to follow them.' And it almost worked!"

That afternoon Bob and his new partner studied their Emersion homework together and after supper the boys retired to the playing field for a little work out. It was an interesting experience, thought Bob. Blaster seemed to have a bit of competition left over for Bob but he was invariably polite and even friendly.

They soon found out what both of them had been wondering about for quite some time, namely, which one was more powerful. As it happened, both boys were evenly matched. Bob getting hit by the Blaster's beam felt just about as painful and exhausting as the Blaster felt when he was getting scrunched and flattened by Bob bouncing on him.

Later that evening Bob ran into Psyche. "Hey, Bobber! Nice going with the submarine race. We tried to beat you to the target like everyone else. You know, Derick is a great friend but he's never going to be a hot-shot pilot- as he'd be the first to tell you."

"Psyche, you old brain box," answered Bob, "how about that new partner of mine! I never expected we could work together at all and yet we clicked like we were brothers or something. I can't explain it."

"I think I can," came the surprising response. "I don't know if you are ready to hear this but our Blaster buddy thinks he's converted you from an enemy into a friend."

"What kind of kooky brain wave are you talking about now?"

"It's true," said Psyche, "Blaster thinks that he took you under his wing that time when you had the sword fight. The way he sees it, it was he who convinced you that competition with him was a lost cause. He's so sure of his superiority that he's actually proud of you for seeing the light and becoming a Mean Blaster fan."

"No!"

"Yeah," Psyche went on, "don't tell him. His respect for you is based on one assumption: you were smart enough to regard the Mean Blaster as 'the better man.'"

"But..."

"That is what you called him. And he believed you. It would be best if he kept on believing you."

"But that's so weird!"

"Ha! And you thought I was weird!"

"That's only because you are. It doesn't count with you."

"Ha, Ha, I like you too, kid."

Later that month something amazing happened to the whole school. It started like any other day. The students were gathered on the playing field trying very hard not to fall asleep as professor Wie was teaching the Leadership course.

"True leadership," he said, "demonstrates more concern for the led than for the leader."

The Crunch whispered to Bob from behind his back, "That's what my uncle says when we go fishing. Always be more concerned with the lead than the leader." Bob had to struggle to keep a straight face.

But just then, very suddenly, there was an interruption and everyone woke up. Behind professor Wie two people were walking on to the field. One of them wore an unfamiliar costume and the other looked like...

"The Thug!" one of the girls called out and pointed. Professor Wie calmly turned around and said, "Well, so it is. Class, we are graced with two visitors today. Most of you already know about Mr. Thug. Let me introduce you to his boss, the Big Cheese."

Nobody knew what to think for a few moments. The professor used those moments to warn the students. "This is an occasion to practice our discipline. No one is to move or speak unless I say so. The present situation will not be dangerous if we keep our heads. Unless I am mistaken Mr. Cheese has come to parley, not fight."

"Surprisingly correct, Wie!" said the Cheese.

As he continued to walk closer the students could see that he was garbed all in orange and yellow. His costume was very strange. He wore what looked like roller skates. Each one had many little wheels instead of the standard four. He had on stripped pants, and a wide belt with two chromium, bell-shaped objects attached; one on each side.

His shirt had stylized holes in it, as if it were made of Swiss cheese. A cheddar-colored cape completed the outfit. But by far the most bizarre aspect of his appearance was his cheese head. His skull was crowned with a yellow helmet that looked like it was carved from a block of cheese.

The man had what looked like two black holes for eyes. It was very creepy to look into those empty orbs. He also had no nose. Bob found out later that the Thug claimed the reason for this was because he couldn't stand the smell. ("Yeah, the boss stinks.")

The Big Cheese spoke, "I am here today for one reason only. I came to challenge you. One day very soon I will invade your school with the full force of my Wheelmen. I hereby warn you: just as I was able to break in on you today, at my whim, I will come and destroy you all!"

He paused and looked around him.

Then he said, "I think that about concludes our business for today."

Chapter XI

When the Chips are Down

"I beg to differ," said professor Wie, "There is much we could speak of, for this is not the first time I have been challenged by your particular brand of insanity."

"No, it isn't, is it? But it will certainly be the last time, Wie! Our last contest will take place inside the four walls of your school. I have my reasons for not making my existence known to the world at large, just as you have your secrets."

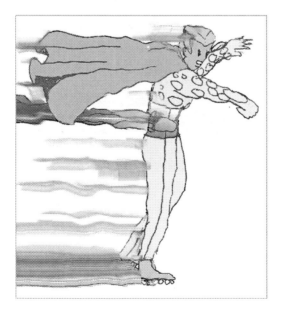

"Give it up, Cheese!" said the professor. We can get you help. There is counseling available; there's psychoanalysis..."

"To my way of thinking it is you who are mad! In any case I have my destiny and you can't stop it! No one can stop it! It is nothing less than the domination of the world. I'll get you Wilbur Wie, and when I finally do, the entire world will be mine!"

Then the Cheese looked up to the sky and maniacal laughter escaped his lips. It sounded like, "Moo, Ha, Ha, Ha!"

He wiped the tears from his eyes, "And now, before you can stop me, I bid you adieu until next time!"

At that, the Big Cheese did something to his belt. The two bell shaped devices on either side proved to be powerful rocket nozzles. These rotated from a vertical to a horizontal position and powerful jets of flame provided thrust to propel the villain's escape on his odd looking roller skates. The many tiny wheels acted as one to distribute his weight as the Cheese sped away.

Bob suspected that the stripes on his pants were really springy steel that helped absorb the shock of riding on uneven surfaces at high speed.

They all watched the arch-villain's departure and then, as if on cue, every eye turned to the ominous, imposing figure of the Thug.

"Hee, Hee," the Thug gurgled his hideous laugh, "You kids want to play?"

"Let him go!" shouted professor Wie! No one is to make a move!"

"Ha, Ha!" the Thug laughed, "I'll come back next time and we'll have fun then." With that, the henchman ambled off after his boss.

"I am gratified," the professor told the students, "The level of maturity and discipline you showed today is of the highest quality." Professor Wie was addressing the class after reaction had set in and the excited talking started to die down. "But this is just the beginning. We have only a little time. In that time you will continue to meet with your regular teachers for your regular classes. However, those classes will now be devoted to the defense of this school. There is much work that needs to be done before we can meet the onslaught of these villains in an organized and professional manor."

"Please sir!" the hand of Bunny Hop was waving for attention, "The Big Cheese acted like he knew you. Why is that, sir?"

"It's because we do know each other. I only recognized him when he showed up here today. I could never forget that profile."

"It happened several years ago. I made the acquaintance of a man who was involved in a tragic accident involving an exploding mechanical cheese maker and some radioactive enzymes."

"I tried to recruit him as a student for this school but he preferred the path of super villainy. Once he was a man I could have called my friend. He didn't go by the name of Big Cheese in those days; his name was Johnny B. Gouda. But he has forfeited that identity in his mad quest to become a crime boss and world dictator. And what we do in the next few days may be all that stands in the way of his insane ambition."

The next few days were filled with frantic activity. Bob, Crunch, Psyche, Moe and Elf had gotten into the habit of holding conferences at ten p.m. each night. Since they were not on vacation, they usually didn't employ their reflection marbles. Rather, they met in the boiler room. They reasoned that Mr. Lester wouldn't mind if he had known about it because he was busy with guard duty at that time anyway.

"I have to tell you guys, I'm nervous," began Psyche.

"Who wouldn't be?" said Moe, "Derick's Uncle and Dad are helping to patrol the grounds every day and night."

"Truly, they are not the only ones," put in the Elf.

"That's right," the Crunch Boy said, "other parents are starting to show up. They are supposed to be helping the school but I think they mostly want to keep an eye on their kids."

"I know," said Bob, "Vortex was telling me that his dad (The Mighty Omni-vac) was always checking up on him to see if he was safe."

"They're all like that," said Psyche, "You can't blame the parents. They look at you and all they see is a baby in diapers.

They can't help it. They are constitutionally unable to see any growth and maturity you have achieved."

"It says that in the constitution?" asked Crunch.

Bob wasn't quite sure if he was joking.

"No, no, no!" said Psyche, "What I mean is that parents aren't built for thinking of their kids as anything but helpless babies who need guidance even to blow their noses. It is physically impossible for a Mom or Dad to relate to their children in any other way except to treat them as children, even when they grow up and become adults."

"Friend Psyche," the Elf spoke in a gentle voice, "you sound as if you were yourself experiencing parental problems."

"Bulls eye, Elf old pal," Psyche answered. "My dad, The Mysterious Mentalus, has been meeting with the teachers every night helping to plan strategy."

"And my Mom, The Eerie Cassandra, is constantly sending me psychic messages. Originally, you know, the teachers asked for her help whenever I had to take a test (just in case I got fancy ideas about reading the answers direct from the minds of the teachers or other students). But now she can't leave me alone for an hour."

"But what's really got me nervous," Psyche continued, "is something I can't quite put my finger on. I got the idea from little things my mom said, about that Destructor character Moe and Bob told us about on vacation. Fellows, I think he's really the Big Cheese."

"The Destructor is the Big Cheese?" cried Moe, "if that's even a possibility I have to call home at once."

"Can we listen in?" asked Bob.

"Sure, no problem," said Moe, "Any classified material will be edited out of the message by the computer anyway."

At this Moe took out what looked like a small bracelet. "I don't usually wear it because it really belongs to my sister and I'm just borrowing it and it looks kind of girlish, you know," he mumbled as he put it on.

The boys huddled closer as the Space Cadet did something to what they now perceived was his wrist communicating device.

"The council generally discourages calls from this time zone, but I think they will take this one. This is Moe du Jur calling the Patrol with information about the Destructor. Please respond."

From the (actually quite pretty) bracelet a metallic voice sounded. There seemed to be gaps in the message that another voice filled in. "We're sorry," (the bracelet said) "the number you have reached is BLOCKED. THIS STATION cannot receive any information about THIS SUBJECT. Please try again in ONE HUNDRED YEARS. Thank you. This message is TERMINATED."

"Well, that's that," said Moe. "Now I'll have to wait until they get my message and call me back or until someone from that time zone visits us."

But the Elf had a question for Moe, "Why did you not leave one of Psyche's magic marbles with your parents?"

"It wouldn't have worked," said Moe, "That stupid brain block wouldn't even let us think about the Destructor, remember?"

"Well, we should tell professor Wie or somebody," said the Crunch.

"But," Bob said, "what if the Patrol or the Council of Unspeakables doesn't want the professor to know about the future, won't you get punished for spilling the beans?"

"Nope," Moe answered, "that's the beauty of this technology. It's self enforcing. If there's something we shouldn't tell anyone about, the conversation will never get started. The block will kick in and we'll just get tongue tied. It's automatic."

When they tried to see the professor the next day it was a great surprise to the boys to find out that theirs were not the only tongues that could be tied.

"I'm afraid it's out of the question, boys," said professor Wie, "It's no use; I just can't talk about this."

"Listen professor," the Crunch called out, "the Destructor is the Cheese; the Destructor is the Cheese!"

"Yes, I appreciate your saying 'please' but I still can't talk with you. Now you boys run along to class."

That day the students found out how their class schedules would be changed now that defense was the top priority. Doctor Unknown chartered no more busses to the secret warehouse. Instead of subs or jets the kids learned to operate backhoes. These heavy equipment mechanized shovels were used to dig ditches all around the inside of the school walls.

Not knowing what kind of attack to expect they spent a lot of time trying to cover all the bases. It was at lunch time especially that the students all put their heads together to consider almost any contingency.

"Well," Captain Eugene spoke up, "if the underground and the sky are covered by devices that will give us fair warning, what about what's left? How do we protect the surface? We ought to concentrate our defense on the grounds themselves. "

At that point Mrs. White entered the cafeteria, "Yes, Mr. Eugene, that's just what we intend."

She cleared off a section of a table and all the students gathered round as she unrolled a large drawing. "Here is a plan of the school grounds."

"Now observe; we're going to concentrate our defense by placing students at the main gate and at the corner of each wall."

While she was still speaking the rest of the teachers were filing in. Mr. Mann and the Professor stopped to collect a cup of coffee. All the students pulled up chairs around the drawing. Professor Wie started by pointing at the depiction of the main gate.

"We will be assigning ten students around the main gate. They will be supervised by Mrs. White and supported by a number of your parents. The students will act as scouts only. They will report on but not engage the enemy."

"The second line of defense will be in the basement of the school building. Here we will assign five students under the direction of Doctor Unknown."

"Far under the basement lies the sub-basement. It is much larger than the basement. Here we will be counting on three students under the direction of Mr. Mann."

"This third line of defense is very dangerous because we believe that the Cheese is going to come after me. And I will be in a room at the center of the sub-basement. That room is called the Infinity Room. In it I hope to confront and trap the Big Cheese along with any of his followers who make it that far."

"We will equip each line of defense with all the traps and deceptions we can think of. Now for those of you keeping count, you will notice that I have spoken of only eighteen assignments for our twenty students."

"The remaining two students will have the most difficult and dangerous job of all. In fact, I haven't spoken to the ones I have in mind; so I want to ask them now if, with the support of the school, they feel they can take on this assignment."

"These two students are among the most powerful individuals in the school and they have demonstrated creative intelligence and courage in tight situations. But most importantly, they have shown that they have what it takes to work together as a team. Each of them proved able to bring out the best in the other; sometimes in spite of their personal feelings."

"For these reasons I would like to recommend for your approval the appointment of the Mean Blaster and the Beneficent Bounce-O!"

It took about two heartbeats – the amount of time it usually takes to make sure of understanding an unexpected turn of events – and then the whole school erupted in applause. Bob was flabbergasted at the show of support.

Kids were hopping up and down. The Wisp was screaming something that sounded like, "WOOOP! WOOOP!" Elf, Crunch, Moe and Psyche started to chant, "Bounce-O! Blaster! Bounce-O! Blaster!" until it was picked up by all the students. Even the teachers were clapping with proud looks on their faces.

If Bob was surprised at the reaction of the students it was nothing compared to how Blaster felt. He had never been popular before (probably because his sharp tongue inspired fear and resentment). But now kids were slapping him on the back and shaking his hand in congratulations.

The smile MB now wore was just about the widest Bob had ever seen.

Professor Wie signaled for quiet. "Boys, we're counting on you to come through for us when the chips are down. The plan calls for you to work as a team. In the time remaining, I will call upon the two of you to help me develop and improve the plan. Your mission will be to keep tabs on the Big Cheese."

"You will be giving me constant reports via walkie-talkie. All throughout the coming battle you will keep me updated with his progress and any orders he gives to his henchmen. Follow him and don't be distracted by the fighting going on around you. Protect each other and don't engage the enemy unless you have no other choice."

"That goes for all of you. Your job is to lead the villains into the many traps we will set. Do not let them harm you. You must run away rather than let that happen. Follow the orders of your parents and teachers and we'll all come through this together."

"Above all you must avoid being captured. We cannot afford a hostage situation."

The days slipped into weeks and still no Cheese. Classes and studies alternated with planning and setting traps. Everyone was getting antsy (and no doubt that was part of the villain's plan). A guarded watchfulness settled onto the school routine. And then, one day, with out any warning, the storm broke.

Chapter XII

Using the Old Noodle

"**S**uper Science can often be defeated by the mere pull of a plug or the destruction of a fuse box."

Mister Mann was in rare form. Unfortunately for his students this meant that he was going to be mind-numbingly boring today. The lecture had already been going on for over an hour. Bob was reflecting on the fact that, as his academic career progressed, so did the amount of lecture time and homework.

"The fundamental thing to look for, even in the most advanced technology, is the good old single-pole-double-throw switch. Disable the power source and even the most sophisticated array of diabolic machinery will instantly become as useful as a flashlight without batteries."

"We will continue our study of the different kinds of technology; progressing from vacuum-tube electronics to the different grades of crystalline and organic machines that aliens favor."

"The question arises: how far can technology evolve? Will we someday encounter beams of light or mind-reading potentialities without instrumentality? Remember our first lesson. Technology is merely the extension of what the human mind can conceive. The lever can extend the power of the arm. The telescope extends the eye; the radio the ear and so forth."

"You cannot over-extend technology with impunity. If you try, the results will be – how do they say it in the comic books – BOOOM!"

The Iguana man said this last so loud that it woke up half the students and caused the rest to laugh. "Perhaps some of you extra somnambulant scholars would care to provide a more accurate sound effect?" he said, "Let's hear you try! Good and loud now!"

This was more like it!

"It's KA-BOOM! Mr. Mann!"

"No! It's more like KRACK – A – TOOM!"

"KA – POWEE!"

"WA – TOOM!"

"BA – ROOM!"

"BA – RACK!"

"POCKITA, POCKITA!"

"BA – TOOM!"

"THRAK!"

"PA - TOW!"

Each student tried hard to excel with all the volume and creativity of which they were capable.

"BRACK – A – BRACK – A!"

"KRAAAKK!"

"THA – ROOOOM!"

Suddenly, there was a flash and a real, live explosion blew out all the classroom windows with devastating force! Boys were shouting and some of the girls were screaming at the stunning noise. Mr. Mann leaped up onto his desk with a hiss and crouched there ready for action.

Plaster fell and dust swirled. Books, glass and papers littered the room. The students looked at Mr. Mann expectantly.

"Well," he said, "I really think KA – BOOM came closest."

Just then, Doctor Unknown and Mrs. White came into the classroom. "The attack has begun," said Mrs. White.

"That's right," said Dr. Unknown, "This is not a drill. At this time everyone is to go to their assigned places right away now."

Bob and the Mean Blaster pushed ahead of the others. They had been carrying their walkie-talkies with them, day and night, for weeks. The boys now switched these on so that they could continuously report to Professor Wie (who was presumably heading for the infinity room).

As they ran out of the building they could see a hole had been blown in the front gate.

"Nobody there!" said the Blaster, then he spoke for the benefit of professor Wie listening in on the walkie-talkie, "There's a hole in the front gate, professor, but no one is around!" It was true. Only rubble could be seen through the fast clearing smoke.

"Take the left!" shouted Bob, "Meet you by the bleachers!"

"Right!" said MB who was already propelling himself through the air with twin beams from his legs. Bob saw that Blaster had learned to use a new technique. He steadied himself in flight with thinner, less powerful beams shooting from his arms. It looked like he was using two thin, greenish - yellow rods to pole his way across the field.

Bob had been practicing his super power as well. The control needed to make his body resiliently bouncy was now second nature to him. Bouncing felt so natural to Bob that it was a pure joy for him to do it. Like a runner

131

in a race, he didn't think of the activity of bouncing as difficult or strenuous. He just did it.

Bob was bouncing in a zigzag pattern towards the dormitory. As he rounded the building he could see that the explosion had been a diversionary tactic. The real assault was coming from just behind the bleachers. "They're coming from under the bleachers!" Bob said for the benefit of his two-way radio.

Some one had breached the wall behind the athletic field using a less noisy method (acid – as it later developed).

Dozens of men were crawling out from under the bleachers. These were the hoards, or minions, who followed the Big Cheese. They were mostly small-time hoodlums and gangsters. The "Cheese Curdlers," as they were called, wore uniforms of black ties and matching yellow shirts and white pants. They all wore yellow, snap – brim fedoras. "They stole that idea from Dick Tracy," Bob thought.

Bob saw the Blaster rapidly closing in from his periphery. The boys rammed their way through and over the bulk of the attacking criminals. Their job was to find the Cheese. As they worked their way behind the bleachers they could see that one of the traps was working.

The students had dug a ditch all around the inside perimeter of the wall and made a kind of moat that could hold various traps for the attackers. About twenty of the Curdlers were snared in a very sticky mud that had been prepared. The traps were not meant to be lethal; so the mud was only about a foot deep.

Bob saw that one of the Wheelmen, National Hank, was trying to free some of the Curdlers. He was using his telescopic prosthetic arm to scoop out the sticky substance adhering to the feet of the assailants.

Just as the boys were about to give Hank their full attention, the Big Cheese tied to run through the hole and sneak past.

"The Cheese has entered the grounds!" Bob yelled into his radio. From the device the voice of professor Wie replied, "Avoid engagement, lead him to me."

"Tag, you're it!" shouted Blaster as he hurtled a power beam to the midriff of the Big Cheese. The villain shrugged off the blow and raised his arm to point at MB.

"Have a taste," the Cheese said, "of my Dart Air Gun. It will put you to sleep; so I call it my D.A.G. napper!" From one of the holes on the arm of his costume a shower of minute darts shot out seeking the Blaster. But the boy's quick reflexes enabled him to easily sweep aside the deadly darts with a wave of his power beam.

"If your weapons were only half as sickening as your dialogue you might get somewhere!" said the Blaster.

Now it was Bob's turn. He bowled the Cheese off his feet with once bounce and quickly got out of the way again.

"This is intolerable!" yelled the crime boss, "You are just children while I am to be the master of the whole planet! You are up against destiny itself, you fools! I'll teach you what it means to insult the Big Cheese!"

Bob and Blaster smiled as they exchanged one swift look, "Thanks, but we know how already!" they said in unison.

If the boys had hoped to enrage the Cheese so that he would follow them, they succeeded on a grand scale. The rocket nozzles on his belt sputtered into life and since the rockets were pointing to the ground, the Cheese flew.

Now began a merry chase.

The boys kept alternating their height above the ground so that they looked like pistons as they progressed across the field. They were offering no easy target for the pursuing Cheese.

Bob thumbed the switch on his walkie-talkie (which was hanging by a strap on his belt). "Blaster," he shouted into the pick-up, "keep taunting him, it seems to infuriate him. We've got to keep him from going after the other kids."

"Rodger that," the answer came. "We'll keep bugging him all the way to the sub-basement."

Now Bob had a chance to take in what was going on below him. The Curdlers had fanned out and were shooting real guns. The Thug was creeping in the front gate and the Hovering Delinquent was helping Joey get over the west wall.

The Silver Baron; Socko, Swashbuckle and Bunny (the students who were more vulnerable to bullets) were scattering for cover. On the other hand the Crunch, Nova, Captain Eugene (using his jet-shield for cover) and Goldie were mopping up the bad guys with vast vitality and vigor. And for some mysterious reason no bullets ever came near Kid Psyche.

Some of the parents got into the act too. Master Cloak was leaping around with the Purp. The Raging Inferno and his wife, Stella Starburst were the parents of Nova Rex. They had assumed the secret identities of Stoke and Stella Dante. Since their superpowers had a lot to do with extreme temperatures they worked together as a "thermo-couple."

Mrs. White was coordinating the defense of the students above ground. Bob could now discern a pattern to the attack. The Thug from the front and Hank from the rear were closing in on the main school building. Joey and most of the Curdlers were coming from the east near the kitchen building. That left the Hovering Delinquent to circle and close in from the west near the Dorm.

Bob became aware that Blaster was doing most of the work of insulting the Big Cheese. "Hey, Dopey," MB shouted, "where did you leave the other six dwarfs?"

"You will soon feel my wrath, you freaky insect!" The Big Cheese was responding every time to the creative rudeness; but he just couldn't catch the Blaster.

"Hey you! Smelly cheese guy!" Bob shouted, "Yeah, I mean you, mold head!" With that, Bob landed on the roof of the dormitory building and the Blaster soon followed. The boys ducked into an open window hoping that the Cheese would pursue them inside.

He did.

They raced each other towards the main school building. They kept taunting the Cheese every few moments to make sure he would keep following

Now, the Cheese was just as eager as the boys to get into the main building. He suspected that Professor Wie was somewhere inside and he wanted to get at Wie more than anything else.

Bob bounced on ahead through the front door and down the stairs, sticking his tongue out at the Cheese for good measure. MB shot stinging bolts at the feet of the Big Cheese trying to herd him down towards the basement.

It had long been a subject of speculation among the students where Wilbur Wie got all the resources to run the school. There never seemed to be a lack of money. If something was needed for a special project it was not only obtained but greatly exceeded expectations in quality. In fact, most of Wie's gadgets and equipment seemed far in advance of present day technology.

Now, as the boys raced into the basement mere seconds behind their foe, the fantastic resources of professor Wie became evident once more.

A large cage of stainless steel dropped from above to envelope the pursuing Cheese. The boys jogged to a halt and looked back in horror. The sinews on the back of the arms of the Cheese were swelling like ropes in water. With a cry he wrenched two bars out of the confining jail. The boys turned and ran down a corridor. They knew that from now on they were working at a disadvantage. Bouncing and flying were difficult in these confines; but it seemed to be just the right thing for rocket powered roller skates.

Yet the boys also had an advantage in that they knew the layout; and the Cheese could only use his rocket in spurts, or risk dashing headlong into a wall on a sudden turn.

As the pair rounded a corner a great wind, like a negative tornado, began pulling at the Big Cheese. The Valiant Vortex Boy and his dad, the Mighty Omni-vac, were on the job. However, the Cheese managed to reverse his thruster belt; and soon he was speeding down another hall.

"After him!" called Doctor Unknown, who had just come through a door, "his mask protected him from my knock-out gas! How do you fight a foe who has no nose!" he asked with some exasperation.

Bob listened to the Blaster reporting all this on his radio. "Don't loose him!" Bob cried. Soon they were joined by the True Believer, the Pink Liberator, Elf and Wisp.

"I tried to hold him while in my Wisp persona but he's too strong," said the Wisp.

"That's nothing!" True Believer was panting and gasping, "I am holding him! He must be related to a bull dozer!"

"Where is he?" the Doctor asked.

"He's dragging me to the staircase," the Believer was turning a sickly hue before their eyes. "I am not fearful," he said - and then he fainted.

They all ran to the stairway. It was clear that the Cheese had entered the sub-basement.

Only Bob and Blaster went on from there. The rest had to stay at their assigned posts in case any of the henchmen showed up or the Cheese doubled back.

The stairs went far underground; sometimes unfolding like an endless fire escape beneath their feet; sometimes snaking and spiraling through dim, dizzying shadows.

They could hear the clank and clatter of the Cheese's roller skates coming up from the steps below them. Bob considered that the Cheese must have some kind of locking mechanism on his skates – either that or he was very, very skillful.

The two adventurers were now descending with more caution; they had learned to respect their quarry. After what seemed like a long time they came to the bottom. Through the open door they could see a large hall with many branching corridors and walkways leading off in all directions. They heard the hushed resonance of air conditioning and no other sound - no clue to indicate the trail of the Cheese.

"Where'd he go?" asked Bob. "Search me," said the Blaster. They both knew that the sub-basement was a real labyrinth, a maze that never stood still. This was because in addition to the many conventional traps that were set, the walls themselves switched and opened and closed in a random fashion. These computer designed tunnels were intended to insure that no one could escape the sub-basement. The only problem was that now it was almost impossible to track the progress of the Cheese.

Just then a hissing, like steam from a radiator, drew their attention to one of the door ways.

"Over here, you two!" the voice belonged to Mr. Mann. Morpho, Moe and Willow-wand were bunched up behind him. "Where is he?" asked the Iguana man.

"Bob and Blaster exchanged a startled glance. "We don't know," admitted the Blaster.

Faster that the eye could register; Mr. Mann's hand shot out and grabbed the Blaster's radio. "Wilbur! We lost him! Watch out, he's probably on his way there."

The receiver crackled with the reply of Professor Wie. "Oh, don't get your tail in a knot! He's here already and we're having a nice chat. Why don't you and the others join us?"

Mr. Mann now took the lead since he was the one who was most familiar with the layout of the sub-basement. Even he had some trouble guiding them in the correct general direction of their goal.

The Infinity Room was positioned in the center of a vast network of deceptive, ever changing passageways.

Through a honeycomb of chambers designed to disorient, they were directed past doors that bore enticing labels such as: "TOP SECRET WEAPONS ROOM," and "EMERGENCY GOLD DEPOSITORY." Bob correctly deduced that these were mere deceptions holding nothing but traps for the Cheese and his minions.

They jogged ahead through a weirdly lit room that was furnished upside-down and another that tilted and spun as they crossed the threshold.

But in a relatively short time they came to the end of a passage that let out into a circular hall of many doors. One of these had the simple label, "THE INFINITY ROOM." Mr. Mann escorted the students to a door almost directly opposite the labeled one.

The kids followed their teacher as one bunched up group. Inside the door they found only a huge, rounded tunnel coated with a mirror surface. Anyone walking down that tube to the other end had to confront an infinite number of reflections. Perhaps that's how the room got its name. Bob watched his other selves reflected in the walls and marching in perfect step: a column of Bobs on either side, rank upon rank, shrinking to an unguessable vanishing point.

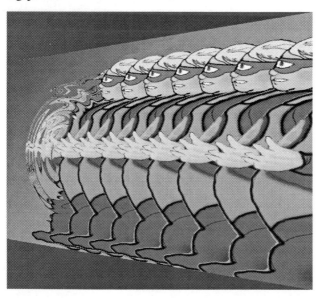

As they came to the end of the massive looking-glass they saw a black and white tile floor stretch out before them. In the center of this there were five or six overstuffed sofas clustered around a few, low, mahogany tables. Futuristic lamp stands illuminated the two figures already seated opposite each other.

The Cheese and the Professor were drinking tea and eating cookies!

"Come in, come in! Sit and help yourselves to refreshments," professor Wie greeted the teacher and his charges.

"Yes," the Cheese put in, "do join us. We're just concluding a little bit of business and then we can get right down to the destruction of everybody here."

Professor Wie responded as the students found their seats. "You will never carry out your plans, you know. Your threats end here, Cheese!"

"Who's going to stop me, Wie? Your band of pitiful, sniveling brats? Your freaky has-been teachers? Your Rube Goldberg defenses? Do you think a few tunnels and mazes can stop the greatest mind ever created?"

"My synapses have all super congealed. My neurons and cerebellum have all ripened for this moment. I have aged since we last encountered each other; but I have not mellowed! I'm sharp! I'm strong! I AM PUNGENT!"

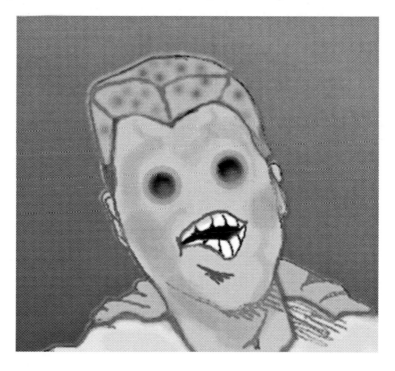

"There is nothing you can say or do to halt me! I will conquer! You first: and then the world!"

137

Professor Wie stood up and walked two paces towards the Big Cheese who also rose to his feet.

The professor looked his adversary in the eye with a steely gaze and said, "I defy you. I oppose you and everything you stand for. I will challenge and resist you to the end."

"Wow!" Bob whispered to Moe who was sitting next to him, "I'd be afraid to stand up to the Cheese that way and I can bounce!"

Moe whispered a fervent reply, "Yeah, even with no super powers, professor Wie is the greatest hero of us all!"

"Stop that whispering over there!" the crime boss yelled as he whipped around and pointed at Bob. "You!" he exclaimed, "You're the same fat kid who dared to steal my plans!"

"His name," said the professor, "is Robert; and I am most proud of him for doing so. Therefore, if you cannot refer to my young scholars with some respect I will have to insist that you refrain from speaking at all."

It looked like the Cheese was just about ready to pop a neck vein; but before he could screech a response, professor Wie continued, "Robert, why don't you bring out the gift we have prepared for our guest?"

This was all part of the plan and Bob had rehearsed it well. He went over to one of the tables and flipped open a lid. From the inside he removed a strange looking object.

"What kind of joke is this, Wie?" growled the Cheese. Bob saw that most of the students had made their way down to the Infinity Room in the last few minutes. They were quietly filing in and forming a circle around the couches.

"It's no joke," said professor Wie, "The room in which we stand has many strange properties. It will magnify the effects of this, our most powerful weapon."

Bob was pointing the sinister looking object straight at the Big Cheese. It looked like a gun, or maybe a portable cannon. It had blinking lights running up, down and around; with bright colored neon encircling chrome and brass fittings. Complex transformers, affixed to the stock of the gun, hummed with suppressed power. It had a stylized atomic nucleus and orbiting electrons painted on the side. Sparks ripples around the muzzle as if they were having difficulty containing themselves.

"Behold the ordinance of the future," said professor Wie.

"I know all about the future!" The Cheese retorted, "You needn't tell me about your connections with certain unspeakable organizations!"

"We will not go into that now," the professor said abruptly, "You will instead surrender yourself to my personal custody. Then we will see about getting you the help you need."

"Moo Ha! I need no help! Not from you; not from anybody!" The villain turned to face Bob. "Go ahead fat boy! Pull the trigger!"

"He will do it if I tell him to," assured the professor, "and if he does, it will unleash forces..."

"Ha! Ha! Moo! Ha! Ha! Ha!" the horrible laugh of the Cheese echoed in the Infinity Room, "Are you a fool or do you take me for one? You're bluffing Wie! You could never do it! Your super weapon is a sham! Go ahead and shoot! Nothing will happen! Shoot, you cursed blob of blubber!!"

Bob's finger tightened on the trigger. There was a loud pop and a jet of white smoke. Instantly, the Big Cheese doubled over as if hit with a ninety-pound cannonball.

"AAAARRRRGG!" the Cheese was spitting and screaming. "You shot me!!! What was it? A death ray? Invisible radiation? Poison? Germs? I can feel it eating at me! But you won't win! I'll beat it, Wie! Whatever it takes!! I have money! I have resources! You aren't the only one with mysterious powers!!"

The Cheese was shaking now- whether with rage or sickness, it was hard to tell. He started to back pedal towards the door.

"I'll have my revenge if it's the last thing I do! Do you hear me? The world can wait! You will all feel my wrath!"

Before the last word was screamed, the Cheese switched on his rocket belt and the yellow Cheese flew.

"Let him go!" called the professor and then he seemed to address the empty floor, "Are you alright, Morpho?"

The spot that moments earlier held the super villain now started to waver and a big letter M became visible. In seconds the M solidified and a boy appeared. Bob put down the gun and helped Morpho to his feet.

"I see that plan B worked," said Mrs. White; and all the kids and teachers clapped while Morpho boy blushed red and rippled in and out of sight.

"Yes," said professor Wie, "We had hoped to capture him. That was plan A. But plan B called for making him fear to attack us again. He may do so anyway. In fact, I believe he will. But today we shook his confidence and his ego. He had to run from us in defeat and he will never forget it."

The professor went on to explain how it was Bob who came up with a plan to build the so-called Infinity Gun with the help of the Crunches and Dr. Unknown. The gun was a fake. Its only power was to shoot out a jet of talcum powder and make a loud pop.

The plan had called for the invisible Morpho (who, was assigned to the sub-basement team for this purpose) to leap and hit the Cheese in the bread basket. It had been easy for Morpho to fade out and get in position while the gangster was distracted with the gun and the professor (not to mention his own impassioned soliloquizing).

"If it turned out that we couldn't stop the Big Cheese," Bob explained, "I had to ask myself, what would scare him away so he couldn't hurt anybody? That's when we came up with plan B, otherwise known as the Infinity

Gun."

Professor Wie congratulated the school on its excellent performance. "I couldn't be more proud of you. We still have more work to do; but today I think you deserve a reward. You are all invited to a pizza-pie party that I will be giving in the teacher's lounge at eight o'clock."

Bob and Morpho and Blaster found themselves in the position of being the new school heroes. Somehow, amid all the celebration, the moment Bob remembered with the most fondness was when Ariel, the Wonderful Wisp, came up to him, shook his hand and said, "Not bad, Bobby Boy," and then she added, "That's using the old noodle!"

Chapter XIII

Bread for Combat

Two days later, deep in the mysterious and cavernous sub-basement, Wilbur Wie crossed the threshold of a room that held one large cage constructed exclusively of M46. The two prisoners stirred and a voice that sounded as ugly as its owner yelled, "How long do you think you can hold us, Wie?"

Inside the cage spotlights revealed the Thug and First Impression Joey.

"Yeah," said Joey "isn't there some jazz in the Declaration of the Constitution or something - some bit about freedom? You never could have caught us in the first place. But that rotten Dr. Unknown used gas on us! It's against the law to hold us here!"

The professor replied grimly, "You weren't so concerned about civil rights when your gang started shooting at unarmed schoolchildren. That's good for a life sentence, boys."

"Don't blame us for that! You can't pin that on us; go after the guys that did it!"

"The police already have them in custody." Professor Wie responded, "I'm not interested in small-fry."

"But I tell you we didn't even have no guns."

"You didn't have *any* guns," the professor corrected.

"That's what I said," Joey replied exasperatedly, "you dumb, stuffed shirt!"

"Now, now, let's have some manners. Or would you rather wait another two days to speak with me? I may find time in my schedule by then."

"Well, what do you want from us? We ain't talking no matter what!"

"You mean," said the professor, "you *aren't* talking."

"Oh, for cry eye!" said Joey; finally comprehending, "a million jails and I gotta get stuck in grammar school!"

There was a distinct lull in the conversation.

"So," said Joey, "what's in it for me if I talk?"

"How about an early funeral?" said the Thug.

"Aw, listen Thug; I wasn't going to spill anything. But, I mean, so what if I do? I thought we were going to let me do the talking?"

"You listen, runt," said Thug, "Maybe you think like I don't have any brains. But the boss appreciates me. He even once told me that my ideas were like poetry!"

"The Cheese said that?" Joey and the professor asked together.

"Yeah," the Thug replied in a hurt voice, "at least he said my ideas were melodious."

"You big booby!" Joey said, "The word he used was malodorous!"

"Boys," said the professor, "I don't have time for the Abbot and Costello routine. You tell me where your boss has his secret hideout and I'll turn you over to the police. I happen to know that the Cheese is a wealthy individual. Maybe he'll come up with your bail. It's worth a chance. Otherwise you stay right hear to entertain each other until I forget to feed you."

It didn't take them long to decide. First Joey talked himself into it. From there it was easy to talk the Thug into going along.

They both submitted to the professor's polygraph machine (one at a time to check if their stories matched). The two crooks went off to jail (as the professor intended all along) and Wilbur Wie had the address of the hideout.

The next few weeks seemed to take off and run around in circles. Certainly most of the students were spinning like tops. They began to realize just how little time was left in their third and penultimate year.

Mrs. White was one of those who helped to remind the students of the rapidly passing time. She conducted a class called The History of Super Villains. The kids really looked forward to these lessons because the only texts that were used consisted of old comic books.

That is, they looked forward until the homework assignments started to pile up. When that started to happen many of the students refused to look ahead at all. Consequently, they were always playing catch up in the homework department.

Unexpectedly, Bob and his Blaster partner had no such difficulties. They seemed to compliment each other's talents so that where one showed an academic weakness the other excelled. Because the boys were doing all their homework as a team they both saw an improvement in their grades.

"But why do we have to remember all this golden age stuff from before World War II?" the Purp asked no one in particular.

"Yeah," agreed Verity Hammes, also known as the Pink Liberator. "My parents were working in the golden age and my grandfather was a pulp hero. But this is now; we're almost in the 1960's! It's the silver age of modern comics. That old fashioned stuff is such a yawn."

"Well, Mrs. White isn't yawning you can bet," said Morpho.

In fact there was no yawning allowed by anyone in Mrs. White's class. "Now class," she warned, "you are in danger! Yes, some of you are in great danger of not graduating. What happens if you don't graduate, Mr. Nova?"

"You flunk!"

The class sniggered and laughed.

"You may think that's all that happens," the teacher said, "but in addition to not receiving a diploma, you will not be approved by the Comics Code."

There was a whispered buzz.

"That's right," she went on, "no one will call on you for help because the other superheroes will regard you as an interfering renegade; and the police authorities will treat you like vigilantes."

"But Mrs. White," asked Bob (and then quickly raised his hand) "if the outside world doesn't know we superheroes even exist, what difference can it make?"

"While it is true that most of the authorities don't know of us," she responded in her frostiest tones, "the few who do make all the difference. You will find that you will not be able to get the cooperation of the president; the chief of police, or the dog catcher if you don't have your professional diploma."

"Now," she continued, "you are all required to negotiate an approved hero to work with as side-kick next year. I know that some of you have already started the process and a few have even completed the commitment agreement."

"I warn you to hurry. Any student who has not signed up by summer vacation may as well not come back. Besides, you don't want to wait until all the good ones are taken."

No one was quite sure if she was joking. Everyone was quite sure that they didn't want to be the one to find out.

Bob had spent a lot of time writing in his journal book (volume three and counting). He liked to write down all the pros and cons of any important decision he had to make. After a bit of thought (and a lot of ineffectual worry) he made a decision to ask Captain Speedball to take him on as apprentice side-kick for next year.

Bob remembered that the Captain had hinted only two summers ago that he might favor such a relationship. When Bob brought up the subject with Derick, the Crunch, he received a surprise.

"I'm sure he'll go for it Bob; he likes you. You can get his permission now and hash out the details when you visit over vacation."

Bob replied, "But I thought you knew I was spending this summer with the Elf. He wants to take me to Elf-land and I promised him I would visit a long time ago. I thought it would be a great adventure."

"So did I buddy, so I asked him if I could tag along. It's all set. We'll spend a few days at my house and then Moe and I are coming with you guys!"

143

"Wow! No fooling? That's great! We'll have a real keen time! But what about Psyche; can't he come too?"

"Not this time. His circus schedule won't allow it. But next summer, after we graduate, we'll all get together at Psyche's home. Or maybe it's a tent, I don't know. Anyway, he's going to use the old magic, marble, reflection, telepathic, telephone thingy like always and we can keep in touch."

Soon enough there came the time for the last book and the last class of the year. Professor Wie said the traditional goodbye and be safe speech. The magic summer beckoned with open-handed promise.

The boys spent four days with the Crunch family. Bob had already gotten approval from both Captain Speedball and the school to be his side-kick for a year. Now that he had completed his third year Bob was officially qualified to go on patrol. Naturally, he was a bit nervous.

"Don't worry about it," Speedball told him, "remember that you already have experience standing up to bad guys. Never forget your fear. Learn from it. You bounce pretty good too, kiddo."

"Yeah, but what if I find I can't stand up to the strain of combat?" asked Bob, "What if it turns out I'm not cut-out to be a superhero?"

"Not cut-out? Listen. This idea of being bread for combat is the bunk. We're all bread for combat: you; me, the butcher and the baker, and my cute little nieces. It's in our heredity. Our cave-man forebears all had to scrape and scrap in order to get by. It follows that anyone can fight in a good cause. Anyone can be a hero. We all have the capacity."

Bob was all for going out on patrol with Speedball right away but the Captain said to wait until after vacation.

"Patrol work isn't all it's cracked up to be, Bob. A lot of it is just mind-numbing foot work and dreary vigilance. You'll get your chance soon enough. Now's the time for fun, not work. Go off to *munchkinville*, or where ever it is your friend hangs out, and we can talk about it when you get back."

There came a moonlit night. The enchanted voyage began in a mysterious enough way.

"At midnight we begin our adventure," the Elf announced to Moe, Derrick and Bob.

"Why can't we go in the morning and get a fresh start?" Moe wanted to know.

"There was much you were forbidden to tell me about the future," the Elf reminded him with a sigh, "now is the time you must follow my lead and trust with good hope."

Well, there wasn't a good answer to that of course, so the boys set off at midnight. The Elf assured them that they didn't have to take along much baggage. All would be provided when they reached their destination.

"How far is it?" asked Bob.

"Beyond the portal of dreams and around the corner of what human thought can achieve."

"Oh, great," Moe mumbled, "We're lost already!"

Bob chuckled, "Come on, Moe! That's just like what you told me when I asked you what year it was last summer!"

"Was not!"

They proceeded down the hill behind that portion of the Crunch's house which showed above ground. Across a field and through a grove of pine and larch trees they made their way.

They were dressed in simple clothes with wide brimmed hats and good boots. Bob thought Derick and Moe looked very different without their costumes (and if he had known it, the others thought Bob looked a little strange too). Each of the hikers carried a knap sack and a canteen.

Before long there was a noise like the wind picking up. But the sound didn't die down. It increased until it was clear that they were listening to fast flowing water. They came out of the trees and found themselves looking at a stream that was a bit too wide to be called a creek and a tad too narrow to be dubbed a river.

The Elf led them to a sandy bank and said, "Here we are."

"Where?" said Moe.

"What do you mean?" said Bob.

"Huh?" said Derick.

"Sit down," the Elf advised, "I want to look at the moon."

145

Sure enough the ginger crown of a full harvest moon was just starting to steal its way above the distant line of trees. It seemed to open out and began to swell as if it were a hot-air balloon mounting to the far stars.

Bob gazed at the moon's wide face. The craters stood out in stark shadows, sharp and distinct. Tyco (the only crater he knew how to find) sat like a spider in the center of a web; or perhaps more like a hole in a window from a BB gun.

Now the mystifying orb had cleared the trees and instead of shrinking it grew as it rose. Bob looked down to see the reflected moon in the water. The bright image danced and shimmered.

Without any transition he could remember Bob found himself looking up from under the water. He was moving downstream and, although he couldn't see them, he knew his friends were right with him.

Ripples undulated. Undulations bubbled. Bubbles gurgled and gurgles rippled with a music sublime. Bob didn't think about the passing of time and was quite unable to concentrate on the dull fact that he wasn't breathing. Nothing was worth worrying about. After a timeless interval, nothing was all that was left.

Bob woke to the sound of singing birds. It must have been near five o'clock in the morning. Or maybe it was near sunset? At any rate the sun was low and the shadows were long. For one disoriented moment he thought he was having another unspeakable dream. But this was something different.

The stream had moved out of sight and so had the trees. The boys were in a broad field of grass high in the mountains. Now Bob wasn't so hot at geography, but even he knew that there shouldn't be mountains for at least a hundred miles.

"What happened?" cried Derick.

"Where are we and how in the name of all the asteroids did we get here?" Moe added.

That left nothing for Bob to ask so he contented himself with saying, "Yeah!"

"My friends, welcome to Elf-land Havenhome."

The boys stared with blinking eyes. Each stone and tree and blade of grass had an extra something that was not easy to define. It was like firefly glow. It was like the beginnings of snow blindness. It resembled the shattered spectrum of dancing colors found in sunlit crystal.

Yet when they looked closely it eluded their vision.

"What is that?" Bob said, referring to the phenomena. "What are we seeing here, Elf? Is there something wrong with my eyes? I don't know if I can take this much color for long."

"You will all soon grow accustomed." The Elf replied, "Maybe too soon."

"What do you mean by that?" Bob said.

"What you perceive here is the life of this land. It is how we know that the earth is alive. Everything is new and full of possibilities just waiting to be uncovered."

"Little children see the world in this way all the time but they misplace their wonder. As they grow older they exchange that which is new for that which is known. And everyone knows there is no need to examine what is already known.

"But you do have a word for that which you are now beginning to recognize as woven deep into the fabric of this country."

The Elf regarded his friends solemnly, "It is a quality you refer to as magic."

Chapter XIV

On a Roll

Bob thought about what it meant to have the viewpoint of a small child. To see the world as forever new, fresh and magical; to never take life for granted, seemed to him a very wise and desirable thing; and he promised himself he would always try to have this outlook.

To disregard the magic potential of life, he supposed, would be like waking up on Christmas morning, or on the first sunny day of summer, and then deciding to stay in bed.

Bob's reflections were abruptly cut off by the sound of a horn blowing in the distance. Keen and impelling as a bugle call, the sound of the horn grew nearer.

A broad smile lit the face of the Elf, "Hark! It is my family signal! The roaming season has started already! See, we have only to watch and wait as they approach."

From a broad pass that lead down into the grasslands the boys could see what looked like a parade coming their way.

First came the young children, dancing and running, arrayed in bright colors. After these, the animal part of the procession wound its way forward with dogs and older children herding the sheep and cows. Next in line were the mule and horse riders. Finally the elders in their chariots and wagons followed the thirty or so men and women who were walking.

And as they walked their voices were lifted in song.

"Come on!" Elf called and began to run to the back of the colorful caravan.

As the boys followed they saw that scouts of elf bowmen had ranged ahead on either side. They were clad all in mottled green and were hard to see until they came closer. One of the horse riders broke off from the group and rode right up.

"Hail, Hawk, of the family Spring-green, my son and my joy returned to me! Moreover, I greet you, his friends, and well met!"

"Hail father!" Elf responded, "My heart is glad indeed to see you well, who are never far from my thoughts!"

Then the Elf turned to his friends and explained, "He's my dad."

The boys introduced themselves one by one and thanked Mr. Spring-green for his hospitality.

Then Derick put his hands on his hips, tapped his foot three times and said, "Hawk?"

Bob broke in, "You never told us your real name was Hawk!"

"It is a family name," said Elf with some dignity, "You are my good friends and may use this name; but it is not for outlanders to know."

"Ha!" cried Elf's father, "The merry companions of my introverted son will now join him in our wagon. There they will meet the rest of our humble family until we camp for the night. Run along, now and I will catch you up!"

Elf's entire family lived in one large wagon drawn by a team of oxen. This only happened during that time the elves set aside for their annual migration. The long and narrow wooden cart was equipped with furniture; a stove and fireplace; and beds. Bob had seen many houses that were smaller than the Spring-green's rolling home away from home.

April Spring-green was the matriarch of the clan and the mother of Elf's mother. Long ages she gathered wisdom and now shared it most of each day with all who would listen. She didn't look a day over sixty.

Bud and Daisy Spring-green were the parents of three children: Iris, Hawk and Sprig.

Hawk, (hitherto known by his friends as the Elf) was the only family member to be engaged in a quest at the present moment.

"I am charged," Hawk said, "with a mission. I must cast away my enchanted spear."

"That's your big quest?" asked Moe, "You just have to throw away an old spear?"

"Basically, yes, that is it," said the Elf.

"What's so hard about that?" said the Crunch.

"I am reluctant to say. I had hoped to speak of this at another time."

"Aw, come on," they said.

"It has to do with where he must leave the spear," piped up Sprig, Hawk's younger brother.

"I will speak of this! It is not your place, brother!"

Moe whispered to Bob, "That kid reminds me of Buster!"

"Well," said Hawk with a deep sigh, "I will tell you. The oracle said that I must depart from my spear and leave it lodged in the heart of a dragon."

"Yes, and we thought all along that the dragon wouldn't like this," said Iris, who was a year or two older than Hawk. Iris was a pretty girl, thought Bob, even if she did have the upside-down pointy ears of her people.

At this point Hawk's mother made it known that it would soon be time for supper. The wagon stopped rather abruptly at this announcement. The elves were anticipating another guest tonight; an important visitor. The boys were not expected to help set up camp (they were regarded as important guests too) but they did have to wash up for the meal.

There was a small lake where the elves chose to set up camp. From the many wagons and carts in the convoy the children now ran to the shore to fetch water.

Bob and his friends proceeded at a more leisurely pace with Sprig and Iris tagging along.

"The procession of the Elf Children," Hawk was saying, "happens each year at this time. It is regarded as part of the great dance of our people."

"So why do your people do it?" asked Bob, "Where do they go? I mean, isn't it hard to settle down and get on with things when each year you have to pull up steaks and go on migration?"

Hawk replied, "There are many reasons why we do so. Do not your people have a custom that the young go to school each autumn and vacation each summer? Why do you go to school every year?"

"To learn things," Bob said.

"And this is why we migrate. You may also say it is an honored tradition of our ancestors: we've always done it this way. Another reason might be because it is in our blood. This is the way of my people, the Children. Thus were we fashioned from the beginning times."

"They do not understand about the dance," said Iris who went on to explain, "The Great Dance of the Children is the way we live our lives. It is a happy celebration. I think your people value lore and learning, and well they should. But there is a higher prize to seek: wisdom."

"Wisdom does not inspect or dissect the experiences of living. It does not suck the marrow dry from the bones of the day. Wisdom itself is a part of what is learned; wisdom joins in the dance."

"Become not impatient with my often windy sister," put in Sprig, "we know well that your customs and habits differ from ours. We have as much to learn from you as you from us."

"Is this not the adventure?" said Hawk, "to find out so as to know?"

"What I'd like to know," said Derick, "is how long before breakfast, I mean, supper? This adventure we happen to be on right now has gotten me all mixed up!"

"I felt the same way," said Bob, "last summer when I visited Moe and had a great dinner for breakfast."

"Well, my hungry comrades, your famine will soon be mended," said Hawk, "We only await the arrival of our special guest, the Chant-weaver."

"This is a very exciting occasion for us," explained Iris, "For the Chant-weaver dwells not with any one caravan. Rather, she rides as the spirits prompt her and can visit any of the Children beyond all expectation."

"Only today did we get the glorious news," Sprig said as he jumped and skipped about, "We will have special treats and can stay up late to listen to the translations of the music!"

"Tell us about this music," asked Bob and Moe together. (The two had developed a real liking for Tchaikovsky last vacation.)

"Don't you hear it?" the little elf said, "The music all around: it's always there. There's music in the wind singing songs for those who have ears."

"That's right," said Hawk, "There is music of rare beauty in the rain-drops that fall and splash their rhythms against the window. Another melody is found in the bombastic crescendo of the volleying thunder."

Iris added, "There's a certain kind of music when I wash my face. Another kind is the wind sighing over the grass. What inexhaustible orches-trations there are! Acorns and leaves falling in the waning of the year. The hush of footprints crunching through snow. There's the silence of the dead cold of winter, which is but the raising of the baton before the symphony of spring. Then comes the chuckling of new life returning as the ices melt."

"Truly, there is music all around," Sprig repeated.

"Aye," agreed Hawk, "Don't forget the melody to be found in the voic-es of friends and loved ones. Endlessly varied are these tones. I cherish the treble of my mother's laugh and the sonorous bass of my father's exclama-tions. My sister is a clarinet and my brother is a reed pipe."

"And my brother is a noisy wind that we love even as it tosses the hair in our eyes!" laughed Sprig.

"There is harmony in conversation that never loses its charm," said Iris, "but now is the time we must hurry back, for I see the feast is ready to begin."

Bob had never thought of these simple things in this way before. Throughout his whole life he had only been listening for people's words and the thoughts behind them. Bob couldn't wait to practice listening for words and music as well. He began to perceive that he would never again suffer boredom listening to people talk.

As Hawk led them back he said, "Of course we young folks have not yet the years necessary for acquiring a developed ear. That is why we are so happy you will get a chance to hear Chant-weaver. She will speak of the one, true story of which all others are merely a part."

"The one, true story; what's that?" prompted Bob.

"There is only one proper story; all the other stories will one day come together in a single pattern to make up the one, real story." said Sprig, "You know of this story; for you yourselves are a part of it. You even have the com-fort of knowing how the great story ends: '...and they lived happily ever after.'"

The feast that night was enough to satisfy even Bob's appetite. Venison stew, wild goose and roast beef were the main dishes; but there were plenty of fruits, vegetables and elf biscuits to compliment the rest. Not to mention desserts and treats - which were not saved for the end but were eaten between courses.

Chant-weaver sat in a place of honor in the center of a semicircle where she could partake of the choicest morsels. The Spring-green family sat next to her alongside of Bob and his friends.

The mysterious songstress looked to be even older than Grandmother April. She wore the simple but brightly colored clothing that her people preferred.

After the meal Chant-weaver laid aside her cloak and placed a carved wooden cask on her lap. The hinges on it opened up into a musical instrument, with keys and strings set in a helix coil. It truly looked difficult to play.

She struck a sweet chord and her eyes opened very wide as she smiled in approval.

"One of you needs a song," she announced. "I know that one of our visitors from a distant land is lacking a song I could give. The music is for healing and learning; it also is pleasant to the ear. Which one of you needs my song?"

Bob began to feel very uncomfortable for some reason. Maybe it was because Chant-weaver's eyes seemed to be drilling through him like twin x-rays.

After a few seconds that seemed like forever, Bob looked away and mumbled something inaudible.

"So!" the weaver lady said as she pointed right at Bob, "You are troubled about who you are. But all boys have this trouble."

Bob didn't know what to say and everybody else waited to find out if Chant-weaver would sing. The campfire crackled making small popping sounds. The wind at least was singing in the trees.

"Ah, yes!" she cried so suddenly and loudly that all the younger children jumped.

"You have been bearing the heavy worry of what others think of you! Is this not so? Have I not hit upon it?"

Bob said a measured nothing.

"I perceive that you are a good boy. I would not discomfort you. I will sing the song you need only if you wish it. There is much else to sing this evening. Do you wish me to sing the song you need to hear?"

Bob had to say something because everybody was looking at him for a response. He said, "If you please, lady Chant-weaver, I would like to hear the song I need to hear."

"Yes!" she exclaimed, and then she started to clap her hands rapidly as if in invitation for all to do the same. Soon everyone was clapping and smiling and Bob found himself doing the same with a surprising feeling of relief.

"The song I have for you is called the Foot Enchantment."

The music began and Bob realized that it was literally an enchantment. For the words of the story were indeed chanted in an ancient mode. And the song seemed to help the listeners draw pictures from the flicker of the fire, and the play of shadow on smoke, until they could visualize what was being sung even as the music unfolded. Here is what she sang:

There was a boy named Billy
Who loved to tend his sheep
He loved his sheepdogs even more
Together they would sleep
And run and eat and rest awhile
Beside a shady glade
And life went on as Billy grew
Until he met a maid

Her hair was flaxen lovely
Her eyes were sapphire bright
Fair Melinda she was called
Her skin was creamy white

One day Billy called to her
And he fell upon his knees
"Come back when you have won your fame,"
She said, and then she teased
"Make sure you wash and comb your hair,
For I fear you may have fleas!"

Now it was known how Billy kept
The company of hounds
And in truth he was no worse
Than other lads around

Rumor cruel took wing that day
Around the village square
"Billy is infested!"
"He has fleas within his hair!"
"Nay!" the local barber said
"No fleas have I found there
By my troth you'll find them
In the clothes that he does wear

But the tailor cried
"It isn't so!

153

His clothes are not to blame!
All should know
The dogs around his feet
Have caused this bane!"

So flea-foot Billy
He was called
By all from that day forth
And Billy didn't like it
But he was not the sort
To try to make things even
Revenge was not for him
Instead he said
"I'll take that name
And fame myself will win!"

And Billy ran the dusty roads
And up and down the lane
Every day his legs would grow
So stiff and sore with pain
But every day he ran the more
'Till after came a day
Billy was the swiftest
And everyone did say

"No one can best our Billy
Champion of the track
And the name we gave him
Once in scorn
We now do take it back
No more shall he be 'flea-foot'
Now 'fleet-foot' is his name"

And with this new respect he won
His girlfriend and his fame

So much for Billy Fleet-foot
Who helped us all to see
A name is merely what you're called
Not what you come to be

The music expired. They took three long seconds to savor the experience. Then the damn broke and they all cheered and banged their hands together with fevered enthusiasm. Bob stood in front of Chant-weaver and bowed in gratitude.

He couldn't figure out how she knew it; but that song really did scratch an itch for him. For a long time Bob had nursed a private grudge against the Mean Blaster. It bothered him that the Blaster, whom he now regarded as a partner, had once taunted him with the name of Blubber Boy.

Bob had tried to confront this in himself and he even pretended that he could make light of the name. But he knew that deep inside, he wanted to get even with MB. And that also bothered him. Wasn't the desire for revenge a sign of villainy?

But now Bob could see that the name which had bothered him so much couldn't really define who he was. He was more than just a "Blubber Boy" no matter who thought differently. The song helped him to feel free of the name. He felt better about who he was. He reflected with a tinge of awe that the song about Billy Fleet-foot was indeed just what he needed to hear.

There were many other songs that night. There were comic tunes and love ballads. There were songs that demonstrated the consummate skill and artistry of Chant-weaver. There were songs that everyone could join in and sing. But Bob went to sleep that night thinking about just one song; and how it was really a gift that could change his life.

The boys slept rather late the next morning, all except Hawk who was used to getting up before dawn. Derick in particular liked to get his eight hours of sleep. Bob felt good about the vacation so far. The previous night had been a wonderful experience. Yet he also felt a bit uneasy.

"I can't quite put my finger on it," he told the others, "but I feel as though I forgot something important."

"Must be breakfast!" said Moe.

"No," said Bob – too distracted to realize he was being kidded, "No, that's not it. Oh well, it'll come to me."

They ate a breakfast of goat's milk; cheese, butter, kettle-bread, wild honey, blackberries and eggs.

"Now my friends," Hawk the elf announced, "with your aid my quest continues. I have a lodestone that will point to where my people will journey and we can meet them after. My mother has set in our packs food enough for many days. Let us ride while the fair morning is young!"

But Derick was tapping his foot again, "Now hold on! Nobody mentioned horse riding! I tried that once and almost broke my –um- my pride."

Moe was laughing, "I don't know how to ride a horse! They're a little hard to find on space stations!"

"Then I will teach you!" Hawk replied. "Before this day is over you shall become riders!"

Now Bob was embarrassed to bring it up, but he knew that the truth would soon be evident weather he spoke or not. So he gulped and said, "I don't think you have a horse large enough to accommodate me."

The realization hit them. Bob was almost six feet wide and who knew how many pounds heavy. It would be a challenge for a moderately sized elephant to carry him.

"Dear Bob!" cried Hawk, "I am at a loss…"

"But I'm not!" interrupted the Crunch. "I really and honestly don't ever want to learn how to ride a horse, but I saw something back by your house that might be the solution!"

What Derick saw was a row of chariots. They looked like wooden tubs with three wheels each and when the Elf saw them he slapped his knee and hooted, "The very answer! Why did I not think of it! Most of our journey will proceed by road and field. We elves maintain a vast network of roads to meet the needs of migration. So Bob can ride in comfort and you and Moe can ride with the extra packs. We can even carry more provisions. Come, let us get started!"

So they bridled their horses and packed their carts. Hawk rode on a horse called Bob, but the elf hastened to assure him that the name came years before he had ever met Bob Blob. "He has this name because of his bobtail," Hawk explained.

Now they started off into the beckoning day. "Looks like we're on a roll!" said Bob with his customary, cheerful disregard for a bad pun.

They rode along at an easy pace; enjoying many an unimportant conversation and jest. As he watched the day open out before him, an idle thought crossed Bob's mind. He wondered what was going on back home. And then he suddenly remembered what had been bothering him.

"Psyche!" he shouted.

They came to an abrupt stop. "Psyche!" Bob repeated, "We forgot to talk to him on our reflection marbles last night!"

Moe said, "We were too busy with the concert to even think of it. You suppose he'll be sore at us?"

"Nay!" said Hawk, "But he may worry at the absence of our voices."

"Hey," Derick said, "Why don't we call him now? We never tried calling him before."

"That's true," Bob agreed, "We always spoke only at pre-arranged times. But it should work because he said we could call him in an emergency."

"We all have our magic marbles;" Hawk put in, "what we lack is the emergency."

"Well," Bob replied with deliberation, "If he thinks we might be in trouble because we didn't call him - that *could* be considered an emergency."

"You've been hanging around with the Blaster too long," asserted the Crunch.

Moe put in, "Bob's right. We should at least try. If he's right in the middle of sawing a woman in two in his magic act or something we can apologize later and call back."

So back-to-back four boys sat on the crown of a grassy hillock while the horses munched grass.

The clouds cast variegated shadows that caused them to slip in and out of the bright sunlight. And along with one of the shafts of light the voice of Psyche was heard, "Wow! You guys, I was wondering about you. Is everything okay?"

"Sure!"

"We're doing fine!"

"All is well!"

"Can you talk or are you busy?"

"I can talk for a little while. How goes the quest?"

"We're having a great quest!"

"Yeah, and we're sorry we missed you last night."

"And I regret you could not be here to share our adventure."

"That's okay, Elf, I'm keeping busy."

Now, as the boys exchanged their thoughts with the aid of the reflection marbles, the voice of Moe seemed to giggle, "Don't call him Elf anymore. His real name - that he's been hiding from his friends all this time - is Hawk!"

"You may laugh," said Hawk, "but the jest is on you. My true name is nothing that could be hidden from the mind of a friend like Psyche!"

"You knew!" the Crunch accused, "You knew his real name and didn't bother to tell the rest of us?"

"Yep," replied Psyche, who sounded indifferent, "It wasn't my secret to share. You'd be surprised at what I know that I have to pretend I don't know."

"Aw, come on," Moe said, "can't you just tell us some little, harmless secrets?"

"How can I judge what's harmless?"

"Just pick one!"

"Very well," said Psyche stiffly, "shall we start with the secrets lodged in *your mind*?"

"Woops!" Moe said, and they all could feel his embarrassment. "You're right as usual. I'll just take my foot out of my mouth now."

"Right as rain," said Psyche, "Look, it's great talking to you guys. You are all great friends. But I can't keep up the telepathic connection much longer. We'll talk again tonight, okay?"

"You bet," replied Bob, "and this time we'll be there, too!"

The marbles went cold in their hands. The boys then started out on the quest once again.

"How far do we ride this morning, Hawk?" Bob asked this because of a private concern. He was habitually uneasy unless he knew the exact time of his next meal.

Before Hawk could answer, Derick added, "And how do we know where we're going? I presume we're trying to find a creature I always thought didn't exist. Do you know where the dragons hang out?"

"They do exist, said Hawk, "but they are not as abundant as in days of yore. In fact, no one I know of has seen one for quite a while."

"So how do we find them?" asked Moe.

"There are two ways that the bards recommend from long tradition. One can follow the trail of death and destruction a ravaging dragon leaves in its wake."

"Great!" said Bob with some irony. "What's the other way?"

"Ah, that is the path we are going to try. We will look for artifacts that will lead us to one of their hive cities. It is much the more dangerous course; but then the glory will be so much greater!"

"Great," said Bob again.

All that day they wound their way through meadow and valley, knoll and gorge. There were worn paths and dirt roads for much of the way. They saw plants and flowers that were strange looking but beautiful. Rock arches and layered sediment rippled on either side of the travelers from time to time. Copper green and carroty, the rusted veins showed great cracks and faults in the granite wall that flanked the mountain.

Soon Hawk raised his voice in song and the Boys joined in. They had fun playing with the echoes for awhile. However, after one particular vocal volley, an echo returned that did not originate with their party. There was the faint sound of shouting and the clash of swords!

Before you could say, "Hark!" the elf's horse broke into a run. The other horses took along a somewhat less willing Moe and Derick in one chariot and Bob in the other. As they vibrated along, behind the dust of Hawk's steed, the trailing charioteers hoped he knew where they were going.

They came to a turn in the road and this slowed them down just as they saw the fight.

It was five against one. Five big guys with swords were trying to kill one frantically darting kid who was using a technique Bob was familiar with. When Bob had fought his duel with the Blaster many months ago, he had kept his opponent at bay by swinging his sword as rapidly as he could in front of him. This kid was trying the same thing. But Bob knew that it was only a matter of time before fatigue would decide the issue.

Chapter XV

In a Pickle

Both attackers and attacked wore masks, or hoods, that concealed half their faces. Hawk arrived a few seconds ahead of the others. He leapt from his horse, cried aloud and brandished his spear. That gave Bob time to bounce from his cart. Moe hopped out of his chariot before it came to a complete stop. It looked like Derick was having some trouble getting his horse under control.

Three of the attackers continued what they were doing but the other two turned to face this new threat. Hawk parried blows from one of them with his spear. He kept jabbing at the man, knowing that if he cast his weapon he stood a good chance of loosing it.

Bob found that his bouncing was greatly hindered by his hiking clothes. His short pants could not take the strain and did not allow for the expansion he needed. He couldn't get high enough to land on top of his swordsman; so instead he tried to find an opening to bowl him over without getting sliced for his trouble.

Moe (who had not taken his ray gun on what he expected to be a relaxing vacation) grabbed a branch to use like a club. All those classes with Mrs. White began to pay off. The boys seemed to be holding their own.

But where was Derick? Out from behind a tall rock strode the Calamitous Crunch in full regalia. He had packed his M46 super costume in his back pack. The construction of the different parts of Derick's outfit allowed for it to be unfolded, assembled and powered up in less than a minute.

The Crunch had time to lift one boulder above his head (it was about the size of a sports car). The attackers broke and fled, one of them with a limp and bleeding arm.

"Pray let them go!" the young stranger was shouting, "Those dogs will never have the courage to return after this!"

"I am Mel Grayson of the Gray clan. My kin dwell in peace here on the flanks of Mount Ryanda. At least we do so until the crow-hearted marauders come up from the valley to raid and pillage. I am also in your debt. You are all braves. But I have never seen the like of yon crimson knight! He can boast of the strength of ten, nay! Twenty!"

"There is no debt to speak of, Mel Grayson. Know that in front of you stand Hawk Spring-green and my dear comrades. They are Robert Rotundus Maximillion Blob, who has earned the name Beneficent Bounce-o; Moe de Jur, a cadet of the Cosmic Patrol; and our brave knight (who, alas! is no horseman) Derick Crunch.

They all bowed and agreed to share supper together so that their acquaintance might have a chance to grow into friendship.

Mel appeared to be a lad of about Hawk's age, though perhaps not as tall. The mask was explained as a precaution imposed by the teachers of their clan on all warriors.

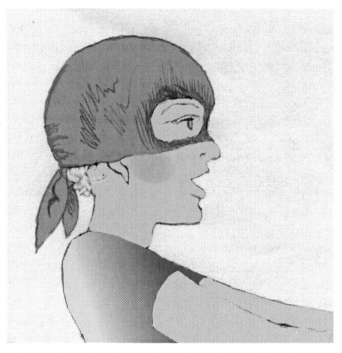

"Thus do we have the chance for adventure and heroism among our own people without the danger of pompous boasting or arrogant bullying."

"We understand, don't we guys?" said Derick.

"Yes!"

"You bet!"

"Aye, our own teachers have much the same rule when we go to school," Hawk said with assurance.

Around the campfire that night they told many tales and exchanged information about their different cultures and customs.

"I would very much like to ask of you a boon," said Mel, "I would join you on your quest, for the adventure of slaying a dragon. Yet I fear great and chivalrous comrades such as you could only scorn the small and humble help, which is all I could offer."

Now Bob had the strong feeling of being manipulated by this speech. After all, what could they respond? Could they say: "You are right, slime beneath our feet, get you gone?" Bob didn't think so. Yet he found he also admired the rascal. It took great nerve to stand against five swordsmen - not to mention skill and luck. They could use these qualities on their quest.

"We will consider this and give answer on the morrow," Hawk wisely answered.

When ten o'clock came around (Bob still wore his wrist watch for this very reason) they got ready to contact Psyche. Mel watched with wide eyes as the disjointed and obviously magical conversation unfolded.

"And after this classic battle," Hawk was explaining to Psyche, "we rescued this kid named Mel who hales from a different clan."

"Huh?" Psyche's grunt of surprise startled the others with its intensity. "You don't know it, but this 'Mel' is going to sleep in a separate camp tonight."

"Whatever for?" said Bob.

"Because I can read from here that Mel is only a nick name. You guys: Mel is short for Melinda!"

They quickly said goodbye to Psyche.

"Let me handle this," said Bob, "Mel, are you, that is, when we first saw you, well, what I mean…"

The Crunch (always one for the direct approach) blurted, "You're a girl! A tomboy girl! You're real name is Melinda! You tricked us!"

"I am guilty of no deception! I spoke no falsehood!" Mel responded with some heat, "You should know that I have been taught to value truth above pure gold!"

Well, to be fair about it, Bob reflected, she didn't exactly say she was a boy. He started to think back on all their conversation together and realized, with a shock, that she had not said one word that might have revealed her gender.

"Is your name Melinda? Moe asked.

"I am called Mel among my family and friends alike. All my words to you were true from the first when I introduced myself. Boys, I am not false and I mean no deception."

And Mel tugged at her mask. A cascade of flaxen hair fell about her shoulders.

"If you're really on the level," asked the Crunch, "why hide behind a mask?"

"I did tell you once of our custom. Also, if you were a maid who had to travel alone through a country that housed marauders, you would not need to ask."

"I will now take my leave of you. It is a shame though..." and here she paused as if undecided, "it is a shame that I know the location of a dragon hive and could tell you - if I were only a part of your quest."

Bob gave one long sigh and then all the boys started speaking at once. In the end they decided to give in. Hawk said that she could save the party weeks of hunting. "We'll let you tag along," said the Crunch boy, "even if you're only a girl tomboy!"

"You speak wrongly! Strange custom can not excuse such ignorance!" Mel said, and they could see fire flash in her eyes, "Have you not considered that next time it may be I who save you?"

"She's right you know," Moe added to Derick's surprise, "Where I come from girls and boys are valued for what's inside, not outside, and not...well, they are equal, that's all!"

Moe was so sincere and Mel looked so angry that Derick mumbled, "I was out of line, I'm sorry."

"Then all is forgiven," said Mel, "but let there not be a repetition!"

"If we're going to go dragon fishing," said Bob after a longish pause, "we'd better get some sleep."

"We have a small tent that was packed in case of rain. You can use that tonight," said Derick, trying to make up.

"There will be no need, sir," Mel replied, "I who have slept out of doors my whole life can fashion a shelter from branch and bough that will weather any storm. Now I bid you dream with joy 'till waking." With that she glided into the night.

The next day they saw that Bob had put on his Beneficent Bounce-O costume. Mel rejoined the boys for breakfast and asked, "What is the meaning of the insignia you wear?"

Bob answered, "It is the letter B; a writing symbol that stands for my name."

"Ah!" she said, "B for brave."

Bob was very pleased with this compliment but, again, he privately wondered if Mel was being sincere, or merely trying to keep in everybody's good graces.

Moe, who may have been thinking along the same lines, asked her, "How is it that you can speak our language? There can't be many schools that teach English in this land."

"This is where you are mistaken. All elves speak English, and many speak no other tongue. This is because we desire above all to accommodate ourselves to the great dance. You may say we have a racial hunger to become one with the surrounding peoples of our land in the world. It is what makes us elves. Alas, it is the old ways that are seldom taught among us."

"Our new companion speaks truth," Hawk said, perhaps a bit pointedly, "For this reason I made the journey to your land and enrolled in professor Wie's school. The elves strive always to understand their neighbors."

All that day and the next they shared stories and experiences that helped to bridge the gap between the two cultures. On the third day of their adventures together they found their first dragon sign. It stood like some stunted, gnarled tree in the center of a grassy field. The artifact was made of stone carved into smooth, strange contours that resembled the patterns that can be found in the swirls of grainy wood.

As they drew closer they saw that it was man high. Perhaps it was intended as a stylized representation of a man. However there was by no means any evidence that the stone was anything but an abstract decoration.

Yet there was something indefinable about it that proclaimed this was no random conglomeration of shape and mass; but rather a purposeful work of fabrication by intelligence.

Moe got out of his chariot to inspect it more closely and the others soon followed.

"What's it supposed to be?" said Moe.

Hawk answered, "This is the artwork of the race of dragons. Their young spend years expressing deep, magic, dragon yearnings with such carvings as the one we have here."

"It looks like parts of it were scoured and chipped," Bob observed.

"That's from the dragon's claws," said Mel.

"This part looks smooth," Moe pointed out, "all polished and glistening,"

"Ah!" Hawk exclaimed, "That shows evidence of much labored burnishing with dragon scales."

"What's this?" Derick asked, "It looks like the surface is scorched and melted into the design."

"Dragon breath," Mel and Hawk answered as one.

The boys peppered them with questions.

"They shoot out fire?"

"For real?"

"How far?"

"How hot does the fire get?"

"What kind of range do they have?"

"Can a dragon melt steel?"

"Friends," Hawk was laughing, "these questions are not a matter of measurement but of survival. Few who have encountered dragons return to tell such details."

"Looks like we'll get a chance to find out for ourselves," Bob said grimly, "Look!"

From the forest, at the far side of the field in which they stood, (but not far enough away for comfort) came the dragon. At first they saw only the

163

head above the trees as it approached. The craggy brows arched expressively over eyes that glowed like hot coals seen thru an emerald. It was possessed of a strange, rugged beauty: it might have been sculpted out of bronze by Rodan.

Derick (who had decided to wear his costume when he saw Bob's attire that morning) shouted, "It's too big! How are we supposed to fight that?"

Moe added, "It's making its way around the trees; but something tells me it could go through them just as easily!"

In a deliberately calm voice Bob said, "Has anyone thought about how we're going to deal with its fire?"

"Running would be good," suggested Moe hopefully.

"Ha!" said Mel, "This one has no fire! Look at its size: it is just a baby! It cannot have had enough time to grow the protective hide it needs to line its throat and mouth!"

"A baby!" said Moe, "I'd hate to see its mama!"

Throughout this conversation the dragon kept coming. Now it looked at the small group and smiled. It seemed to be following the discussion, because it laughed as if in reaction. The laugh reminded Bob of an air-raid horn – but pitched in a bass register. There was a slight hiccup quality to the sound.

"I think he understands what we're saying," Derick said, "can he talk?"

"Nay," answered Hawk, "such speech as dragons have is not for mortals to hear. Its mouth is not made for speaking our tongue, but this one knows well enough our intent.

Indeed, the dragon sat back on its massive haunches and cocked its head as if listening.

"He's just like a big puppy!" Derick said.

"What makes you think it's a 'he'?" asked Mel.

Derick, the Crunch, put his hands on his hips and tapped his foot. But he said no word.

Now, strange to tell, this is just what the dragon started doing. It was mocking Derick! Its face and posture seemed to mirror the attitude of the Crunch so faithfully that they all marveled and giggled at the same time.

Bob became very intent on trying to communicate with the behemoth. "Can you understand me?"

The creature gave a solemn nod.

"Is this your artwork?" Bob continued, "Did you make this?"

Another nod.

Mel began to look like she was having trouble restraining herself and she broke in, "This is folly! Dragons and elves must ever be deadly enemies! We must slay the beast!"

The dragon lost its smile and swung its head from side to side.

"You mean you want to be friends?" Bob asked.

This time there was an emphatic nodding.

"I wonder if he's related to Mr. Mann?" Moe commented.

"Hush!" the sharp remark came from Hawk, "Do not jest! The creature is playing a ruse to take us off guard. Speak no more words to it, I pray you."

"Why not?" Crunch asked, "If there are more dragons out there we will have plenty of time to see them coming. He could have had us for breakfast already if he wanted to, couldn't you, boy?"

The Crunch held out one gauntlet before him and slowly approached the monster. "Nice dragon, good dragon," he called softly, almost singing the words. Under a jaw the size of a garage door, the Crunch put his hand and scratched the knobby scales.

And the monster was no longer a monster; it was humming a melodic purr of contentment.

"Ye heavens, can I bear such foolishness?" Hawk was beside himself in frustration. "Long have I dreamt of the glory of this day. The end of my quest sits passively before me. All is over with but the cast of a spear. And now is my foe to be tamed at the touch of a friend? Nay! All who hear of it will laugh!"

The dragon picked this moment to break into a wide smile.

"Clown!" Hawk shouted, "Your eloquent pantomime shall cease with the stilling of your fowl heart!"

The moment teetered.

Magically, a look of infinite sadness crossed the face of the dragon. It gestured, pointing with both hands to its scaled and segmented breast. Next it pointed to the statue behind as if to say, "Here is my soul and my heart." Then it slowly opened both arms wide.

"Spawn of woe!" cried Hawk, "Do you bid me strike? Know then, that this is no ordinary shaft. The enchanted spear shall now end my quest and break the spell! Destiny's decision declares thy doom!"

And Hawk Spring-green drew back his arm; but he faltered. With a curse he threw the spear not at the dragon's chest but past its shoulder striking the carving behind. Such was the force of the throw that the shaft lodged deep in the stony statue.

The magic weapon vibrated there. But instead of dieing, the quivering only increased until the spear blurred and seemed to turn to gold. The glitter became dazzling. The shaft broke into shards which flew up and out. And as they floated into the blue sky, the ruminants of Hawk's spear appeared to diminish, on the edge of sight, like tiny birds fluttering off afar.

They heard a shuffling noise behind them and all turned to see the dragon stalk off; perhaps in irritation at such critics. Maybe it would return in a few dozen years when it was sure the coast was clear. But who can fathom the alien motivations of a dragon?

"That is the creepiest, kookiest story I ever heard!" It was ten o'clock and Kid Psyche was sending his skeptical thoughts to Bob and the boys through the medium of their reflection marbles.

165

"If I didn't know you guys so well, I'd say you were either very bad liars or very good candidates for the funny farm!"

"I don't blame you," Bob's thought replied, "I don't believe it myself and I was there!"

"So what happened to Elf's, I mean Hawk's, spear?" Psyche asked.

"As we later spoke, and the wonder in my heart had time to fade, I thought of a possible explanation," said Hawk. He continued, "As you may know, my quest was revealed by an oracle. My parents spoke of that day. The oracle came and placed the magic spear in my hand, when I was but an infant. The prophecy said that the magic spear would give me power that would grow as I grew."

"I was told that I would find the end of my quest only when I could cast away the spear, never to be recovered, into the heart of a dragon."

"But you didn't," said Derick, "You ended up sticking the statue instead."

"Aye and that is where the misunderstanding comes in," said Hawk, "for well can I recite the exact words of the prophecy:

Seek to end the quest,
From thy spear depart,
There to ever rest,
Lodged in dragon's heart

The heart of this dragon was clearly in his work. He loved his craft and when I struck, the blow touched his heart."

"It may be," said Bob slowly, "But I have an alternative suggestion. I think there may have been a misunderstanding alright, but it was an audio one. The real words of the prophecy were meant to be heard in a different way. What if the oracle originally ended with different words?"

"Don't be dramatic," said Moe, "Just tell us!"

Bob said, "What if the real words were to go: *Lodged in dragon's art*"

"Aw, come on!" cried Derick, "Are you seriously proposing that a magic spell can have a speech impediment?"

"I think this one did."

The next day began frolics and carefree play after the fashion of elves. For day after endless day the party rode and walked, ran and swam, all without worry or purpose, other than merry-making and fun.

As the time drew close for vacation's end the companions came at last to rejoin the migration. Bob remembered the afternoon when they topped a hill and saw before them the long lines of carts and rolling homes all converging into a mighty stream from smaller tributaries. The portable homes were being put into storage for the summer. And the place of their resting became the wall of the city of Havenhome.

"Next year the city will move again," said Hawk, "and the hearts of my people will skip to the beat of the great dance once more."

"Alas!" said Mel, "Here must a happy adventure end. The city of my kin lies in another direction on a different road. I sore miss my family but I will henceforth look to the place in my heart for you, my friends, and find only sweet memories. Yet I vow these will ever remain while I live!"

"We won't forget you either, Mel Grayson," Hawk spoke for the others, "When we first met, you went from lad to lass before our eyes. Yet from now on we will think of you only as our true friend. Farewell!"

There came a moonlit night. A quiet stream and a silence that never the less spoke. Star glint powdered the night sky. Bob saw the spaces in between the stars expand into other stars and still more suns. It was for him as if he was back in the Infinity Room, watching endless reflections cascade into nothing and everything all at once.

And just as the tiniest spaces between one point and another opened up into infinite realms, so it was with time. Between one moment and the next were hidden epochs of duration. Enough to hold all the adventures that could ever be imagined. It was for this that Bob had been born and had grown to an awareness of people and places with which to interact. He had found the key to the purpose for which he had been made: to dance the great dance; to be at one with life and a vital part of the story of stories.

Bob felt keenly that he was swimming through the mystery of life.

When the mystic spell expired the four boys heard the gurgle and gush of the creek near Derick's house.

Without a word they each sought their beds to pursue dreams hardly more fantastic than their waking lives. Summer vacation had come to a close.

"If your automatic response is to repay evil for evil, then you will find that you are locked into that and can be manipulated by anyone else who is evil. Instead, you must always remain free to choose to do good - which is much more constructive anyway."

Professor Wie was beginning his lecture and the new school year with a class called Time Warp and Multidimensional Integrating Seminar.

Bob was excited at the near prospect of graduation even as he feared the final exams, projects, tests and thesis. Bob was determined to face this challenge as he had so many others. He had written in his journal, "no one can do everything, but anyone can do better."

He was also more than a little worried about how good a side-kick he would make. The students were all official side-kicks now and could even be featured in comic books (but not on their own. They could only appear with their sponsor super hero. They had to finish this last, all important year before they could be regarded as heroes themselves.)

Bob had spent quite a bit of time talking with Derick about his new apprenticeship with Captain Speedball. Derick expressed regret that the rules had prevented him from working as an apprentice with a relative. The Crunch would instead be functioning as side-kick with a hero called Doctor Jolt; and he was very nervous about it.

The good Doctor Jolt was the father of Morpho Lad (many of those helping to train side-kicks were school parents). Derick had some cause to worry. Not only was the Jolt regarded as a first class super hero, but it was said that he used his powers to give mild shocks to his students when they forgot their lessons or didn't obey orders to the letter.

"The difficulty with using intuition alone to solve a problem," continued professor Wie, "is that when you figure it out, before you actually are able to figure it out, you'll never be able to figure *that* out."

Sometimes Bob suspected his teachers of saying obscure or ridiculous things on purpose just to get *some* response from the students. But he wasn't really sure. Bob found his mind drifting back to the events of his vacation. In this he was probably in synch with all the other students. Bob had been worried for his friend Hawk (he must always remember to go back to calling him Elf when others were around who were not privy to his real name). Bob was anxious that Hawk might find it difficult to graduate, now that he had lost his greatest weapon.

"If loss of arms can so weaken or diminish me," the Elf had asserted, "I had better not come to rely on them in the first place. Besides, the oracle said that I would grow in power from possession of the magic spear. It said nothing about loosing the power when the weapon was lost."

Bob became aware that the professor was ending his class with a warning, "Remember that the Big Cheese is still on the loose and he has vowed revenge. Because we must always be on guard against another attack, the time you spend on homework assignments will be more important than ever."

"I will not compromise your safety or the academic standards of this school. There will be emergency drills and patrols like last year. But the schoolwork must not be allowed to slack off. You will be busy with the demands of your sponsor in your side-kick duties. You will be busy getting ready for your thesis and its defense. The requirement will be no less than a hundred and fifty pages for your final paper."

There was grinding of teeth at that announcement. It was the first of many academic shocks they would receive that year. A few weeks later found Bob in the cafeteria getting ready for lunch. Just as Bob was sitting down to his hot dogs, beans, soup, grilled cheese sandwiches, and assorted deserts, the Endearing Bunny Hop ran in and shouted, "The papers put out an extra! Bobby is being blamed for everything the Big Cheese did!"

It was all too true. The students read a description of everything the Cheese had threatened to do. They read an account of the threat to "blow-up" Chicago. But the blame for all this was put on a mysterious and monstrous new menace named "Blubber–Boy."

"Where did they get that name from?" Psyche wanted to know.

"There's an artist's depiction on the editorial page," said Bunny. Sure enough, there was a cartoon showing a perfectly round monster big enough to knock over buildings. The monster was even wearing a close version of Bob's costume. The caption read, "Evil Blubber-Boy Peril Could Make Us All His Size!" The editorial called for the immediate arrest of anyone wearing a strange costume or possessing unusual powers.

"They can't do this," said Psyche. Bob didn't know what to say.

"It's written by a cub reporter named Olsen," Bunny Hop pointed to the byline. "I've read his stuff before and it was always very interesting and accurate."

"How can you say that?" Psyche wanted to know. "He got the Big Cheese mixed up with Bob! One's a good guy and one's a crook! How accurate is that?"

"Now you don't want to get all upset with little me, do you?" Bunny asked in the sweetest tones.

"Don't try it, sister," Kid Psyche grated.

"I'm sure I don't..."

"I'm sure you do!"

"But you..."

"Not like that!"

"Wow!"

"Ha!"

"So?"

"Cut it out!" Bob cried, "You two should really learn to talk with words like the rest of us!" And then Bob did something that was extremely rare in his life. He walked away from an uncompleted meal. But he didn't get far before Mrs. White found him. "Robert, there you are! We have been looking for you. Professor Wie wants to see you in his study."

So the two made their way from the cafeteria to the school building. On the walk there Bob had time enough to reflect that the professor had probably read the paper too. "Mrs. White, what does the professor want to see me for?"

"Doubtless, he wants to remind you not to end your sentences with a preposition." Then seeing the expression of worry on Bob's face she added, "I'm not really sure, Robert, but I'll go in with you and we'll find out together."

They knocked and entered one of two massive oak doors. The professor was sitting behind a desk that curved around him like a horseshoe. Behind him, stretching and arching to the high ceiling, dark paneled walls framed a walk-in fireplace. The lively flames sent dancing shadows around the faces of the professor and a boy who was sitting alone, in one corner of the room, almost completely lost in a high leather chair.

169

The boy was the Mean Blaster. He wore an expression that was poised half way between subdued contrition and suppressed belligerence.

"Please sit down Mr. Bounce-O. Thank you, Mrs. White that will be all."

The heavy door closed. The muffled ticking of a grandfather clock tallied more than twenty quiet seconds.

"You have read the paper?" Professor Wie addressed the question to Bob.

"Yes sir."

"In that case, I believe Mr. Blaster has some further news for you."

Bob was surprised to see the Blaster boy actually squirming in his seat. "It was my fault," MB blurted, "They wrote all that because of what I said about you and I'm sorry."

"I don't understand," said Bob who really did not want to understand.

"Your partner," the professor said while MB flinched at the word, "Your partner gave an interview to the paper revealing to the public the existence of this school. He also told them about the threat of the Big Cheese's enlarging gun. He neglected to mention the Cheese or his henchmen by name. Instead he ascribed the menace to a new super villain called *Blubber-Boy*."

"Now I was under the impression that you two had a gentlemen's agreement not to call each other hateful names. I was also under the impression that Robert has lived up to his half of the agreement in every respect. Am I mistaken?"

"No sir." It was a barely audible mumble from MB. Then the Blaster added with emphasis, "But there is no such person as Blubber-Boy, really. So I figured that making up a story that sounded like Bob did all those things - I thought that would draw out the Big Cheese. He's the kind of guy that wouldn't be able to stand the idea of someone stealing his thunder. And he hates Bob already anyway for swiping his plans."

"You never stopped to consider that you put Robert in danger?" Wie asked.

"No! I never thought he could get at Bob."

"Well, Mister Blaster, I think that what you actually accomplished was to paint a big target on the whole school and especially on your partner's back."

"But," said MB, "this will make the Cheese come out of hiding where we can get him!"

"I happen to know exactly where the Big Cheese is hiding." said the professor, "Your interference has forced me to alter my plans. Didn't you think to come to me or one of the teachers before you pulled a stunt like this? You didn't even bother to tell your partner!"

"But there wasn't any time. That reporter got me talking and I had to tell him something. I didn't call up the paper and ask for an interview, you know!"

"No," said the professor slowly, "I did not know that. Just how did it happen?"

"I was working as apprentice side-kick with Red Ranger." Bob remembered that Red Ranger, a popular radio hero, was the father of the Pink Liberator. "We were out on patrol and Red sent me to cover my patrol route. Half way through, I saw this reporter waving at me (although I didn't know he was a reporter right away.) He was about twenty years old; had a red crew-cut, freckles and a bow tie. He said he needed my help. That's what we're supposed to do out on patrol, isn't it?"

"You won't be going out on patrol for awhile," said Professor Wie. "I appreciate the fact that it is hard to participate in an interview if you have had no experience and the reporter is a skillful questioner. I am also gratified to learn that this was not a premeditated character assassination directed at Mister Bounce-O."

The professor sighed, "I have decided to place you on suspension for two weeks, mister Blaster."

"But I said I'm sorry," said MB.

"I am sure you are, given the outcome of your actions," the professor said, "You are now on probation. I have had cause to suspend you once before. There will be no third time. Do I make myself clear?"

It was very clear; Bob thought to himself, "Three strikes and you're out."

Chapter XVI

Hamming It Up

"The Mean Blaster is missing!"

"What? Who says?"

"I heard it from Bunny who got it from Mr. Lester!'

"The Blaster has the bunk right underneath me, and his bed wasn't even messed!"

"He got bawled out by Professor Wie and decided to quit!"

"You mean he ran away because he was too ashamed to face his partner after this!"

"No! He was just suspended. He'll be staying at the kitchen building, like last time."

"It's not like last time; no one knows where he is."

"Maybe Professor Wie changed his mind and decided to kick him out after all!"

"No! Mr. Lester says he saw MB get into a car right outside the front gate last night!"

"That's right; it was a big, black limo."

"Maybe his parents took him home."

"He never talks about his family."

"It wasn't his parents! Mr. Lester said he saw someone in the back seat who looked like the Big Cheese!"

"The Cheese! Why didn't he sound the alarm?"

"He wasn't real sure because it happened so fast."

"So the Cheese captured Mean Blaster?"

"He wasn't sure!"

"Come on, Bunny, tell us the rest!"

"Well, it's not for sure, but Mr. Lester thinks MB got into the car willingly, like he was just waiting for it to show up!"

"What do the teachers say?"

"Nothing, and lot's of it. There's supposed to be an announcement later."

"The Blaster captured! Do you think he'll betray the school's secrets to avoid being harmed?"

"Are you kidding? I would!"

"Me too, and when I ran out of secrets I'd make up some!"

"I don't think he will betray us. They won't get anything out of him."

"Oh, Bobby, you're too loyal - just because he's your partner!"

The official announcement took place later that day. By then the students already knew almost everything that was announced.

"Getting back Mr. Blaster will be our first priority." Professor Wie was addressing the student body and almost all of the parents who were crammed into the small auditorium.

"I will now read a telegram that I received early this morning."

'My dear Wie, by now you will have learned of my new recruit to crime. He's working for me now, but I will consider a swap. I'll trade one Blaster for one Professor. I realize I will be trading down but I have almost made all the use I can of the kid. My associates tell me that you already know where my secret hide-out is. So come and get him before it's too late. Your true nemesis, The Big Cheese.'

"So now we are going to recover the Mean Blaster. I will lead a rescue party consisting of Mister Mann and Captain Speedball."

"I can promise you that I will not return with out Mister Blaster. If I should find it necessary to surrender myself to the Cheese in order to save one of our students, I will do so. If that happens, I expect you all to carry on."

"No!"

The cry came from the back of the auditorium. No one was more surprised than Bob, for it was he who had unexpectedly shouted.

"What is it, Robert?" the professor said in a kindly voice.

"I have to go with you. He's my partner and I have to go too."

"We all appreciate..." began professor Wie.

"No!" Bob repeated even louder. "You don't understand. I am not asking permission. I will follow you. I will go on my own, with or without you. I have to do this!"

The professor looked at Bob and realized that he meant it. The professor was a good judge of character. Bob did mean it.

It was just after dusk. The entire third floor of a downtown office building had been rented by the Big Cheese and converted into his headquarters. Speedball remained on guard outside. The professor, Mr. Mann and Bob entered a freight elevator. The doors closed down from the top and up from the bottom; clanging shut like the jaws of a steel beast.

It seemed a very slow ride to the third floor. When the doors opened they saw one lone figure in the center of the floor, picked out by a single, bright spotlight.

It was the Mean Blaster. He was imprisoned, his body was stretched out and hanging on a dangerous looking rack of chrome steel. His arms were enclosed up to the elbows, and his legs to the knees, in blocks of metal. These devices were blast absorbers, designed to keep the Blaster's force beam from functioning. He appeared to be asleep.

"That's as far as you go, Wie!" The Big Cheese stepped out from an alcove at the other side of the dimly lit room.

"You will now release the boy, Cheese!" said the professor.

"Oh, you can have him now. He's served his purpose and I'm through with him. Now that you are here I am no longer concerned with the Mean Blaster!"

The Big Cheese walked up to the imprisoned boy and pulled his head up by the hair. Bob drew a sharp breath. The Blaster's mask and helmet had been removed!

"Doesn't look so mean now, eh?" and the villain cuffed MB across the face.

A cry of rage escaped from Bob and he bounded forward. He bumped against the Cheese so hard that the gang boss flew and bounced off a near-by wall.

But Bob wasn't thinking about the Cheese. He took one of the imprisoning blocks and, with teeth that had grown to diamond hard density, bit through the clasp that held it shut. In three more bites the Mean Blaster was free.

"Get him out of here!" Professor Wie shouted to Bob.

But it wasn't that easy. MB shot up to a height of fifteen feet, just below the ceiling. The greenish-yellow force beams were supporting him as they blasted from his legs. Now his arms were lit up and he looked like he was throwing force beams: as if they were bright green plasma medicine balls.

"Blaster, disengage!" shouted professor Wie.

The Cheese had time to activate his belt rockets.

"I can get him!" snarled the Blaster boy and he struck with twin bolts of pure energy. The Cheese was hit in the stomach and pinned against the wall. MB held him there. The beams grew brighter and wider. A cry of pain escaped the lips of the Big Cheese.

"That's enough, Blaster!" shouted the professor.

"Stop!" Cried Mr. Mann, "Stop blasting, Blaster, blast it!"

"No!" MB screamed, "He has to pay! I can get him! I'll kill him!"

"Let him go. We are not killers!" professor Wie's voice was harsh.

"But he is! He was going to kill me! He said so!"

"And now you will become just like him!"

The Blaster advanced, arms rigidly locked in front of him, and his force beams grew in power. The Cheese was having difficulty breathing. The lurid glow from his own rays lit the face of the Blaster and transformed it into something hideous.

"He has to pay for what he tried to do to me! I'll get even, I swear it! I hope it hurts, Mr. Big Cheese. You're the one who doesn't look so big now!"

"Stop this at once!" the professor bellowed.

It didn't look as if MB was going to stop for anything.

Suddenly, the hand of the Big Cheese (which had been slowly moving into position) pressed a control on his belt. Emergency booster rockets exploded and the Cheese flew sideways several yards. He smashed through a window and went howling off into the night like a defective firework.

"He got away! We've got to go after him!" The Blaster was sobbing with frustration, "What are you waiting for? Bob! Don't just stand there!"

"No one is going anywhere," professor Wie was shouting as he turned to MB.

"You truly are the Mean Blaster! When you chose that name I allowed it as an expression of boyish enthusiasm. But you really are mean, aren't you? Aren't you!"

There was room for an answer but none was forthcoming from the Blaster's open mouth. Bob too, was surprised and a little awed at the intensity of Professor Wie's scarcely restrained rage.

"You are a danger to yourself and to those around you!" The professor's finger was pointing at the Blaster, but it was shaking. "You disobeyed orders! You disregarded the danger to others just to satisfy your own thirst for revenge! Revenge will eat you alive! If you learned anything at my school you should have learned that lesson!"

Professor Wie took a deep breath as if readying himself to jump into water, "You have never been able to conquer that mean streak! Now it becomes a matter of security! Real heroes hate violence. They hate hatred! You've used up all your chances with me! We have no room for a Mean Blaster! For your safety as well as that of the school I have no choice now but to expel you. The Mean Blaster can never again be a part of us!"

"Fine!" the Blaster was crying now, "That's fine! I'll go after him myself. You just wait! I'll show you all!" Before another word could be spoken the Mean Blaster ignited his verdant tinted beam. It vibrated through the souls of his feet to push against the floor and send him rocketing out the window.

The Mean Blaster was gone for good.

The tragedy of this turn of events did not stop life from proceeding with all its demands. And although this could be said of all tragedies, it was especially hard on two people in particular.

Professor Wie felt that he had failed and that the expulsion of the Blaster was just an expression of his failure as a teacher.

And Bob felt that he should have done something more to prevent what had happened. He could have made an extra effort to get closer to his partner.

Although he had tried to be friendlier, he knew that something was bugging the boy. Some secret hurt, some circumstance in the Blaster's past, was always haunting him; never letting him alone. Just when things seemed to be going better for him, the Blaster would inevitably do something or say something, well, mean.

Life at school went on even though something seemed to be missing. The Cheese was still at large and the local citizens, while still worried about the Blubber-Boy threat, started to give their attention to other things. Fortunately, while MB had revealed to the press the existence of a super hero school, no one knew where it was or anything more about it.

The students at Professor Wie's school also had to give their attention to other things. There was a series of tests leading up to final exams and the thesis - that hundred-and-fifty-page paper that would help determine their final grade.

Escapology II, Advanced Intuition, Tactics - the subjects danced in Bob's head with the intensity of Rhythm and Blues.

Days turned into weeks. Finally the day of reckoning arrived. Bob had one final test to pass in order to graduate. In the weeks leading up to this day Bob had stayed up late every night and sometimes all night. He tried to concentrate on his studies but he found that he was now haunted by the Mean Blaster.

Bob tried to answer a true or false question about what to do when a side-kick is captured by the villain. But Bob could only see in his memory the Mean Blaster hanging in the Big Cheese's trap.

When Bob came to the essay part of the test he almost filled in his name as "Beneficent Bozo!"

He could almost hear the voice of his former partner.

"I'll teach you to insult the Mean Blaster!"

"Man, you should be on television!"

"...and you can call me Admiral!"

"That's a plan, man! Let's go!"

"Bounce-O! Blaster! Bounce-O! Blaster!"

Bob found himself trying to erase a perfectly good answer when the bell rang.

"Time's up!" said Mrs. White. Turn in your answer sheets. Your final grades will be posted in the cafeteria tomorrow at supper time. It is this grade that will determine who will be graduating next week and I expect to see all your names on the final list."

Bob wasn't so sure his name would be on that list. He felt that he had probably flunked his critical final exams, because he couldn't remember any of the answers he had put down. But the next day, to his astonishment, he found that it was at the top of the list.

"Bobby! You made first place!" The Wisp was excited for him. "Not bad, Bobby," she was hopping in place enthusiastically. "The head of the class gets to make the valedictorian speech at graduation! Congratulations!"

All the kids were congratulating him and Bob was bemused to find that none of them seemed to be as surprised as he was.

Mrs. White walked in just then, "Yes, congratulations, Robert! I am very proud of the way you have applied yourself. After all, you did have a less than auspicious beginning to your efforts here, you know."

That was true, Bob reflected. At some point in his second year he had reformed his study habits and his grades improved to the point that he could really shine in this last year.

He realized with a start that he owed much of his success to his study partner. He felt guilty that now he would be graduating and the Mean Blaster would not.

The voice of Mrs. White interrupted his thoughts, "You will be delivering the valedictorian talk at the commencement ceremony. The talk shall not exceed fifteen minutes in duration and I will expect to see your final draft on my desk by noon on Friday."

"Wow!' said the Crunch when Mrs. White departed, "That's not a lot of time to write a talk for the whole school!"

"Yeah," agreed Moe du Jur, "and don't forget all the parents and teachers hanging on your every syllable! Better you than me, buddy!"

After some more backslapping, Psyche signaled with a toss of his head that he wanted to speak to Bob alone. The two boys met outside the cafeteria.

"Nervous?" said Kid Psyche.

"I am," confessed Bob.

"I thought something was going on. You're up to something again."

Psyche, I would trust you with my life, you know that. But this one I have to work out all by myself, okay?"

"I kind of figured that would be your answer. Just wanted to remind you that help is just a reflection marble away."

"Thanks. You're a good friend, Psyche."

"Right as rain, Bob-O! I just wanted to make sure you knew it."

Psyche flashed a smile and was about to walk away when he stopped as if something had just occurred to him.

"Listen, Bob," Psyche said with some earnestness, "When you write that speech – well, I know how much you like to have fun and how much you enjoy puns and stuff."

"What are you getting at now, O Brainy One?"

"Well, don't take this the wrong way, but try not to spend the whole fifteen minutes hamming it up."

The next few days all the students were in the mood for nothing but fun. They had nothing to do but goof off and go to parties until Saturday afternoon when graduation was scheduled to take place.

If it didn't rain that day, the ceremonies were going to be held outdoors on the athletic field near the bleachers. A local high school marching band was engaged to provide entertainment.

The high school teacher involved in arranging for the band's appearance was happy for an opportunity to practice in front of an audience (especially after professor Wie's generous donation to the band's music fund).

In fact they were under the impression that Mr. Wie's establishment was a school for the arts specializing in costume drama.

This misapprehension might have the effect of preventing a lot of embarrassing questions from being asked when nineteen super kids marched up for diplomas in their gaudy costumes.

Bob spent a lot of time working on his speech. He also spent even more time writing in his journal. As the weekend approached Bob seemed to grow less nervous and for some strange reason Psyche started getting jumpy.

Thursday night Psyche called an informal meeting in the boiler room with Elf, Moe and Crunch.

"I'm worried about Bob," Psyche told them. "The other night I was at his table for supper and I ate more than he did!"

"We've been meaning to talk to you about that," The Crunch put in with a chuckle, "a pot-belly would really stick out in your costume!"

"I'm serious!" Psyche said. "I don't know what the trouble is, because I refuse to probe, but Bob is up to something. I'm picking up perturbed vibrations."

"Are they heavy?" Moe asked with a straight face; but then a snort escaped and it became evident that he wasn't taking Psyche seriously. It was really hard to take anything seriously now that the relief of graduation time had arrived.

"Friend Psyche," Hawk said, "long have we known you for a true friend. But you are also a worry wart!"

However, it became evident that psyche was on to something because of what happened that very next day at breakfast.

"Bounce – O is missing!"

"What?"

"Don't tell me that he took a ride with the Big Cheese!"

"Here we go again!"

"No! It's not like last time. No one even saw him leave."

"He was working on that talk of his."

"Do you suppose he got cold feet?"

"Hey, yeah, that must be it! If I had to make a speech, I know I'd run away!"

"If *you* had to make a speech, *we'd* run away!"

"Ha! But Bob's not scared of anything! He took on the Cheese himself, remember?"

"But where is he?"

"Search me!"

"Well he better get here on time; tomorrow we graduate!"

"Anyone see him at breakfast?"

"No! And I was the first one here!"

"If he missed a meal, it's serious!"

"Do the teacher's know he's gone?"

"Yeah, they've looked everywhere!"

"So where is he?"

At that particular moment Bob was nine miles away from the school and he was making news. And he was doing it by visiting the local newspaper.

There, in a fifth floor office suite, the editors who had decided to run the Blubber-Boy story were having a meeting. Suddenly, the door opened and there he was; big as life (and maybe a tiny bit bigger).

With a voice that sounded like Orson Wells pronouncing words of doom from a tomb, Bob spoke, "I am the one you called Blubber-Boy. I am the 'perilous menace!' I am the 'threat to the city!' that you wrote about." Bob was using words from the newspaper story. "I want you to tell me who called me these things! I will depart and leave you in peace only if you tell me how to get a hold of him!"

One of the editors spoke up, "We can't tell you that, we are bound to protect our sources!"

With a very casual gesture Bob pushed a heavy desk up against the door, as if to prevent anyone from leaving.

"I could get you a free subscription!" the editor said.

"You!" Bob yelled and pointed to a young man who was trying to make himself look unobtrusive. He had red crew-cut hair and a bow tie. "You know where he is!" Bob said.

The man started to plead, "Don't eat me!"

Bob smiled and said, "That reminds me, I haven't had breakfast yet."

Fumbling in his haste, the man handed Bob a yellow note pad. Circled were the instructions to publish these words: *M.B. to B.C. I left my hat at your party. It was a blast, but to say I had fun is a stretch. I know why and I know where. Call me mean but call me at EV – 4165.*

Bob understood that the Mean Blaster had put together a clever code to get the attention of the Big Cheese.

"Take the whole notepad," Bob was told, "The guy you want is M.B. and that's his phone number."

Bob asked him, "Did you run this ad already?"

"Yes, sir," said the reporter, "It's in this morning's edition."

"Good!" said Bob, and he jumped out the window.

Bob had been thinking so much about the Mean Blaster in recent days that he was beginning to think like him.

"What would MB do?" he asked himself. MB would go after the Cheese. He said so. How would he do it? The Blaster would first have to find the Cheese before he could go after him.

And then Bob remembered how the Blaster had made up the Blubber-Boy story in order to make the Cheese come out of hiding. And it had worked!

So now, if using the press worked once, Bob thought it might occur to the Blaster Boy to try the same trick again.

Bob's guess had paid off to the extent of gaining a phone number. He hoped that it would lead him to the Blaster.

Bob went to a nearby phone booth. He couldn't fit inside. So he reached in, took the receiver off the hook, put in a dime and called the number.

One ring.

Two.

Three.

"Hello?"

The voice sounded like MB.

"Blaster, don't hang up! It's Bob Blob!"

"Bob?"

"Don't hang up, please! I have to talk to you!"

"This isn't some trick of professor Wie, is it?"

"No, honest!"

"You were always a straight shooter Bob. I'm going to trust you. Meet me at the Comic Shop in one hour."

The phone clicked and hummed.

One hour later Bob was looking through old copies of Red Ranger's True Tales of the Old West. A boy with tousled black hair and a wide mouth came up to him and said, "Let's walk."

It was the Mean Blaster. He was dressed in blue jeans, Red Ball Jet tennis shoes, and a white T-shirt. He looked smaller and skinnier than when he wore his Blaster costume.

It was a fine June day so they walked to the park.

"I want to help you catch the Big Cheese," said Bob. Before MB could reply he continued, "I know we can get him if we work together. We're a great team and we've already proved we're more powerful than he is. I have a plan all worked out. But I'm going to need some special cooperation from you."

The Blaster boy looked thoughtful.

"Tell me about this plan," he said.

Later that afternoon a phone in a booth rang. The boy who was the Blaster was alone. He had been waiting for this call for hours. The number of the phone was EV – 4165, the number printed in the paper.

"MB here," the boy said.

"And you know who I am, don't you?" It was the Cheese.

MB spoke quickly, "I can help you get Wie. I have Bob Blob, the Bounce – O boy. You know the one I mean. He thinks he's helping me," he took a breath, "Meet me in the park at midnight. You can have him. You can hold him hostage like you did to me. It's the only way to catch professor Wie."

"And you can deliver him to me?" the Cheese grated.

"For $10,000 I can," MB assured him, "Wie kicked me out. I have no use for any of them!"

"If you dare to betray me…"

The Cheese's warning was cut short by MB's reply, "I am on your side now. For ten thousand, you have the word of the Mean Blaster!"

The birds were shining and the sun was singing! The next morning, Saturday, had revealed a bright and cloudless azure sky. Everything looked picture-postcard perfect. The students at Professor Wie's school were very excited. In no time at all commencement would commence.

The high school marching band glittered their way across the field with brass and spangles and chrome flashing in the sun. The rhythm of a Sousa march altered the pulse of more than one listener.

But there was worry too. No one had seen or heard any sign of Bob. In a few minutes he was supposed to give the valedictorian address. If he didn't show up soon he couldn't graduate.

The stands were filling up with parents and a number of super heroes who were not affiliated with the school but had accepted professor Wie's invitation. Electric excitement filled the air.

Meanwhile, the graduates to be were lining up just outside of the dormitory. In fifteen minutes the band would play Elgar's *Pomp and Circumstances* and they would march across the field away from their status as mere students into the glorious future of being certified and graduated super heroes.

"Line up in alphabetical order," Mrs. White instructed them. She read the names: Baron, Believer, Bounce-O…she really didn't expect to hear a response to that name and so she wasn't surprised when there was no answer.

She felt she had to make every allowance in case Bob showed up at the last minute. She remembered with a pang of regret that the Mean Blaster would have been in line right before Bob.

She looked with pride at all the remaining students. They looked crisp and colorful in their super attire.

Bunny Hop was really excited but trying to look sullen because she had failed to talk Mrs. White into letting her be first in line.

"My name starts with a 'B,' and sometimes my friends even call me 'B.' I sign my name B. Hop..."

Mrs. White was firm and Bunny had to take her place between Goldie and the Pink Liberator. There was another gap at the letter 'L.' The Absolute Locus was out in the stands with his parents. His study of the new discipline of *Inter-dimensional Scrutinization* was taking him away from a career as a super hero in the conventional sense. But he was there to cheer on his old friends.

Many people who are not official super heroes lead good and productive lives, Mrs. White reflected. They do good work, often difficult and dangerous work, without all the recognition.

Her thoughts were cut off by a blaring of trumpets. A short fanfare sounded and then the March of the Super Heroes began.

Graduation had arrived at last, and Bob Blob had not.

Chapter XVII

Duck Soup

Every light was flashing on the Crunch's costume. There was spit and polish evident in Moe's Patrol uniform.

Here came the Elf with a brand new, buffed up and gleaming spear. Captain Eugene's jet shield shone with patriotic pride.

Bunny Hop managed to look pretty as well as cute, even as she tried to hide her annoyance at having to dodge Goldie's flowing and flapping cape.

Next came Liberator, Morpho and Psyche (who had the best posture. He had decided that this was really the only way he could look special today).

The end of the parade consisted of Punisher, Rex, Socko, The Swashbuckle, Vortex, Willow-wand and the Wonderful Wisp.

They took their seats in folding chairs arranged in four roes near the speaker's platform.

The band ground to a halt and all that could be heard was the occasional snap and rustle of flags and pennants; capes and cloaks.

Professor Wie rose to speak, "May I have your attention please."

The microphone caused a howl of feedback that was quickly squelched by Mr. Lester. If the professor didn't have their attention up to that point, he certainly did now.

"I regret the necessity of having to make this announcement," he began. "As you know, the program for this afternoon calls for the valedictorian address to be delivered at this time. The valedictorian is that student who has achieved the highest academic marks."

"Unfortunately I find myself in the position of having to cancel the valedictorian speech this year. Our valedictorian is not present. So it is with a very heavy heart that I..."

The professor's voice trailed off. There was a disturbance from behind the bleachers. Three of the band members were scrambling from their benches, clutching hats and horns, to make room.

It was the Beneficent Bounce-O! He was pulling on a rope. And tugging and dragging on the other end of the rope was the Big Cheese! Bob had captured their greatest enemy!

There was cheering and relieved applause from everyone present as Bob hauled the villain up to the front. The gang leader's every weapon had been removed or disabled. Something violent had been done to his belt and costume.

He was manacled, hands and feet, in chains forged of M46.

One of the trumpeters in the high school band whispered to a fellow musician, "I saw this scene in a Shakespeare play one time. The fat guy's supposed to be Falstaff."

After several attempts Bob succeeded in signaling for quiet.

"Professor Wie, I present to you the Big Cheese!"

The crowd exploded with clapping all over again.

"Please!" Bob said, and the microphone howled, "Please allow me to tell you. I did not capture our foe all by myself as you seem to think."

"I had help: first class help. With out the help of which I speak, I would not be standing before you today and the Big Cheese would still be free."

"With your permission, professor Wie, I would like to introduce to you the hero who helped me catch the Cheese."

The professor nodded and Bob waved. From behind the bleachers came a boy. He wore a green and black uniform that seemed to be inspired by a triangle motif. The large letters G.B. were embroidered on his breast.

The trumpeter whispered, "And that guy's Richard III."

It was the Mean Blaster, but he was wearing a new uniform. Bob handed him the microphone.

"Professor Wie, teachers, parents, students and illustrious visitors, some time ago a student named the Mean Blaster enrolled in this school.

"He was possessed of great powers but also a great ego. He was loud, opinionated and undisciplined. This last attribute got him into trouble many times."

He paused for a moment. "...and he was mean."

Here the boy stopped to collect himself.

"I am here to tell you that the Mean Blaster, who was expelled – and he deserved to be expelled – that Mean Blaster no longer exists. With the help of the Beneficent Bounce-O I have not only defeated the Big Cheese, but I have renounced the Mean Blaster and the person he was becoming.

"From now on I will be called the Green Blaster. I have come to realize just how much a pain in the neck that Mean Blaster kid was. Believe me; sometimes even I couldn't stand him!"

That got a gentle chuckle from the listeners.

"With the permission of professor Wie, the tolerance of the students, and the forgiveness of you all, I will try to repair the damage I have done.

"It is my hope that, with your help, I may be able to complete my studies and take my place among all of you who resist the kind of bully I was. I have learned that bullies are the weakest among us.

"I am sorry and I apologize to you all. That's all I have to say."

There was a significant period of complete absence of sound. Even the wind died down. The birds held their breath.

Professor Wie came to the microphone. "I have always been proud of my students and their accomplishments. For example, I am very proud of the Beneficent Bounce-O.

"On the other hand, when I said that there was no room in our school for a Mean Blaster I meant it. I had to...to do what I did."

He took off his glasses and cleaned them. Every one waited.

"However, I am always on the look out for new talent. I would be honored and proud to accept a new hero. Welcome home Green Blaster!"

The place went nuts. That is to say, they all cheered with wild abandon. The professor had one arm around the Blaster's shoulders and Bob was holding up his other hand as a sign of victory.

It took a few minutes for the surging tide of emotions to recede.

The professor took the microphone but he was looking at Bob as he did so. "I was about to announce a change in the program. I wonder if this is now really necessary?"

Bob said, "Huh? Oh, yeah, I have it in my pocket!" and everyone laughed as he took out his speech. Everyone but the Big Cheese, that is.

"You frauds!" he was screaming at the peak of his vocal volume. "You're high ideals and morals mean nothing after all! You are going to torture me in public!"

"We do not torture," said professor Wie with a touch of weariness.

"Wrong, Wie! You are going to make me listen to a speech by that Blubber-Boy of yours! If that's not torture, I don't know what is!"

"You can put your mind at ease, Cheese," the professor signaled to Captain Speedball and Dr. Unknown to come forward, "You are not worthy to listen to this brave lad. There is a comfortable cell waiting for you in the Infinity Room and no earthly power can free you from there! Take him away!"

Speedball took the rope and Dr. Unknown followed with what appeared to be a giant cattle prod. He had constructed it from left over science projects in the school laboratories just in case the Cheese should ever attack again.

"Moo Ha, Ha, Ha, Ha! You may have captured the magnificent Big Cheese, but you'll never hold me, Wie! Do you hear?" Then he turned to the audience, "You fools! Don't you know that the super villain always escapes? You can't ever kill him off! Even when he dies, he comes back! Always!"

The mad laughter and pure hatred in his voice riveted the attention of all in the crowd (with the exception of one trumpet player who started clapping at the performance).

185

As he was dragged across the field the Cheese tried to continue his exit speech. He saw that he wasn't going to make it so he began an attempt to lead the spectators in a kind of football cheer: "The Cheese is great! The Cheese is great! Great Cheese! Great Cheese!"

Bob started his address as the voice diminished in the distance. "Thank you Doctor Unknown and Captain Speedball, he was beginning to grate on the nerves."

In the third row Psyche clapped a hand over his face as if to say, "Oh no, here we go!"

"The dictionary," Bob continued, "says that a valedictorian is supposed to bid farewell on behalf of his class. I had always assumed that the word had something to do with bravery because it sounded like the word valor. Things don't always turn out the way one expects. However, I believe my classmates and I have learned some thing of bravery in our four years at this school."

"Such lessons are best learned by example. And we have had the benefit of great examples from teachers and parents."

"So today, as I look out at the bright and brave colors of these superheroes, some who are brand new and some who have been tested in the crucible of many trials, it is with pride that I remind you to do your colors proud!"

"The colors of a super hero can inspire hope in those who wait for help and rescue. They can stir the sleeping courage of the complacent and help reaffirm the confidence of people everywhere in the goodness to which we are all called. To help the helpless, to defeat evil, yes, but also to set the example of extra ordinary effort that can lead to success."

"We have learned something of how extraordinary effort can lead to success. More important than super strength is the capacity to believe in yourself. More vital than vast powers or strange skills is the quality that we call faith. Faith in God and in one's self. And faith in all people. For there is a hero hidden inside every man and woman, girl and boy, just waiting to get out and to show the world what glory really means. We, the super hero class of 1960, have heard the call to show our true colors. So I say, do your colors proud!"

"My heart is filled with gratitude today. Thanks to the teachers. For red ink that made us think. Thanks to you, fellow students –I should say fellow graduates- for giving me what I could never have achieved on my own. You gave me a sense of normalcy, a feeling of belonging, and the ability to think of myself as just one of the kids. That's worth gold!"

"I'm blue because I have to leave. Thanks to Professor Wie for a green light. His permission enabled us all to participate in his dream."

"Thanks to Mrs. White for the bright possibilities she always encouraged in me. Thanks Mr. Mann, for your love of purple prose and passing along to us your love of learning. You helped us scale the heights."

Psyche shook his head.

"Doctor Unknown, yours was the precious platinum of experience, burnished and never tarnished through tough times. Indeed we owe all the teachers our gratitude for those things we unwillingly read."

Here, Kid Psyche smiled and thought, "That ones just whizzed by!" because he felt no one else would discern at least one of Bob's puns.

"Thank you, Dr. Martini, for keeping us all in the pink."

"And last but not least, thanks to Mr. Lester; orange you glad I couldn't think of a color for you?"

This got an appreciative chuckle, to Psyche's disgust.

"So now the time is here. Let us turn our faces to the future with an optimism that will require of us no heroics to sustain, only fidelity."

"Class of 1960: do your colors proud!"

Counting parents; graduates, their relatives and friends, there couldn't have been many more than one hundred people in attendance. But the applause that now burst forth would have done credit to the enthusiasm of a thousand.

As the waves of affirmation broke over the stands, Bob was seen whispering something to professor Wie who nodded his head.

"I must ask for your attention one last time please," said Bob, "Please, I have an important announcement to make." The assembly reluctantly complied with this request and they quieted.

"I must announce that this occasion will mark the last appearance of the Beneficent Bounce-O."

A stunned silence gripped the crowd.

"No," Bob continued, "I am not leaving to start my own restaurant, as some have speculated. Even though my name is Bob, and I happen to be a Big Boy, I am not going to end up selling hamburgers. I want to assure you that I fully intend not to waste the opportunity that was given to me. I am committed to the super hero profession."

"Today I take up a new name. Like my friend, the Green Blaster, I feel a need to change my professional name. Among the many lessons I have learned is that a person can be more than the name he or she is called."

Hawk, Moe and Derick exchanged knowing glances.

"With the permission of the one who invented the name, I have decided to call my self Blubber-Boy."

Since the crowd was already in the grip of stunned silence, that silence merely grew more profound.

"I feel a responsibility toward the public who has been terrified by this name. I intend to take that name and transform it into a force for good and an even more fearsome appellation in the ears of evil-doers."

"In this way I can also demonstrate my support for the Green Blaster." He turned to where GB was sitting, "This is so you won't be alone in your struggle to achieve a good name."

187

The Blaster Boy got up and walked over to Bob so he could speak into the microphone, "I want you all to that know this was *his* idea!" They all laughed and clapped as GB added, "He *likes* the name now!"

Bob held out his hand but GB quickly embraced him (although, since it was difficult for anyone's arms to encircle more than one third of Bob, it might be more accurate to say that GB was engulfed in Bob's hug).

Soon professor Wie was handing out the diplomas. The band crashed into an excerpt from *Les Preludes* by Franz List. Parents were beaming with pride.

Bob saw that the Wonderful Wisp was sniffling and the Pink Liberator was crying openly. He was startled to see a trickle of tears on Psyche's cheek. "He's a sensitive guy," Bob reminded himself. Come to think of it, Bob's eyes were starting to water too.

Later that afternoon, there were parties to attend. Bob met a lot of the parents of his classmates for the first time. He also had another long talk with the Green Blaster.

In exchanging stories, the two new super heroes found out something else they had in common. Namely, the Blaster had no parents. They died when he was five years old. They had met their tragic end saving an entire city from destruction.

The Blaster had been spending his summers at an orphanage (and this explained why he felt he could never get enough to eat during the vacation months).

Bob in turn told him all about Julio and Tiffany. Bob, too, felt like he was an orphan.

That night, Bob and the Blaster accepted an invitation from the Crunch family to be their guests at a fancy restaurant. Moe, Elf and Psyche also came along.

Somehow Mr. and Mrs. Crunch must have known about how the Green Blaster spent his summers.

Mrs. Crunch said, "Filbert and I want to invite all you Boys to stay with us and visit over the summer vacation. Now, before you say anything, we know that most of you had planned to visit the Psyche family. That's fine with us. If any of you want to spend a day or a few months, or even longer, well, we want you to feel that you always have a home with us."

"I can't speak for the rest, Mrs. Crunch," responded GB, "but I'm sorry, I have to turn down your generous offer. I can visit for a day or two, but I have promised to continue my intern work over the summer with Red Ranger."

"I think," he went on, "that I could use a little peace and rest out on the ranch. It's a good deal for me. I don't need to develop my powers anymore. I got power to spare. Red is going to teach me about the Code of the West. It sounds like just the ticket for this city boy."

"It's too bad you'll miss the circus," said Psyche, "but maybe next summer? Anyway, you have an open invitation any time you can get away."

"Thanks, Psyche," the Blaster replied, "Professor Wie said that if I apply myself this summer, graduation next year ought to be 'duck soup' for me. After that I can travel a bit if things work out."

"Speaking of traveling," Moe said, nudging Bob in the side.

"Oh, yeah," Bob dabbed his chin with his napkin; "Mr. Crunch, the guys and I were talking and while we were making plans for this summer, we decided not to spend the whole time at Psyche's place."

"Yeah," Kid psyche agreed, "We're running a short season this summer anyway."

Derick continued the discussion, "So we thought, if it would be all right with you, that we might do a little traveling on our own this summer."

"Tell me about it," suggested Mr. Crunch in a most non-committal sort of voice.

At this point Bob picked up the ball, "Well, Mr. Crunch, Derick mentioned to me that you were thinking of getting rid of the family car."

"I think I see where this is going," said Mr. Crunch.

"Filbert, Crunch," said Mrs. Crunch, "Let the boy finish!" You just go on, Bob dear."

"Well," said Bob again, "Professor Wie has given me a scholarship loan to help me get set up in the super hero business. Frankly, it's more money than I ever hoped to see in my life.

So I thought, as long as you are selling the Impervo-car anyway, I might be able to buy it and convert it. I figured that I could pay you in monthly installments. I was thinking of calling it the Fat Mobile."

"Ha! That's a clever play on words, Robert. I like that! You know, I think we might just be able to arrange something. Fins are out this year, anyway. So, now, where are you boys planning on driving this summer?"

Mr. and Mrs. Crunch were well aware of the curriculum of professor Wie's school and that all the boys had to be fully qualified to drive or fly any vehicle before they could be allowed to graduate. Even though Bob was only thirteen years old, and wouldn't normally be granted a license in most states, the training he had received in classes like Vehicle Emersion made him a safer driver than most.

Along with the diploma, the graduates had received certain federal permits, wavers, secret classifications and other papers that enabled them to legally do things other boys their age could only dream about.

"We're going to drive to Europe!" Derick blurted out in his excitement.

"Um," said Mr. Crunch in a voice that was even less committal than before. "Have you fellows looked at a map?"

"Aye, we did, Mr. Crunch!"

"Oh sure, dad."

"You bet!"

"Actually, we did quite a bit of study on this, Mr. Crunch," Moe du Jur said, "We start off from Chicago and go north through Wisconsin into Canada. Then we go through Winnipeg, Port Newman, Churchill..."

All the other boys, except GB, started to chant the names together in a demonstration of just how well they had researched their route, "...Eskimo Point, Boothia Peninsula, Igarka, Syktyvkar, Kostroma..."

"Hold on!" said Mr. Crunch, who apparently knew something of geography, "How'd you jump over to Russia?"

"We wouldn't jump, dad," said Derick, "The ice flow should be solid enough this time of year to carry us over the North Pole."

"Should be is right! What are you modern Magellans going to do if you run into open water?"

"Dad! We'll turn back of course!"

"Hmm," said Mr. Crunch while Bob thought privately, "He's real good at that!"

"And where do you go after Kostroma...Minsk?"

"That's it, dad, we go through Moscow first, then Warsaw, Berlin, Frankfurt, Luxemburg, Reims, Paris - anywhere we want to go in Europe from that point."

"I suppose the State Department fixed you up with passports, eh?"

"Sure! We plan on meeting up with Professor Wie in France. He's going to be looking for new students again."

Since everyone had to wear regular clothes and not costumes that night, Mr. Crunch was able to exchange a most expressive glance with his wife. Mrs. Crunch just smiled in return. After some moments of this he sighed.

"I guess you'll remember to send us postcards?"

Chapter XVIII

Going Crackers

"**S**tep right up, folks, to the biggest little show in town! It's all on the inside! For one thin dime, one tenth of a dollar, see exhibits from the exotic corners of the world!

"Meet Kid Psyche who can see into your past, present and future as if he were reading a newspaper. In fact he will do it *while* reading a newspaper!

"Feast your eyes on the Robot Man of the Future! Watch him bend steel as if it were licorice! See him play ten games of checkers or chess at the same time!

"Meet the unbelievable Blubber-Boy! Tons of fun; he will bounce his way right into your heart! One hundred dollars will be awarded to any twenty men who can manage to throw him to the ground or defeat him in the tug of war contest!

"Meet the mighty Moe, strange visitor from another planet with powers and abilities far beyond those of mortal men!

"And from the tales and legends of the past, by special engagement, we bring you the magical Elf! He sings! He dances! And, I myself have personally witnessed him put a spear through a donut at thirty paces!

"Hurry! Hurry! Don't crowd! The show is about to start! It's all on the inside!"

The boys had spent a week with the Green Blaster at the Crunch's and this was their second week at the Psyche Brothers Circus Extravaganza Extraordinaire.

"Another week of playing the 'Mighty Moe' and I'll be going crackers!"

"That's nothing!" said Psyche, "I used to do five shows a day and seven on weekends!"

"But Moe speaks for me as well," said Hawk, "The customers (or 'marks', as your custom names them) are rude and uncouth. They care nothing for forging friendships or crafting community. Let but my voice or feet falter and it's: 'Bring on the dancing girls!'"

"Hawk's right," said Bob. "We need a break or we'll all go crackers! The first few days it was a lot of fun and we all thought it was great to have our own acts and be applauded and all."

"Yeah, but that wears off pretty quick," said Derick, "I thought circus work was glamorous. But the glamour doesn't last and all that's left is the work!"

"Well," said Psyche, "I could sense your discontent. So I talked to my folks. They made enough these past two weeks that they agree we can leave early on our car trip."

"No fooling?" said Moe.

"Not only am I not fooling, my mom said she predicted this would happen all along. If you celebrities of the big-top are all okay with taking a final bow, we can leave early tomorrow morning."

"Hurray!" they all shouted.

"Why do we always have to get up early?" Derick asked, but he didn't really mean it.

"I was thinking of getting a new paint job but I found out it just can't be done." Bob was helping his friends pack supplies into the commodious trunk of the Impervo-car. It was the crack of dawn and Derick seemed only good for blinking and yawning.

"That's right," Derick said. "You can't paint M46. Paint won't stick to the surface. It's like trying to paint an ice cube. The only way you can change the color is by a bombardment of high energy electrons."

"Then you got it made, Bob," Moe said, "All you have to do is find a drive-in cyclotron!"

"Well, that's the last of it," said Psyche as he slammed the trunk and ran to the passenger seat in the front.

"Good! Everybody strap in!" Bob was driving the first leg of the journey, "Deflection mode is green! Blast off!"

Even Derick, who was most used to travel by Impervo-car, felt a little apprehension at how quickly Bob gunned the rocket engines.

"Hey! A little less enthusiasm in the gas pedal, Bob!" said Moe.

"Verily, we fly!" said Hawk.

"We ought to go back for my stomach!" said Psyche.

The ability to sustain speeds that were almost twice as fast as the surrounding traffic had its advantages. The car was equipped with fold-out beds and every convenience one might expect to find in a large camper.

The boys sang along to songs on the radio. They took turns driving the "big bus" as Psych called it.

They navigated with the aid of onboard computers that compared detailed maps with their real surroundings. The exterior TV cameras captured images for the computer to read and convert to an electronic model that could be superimposed over the map.

"This car knows where we are better than we do!" said Psyche.

"Yeah," said Moe, "I think we ought to just let it drive, too!"

Some time later Psyche asked, "Did any of you guys bring along your reflection marbles?"

"What for?" said Moe, "You're two feet away! I can hear you just fine!"

"I did not want to risk loosing your magic gift," said Hawk, "so I left it safe at Derick's house."

"Here," said Bob, as he handed over the mystic amber sphere. "When you first gave it to me it was so cool to look at that I promised myself I would carry it always."

As soon as Bob dropped the inscrutable orb in his hand, Psyche sat up straight as if he were propelled by invisible springs.

"That's it!" he cried, "That's what was wrong! I felt uneasy all day! Some one's been urgently trying to contact me and my subconscious was trying to tell me about it in the only way it could. I was a fool to leave my marble back in my tent!"

"Never mind all that!" said Moe impatiently, "Get in contact! And every one else shut up!"

The eyes of Kid Psyche glazed over and he started to mumble something that sounded like, "I don't know...why? Why?"

Suddenly, he came out of it with a shout, "This is bad! We've got to get back to school, full speed! Now! Hurry!"

Bob took him by the shoulders and shook. "Take it easy! Tell us what it is! What's bad?"

Psyche looked as pale as the landscape. "Everyone - all the kids are cutting their vacations short and heading back to school! Teachers, too!"

"Why?"

"Yes, that's right! They've captured professor Wie!"

Less than two hours later Bob and his pals were back at school. The rest of the kids had been waiting for them to arrive.

Doctor Unknown said, "We're all here now."

"Let's get down to business," Mr. Mann suggested, "Show them the card please Mrs. White".

"This came to the school by special delivery about twelve hours ago." She passed a handsomely engraved card around so every one could read it.

His Magnificence, the Big Cheese

Requests your hated presence

At a party to be given

In memory of

Wilbur Wie, the Mean Blaster and the Beneficent Bounce-O
(You supply the latter two)
Third Street Warehouse
City
Midnight

"It's seven pm now, that's only five hours!"

"That's not much time to devise a plan."

"You devise if you want, I'm going over there!"

"No! We have to work together on this!"

"But what is he doing to the professor while we sit here and talk? The card says "In memory"!"

"What if he killed the professor? I can't stand thinking about it!"

"Take it easy! It says "In memory" of Bob and Blaster, too! He's too experienced to allow anything to happen to a hostage before he gets what he wants."

"But how did he escape? We thought he was in an escape proof jail in the Infinity Room."

'So did we," said Mrs. White. "When we got this card that's the first place we looked. But his Wheelmen must have been able to sneak in and spring him."

"We were so sure the M46 would hold him, that we didn't pay much attention to protecting the prison itself. It turns out that they didn't need to break or bend the bars of the cell to get him out. We found the door of the empty cage had been expanded to one and a half times its original size!"

"He perfected his Blow-up gun!"

"And he just slipped through the enlarged bars!"

"So the Cheese not only escaped, but he captured professor Wie for dessert!"

"I say we ought to go in there full force, with everything we have and rescue professor Wie!"

"No! That's what he wants! We need someone to divert his attention while the rest of us spring an attack!"

"I think Bob should go!" Everyone looked with surprise at the Green Blaster, "Yes, Bob's the most powerful of us all, even of the teachers!"

"Blaster!" said the Pink Liberator, "that's no way to talk!"

"No, He's right!" said Dr. Unknown. "We don't have time to pussy foot around and sugar coat the truth. I have more experience than anybody in this room. I was fighting crime before some of your parents were born. The heroes of my generation never had to cope with someone like the Cheese. I wouldn't get to first base with that guy."

"What I'm trying to say is this: if you don't know it yet, our Mr. Blob is the goods. He should go."

The Green Blaster added, "I owe my life to professor Wie, but I am not the man for the job. You need someone who won't blow his cool like I did. I don't trust myself. When I see that Cheese again I may just loose it, and you can't afford that. Bob will keep his head."

"Well," Bob replied slowly, "if the Cheese is interested in seeing me. I think I should accommodate him. But not the way he expects."

Chapter Nineteen

"How dark was the night!" This is what Bob thought to himself as he waited to go into the warehouse to face his enemy all alone. This is also the point at which we began our story way back on page 1. Now you understand why this particular night seemed so dark to Bob.

He was about to journey into the future again. But this time it would be his future that was dark. He knew that. The odds were against him having any future at all an hour from now. Bob knew that this would be his final encounter with the Big Cheese, one way or the other.

"Well," he thought, "if the bad guys get me I can at least give the other kids a chance."

Bob was not about to go in through the front door. That would be where all the traps were. He took a skipping jump. As he landed, his legs looked like they were retracting. In fact they were being swallowed up into billows of flexible fat. The fat engulfed the legs entirely as he struck the pavement and then rebounded.

Now Bob's body took on the properties and behavior of a hard rubber ball as he bounced ahead in a wide arc. He had once boasted to Mrs. White about how easy it was for him to crash through a wall. It turned out to be no idle boast.

Wham! Bricks broke, fragments flew and plaster got plastered all over!

Bob peered into inky darkness. What light there was spilled through the hole Bob had made in the wall. He felt very alone and then abruptly remembered that he wasn't.

"Psyche, are you there?"

"I'm here, I'm here. Are you okay?"

"Yeah, nobody home so far."

"You know the reflection marble works better if you hold it in your hand while you send out your thoughts."

"Sure, okay, but I'm going to need both hands soon if I'm not mistaken."

"Should I call in the cavalry?"

"Not yet. My watch says twenty to twelve. Give me fifteen minutes. But be ready if I holler."

"Right as rain. I'll stand by. Be careful, Bob."

As his eyes adjusted to the dark, Bob could see many shadowy forms take shape. They looked like boxes and crates made ready for shipping. Nothing moved except Bob as he made his way deeper into the trap.

Suddenly the lights blazed on with a loud clack. There stood the Big Cheese about a dozen yards ahead. His arms were folded in an attitude that spoke of supreme confidence. Just behind the Cheese a complex mechanism, a giant cannon, tilted its technological snout to the ceiling.

"It must be the enlarging gun!" Bob thought.

But something - no someone - was stuffed into the barrel as if ready to be shot out of a circus cannon.

Bob edged forward slowly to get a better look. The man inside the gun was sticking out from the waist up. His hands were tied and he was gagged. Bob looked again.

The Big Cheese spoke, "Yes, you oaf of obesity, you lack-brained lump of lard; it's your precious professor, all ready to be shrunk down to size along with the rest of the city."

"That's right, I said shrunk! I have finally perfected my enlarging ray to the point where it can enlarge or shrink anything in its path! At the stroke of midnight the day of the Cheese will dawn!"

"When I am done with the city, I will shrink your lifeless body down to paperweight size! A fitting memento, don't you think? Perhaps I'll have you bronzed. I must kill you first, of course. Not even my fabulous wealth could afford the amount of bronze it would take to cover you at your present size!"

The Cheese continued, "We have a few minutes before zero hour. So, now, before you taste your final defeat, let me introduce you to the one who masterminded this entire operation; the only genus ingenious enough to be my partner. She planned the defeat of civilization as you know it in two time periods at once! Meet the one who will sit beside me on the throne when I rule both worlds! Step forward, Cheese Louise!"

From behind the gun stepped a young woman. She wore an insignia above her heart that was a stylized representation of a cheese. Her costume was tinted yellow-orange and it seemed to glow with an unearthly light. Her long cape was gold, flecked with silver, and her hair was like the cape.

She looked both beautiful and dangerous as she smiled and walked to a control panel at the base of the gun.

"Yes, we came from the far future! We didn't like how things turned out in our time zone, so we decided to come back and change it all! In just a few minutes she will pull the trigger that will change history forever!"

197

Bob realized that he had to do something right away.

So he said, "Well, I knew you were too scared to face me on your own, Cheese! Even someone as stupid as you could figure out that you wouldn't stand a chance! I'd eat you up and spit you out but you're too yellow: like a lemon!"

The Cheese responded, "Don't egg me on!"

"Ha!" said Bob, "Okay, let's chew the fat!"

"So? You suggest a meeting of minds?"

"Lettuce!"

"I'll cream you, you know!"

"Don't try to butter me up!"

Bob was stalling for time by engaging the Big Cheese in a verbal duel. The Cheese recognized in all the punning a challenge to his quick wits. What did he have to loose? He had the upper hand.

So the Cheese said, "I don't carrot all if I do!"

Bob came back with, "I've never seen a rutabaga than you!"

"You're full of bologna, you know!"

"Now we're cooking!"

"You got a beef with that?"

"Let's just say I resist assault!"

"I suppose you tried a steak out?"

"You could say I play the roll of an unofficial peas officer!"

"But this might not bear fruit!"

"I have an appointment to tie you up like a pretzel!"

"I'll have to see if I can sandwich you in!"

"And I'll see you get your just desserts!"

"Your thoughts are peppered with inconsistencies!"

"Nuts!"

"Fudge!"

"Shrimp!"

"Crabby!"

"Turkey!"

"Enough of this!" shouted the Cheese in exasperation, "This could go on all night! I don't have the time to deal with you as I would like! It is nearly midnight and I have an appointment with destiny! Let's end this once and for all! My gang has been itching for a chance to take a crack at you!"

As if responding to a prearranged signal, the Wheelmen stepped from behind the stacks of boxes that stood in rows on the warehouse floor.

"You see my fat fool, my hoards may have been taken from me, but my Wheelmen have not! Take him, boys!"

Joey came from one side and the Hovering Delinquent from another. Bob knew that Joey could only act as a decoy, so when the Delinquent fired his gun Bob was ready for it.

He bounced out of the line of fire and grabbed the line that was still snaking out of the Hovering Delinquent's gun.

Now Bob began a series of short, frantic hops. He was bouncing off the ceiling, walls and every surface he could. Taking the cable from the gun he tied up the two crooks just in time.

National Hank shot his fist out with such speed that he caught Bob a good one on the jaw.

Using his natural resiliency, Bob rolled with the punch and grabbed the prosthetic arm. Yanking on the arm, Bob forced Hank to follow him. Bob rammed the arm between two large water pipes hanging from the ceiling.

Holding on with one hand, Bob forced Hank's artificial arm back until it bent nearly double. Hank was now unable to retract it from its extended position.

Bob dropped down to the floor leaving Hank to hang there. Suddenly, Bob was aware of two arms clutching at his legs.

It was the Thug. There was no time for the opponents to size each other up or exchange insults. The two of them wrestled and rolled over and around the floor. From the back of his belt Bob pulled out a noose made of knotted and twined M46.

He was forcing the Thug's arm behind his back. The Thug was trying to gouge and bite at Bob. (I refuse to write down the names Thug called Bob at that point).

Out of the corner of his eye Bob saw that Cheese Louise had started up the power for the big gun. It lit up and crackled with energy. A subsonic hum started to rise at the same time a supersonic tone began to fall. The waves of sound produced overtones that seemed to move Bob's hair and tingle his teeth.

He saw Louise shouting and gesturing to the Big Cheese, "I need ten minutes more!"

Apparently, the gun needed time to warm up and build up a charge.

Bob slammed the Thug into a freight elevator. He took the improvised handcuffs of M46 and looped the Thug's hands through a thick steel strut. There he had to sit imprisoned while Bob closed the doors of the cage with a clang; cutting off the Thug's bellowing voice.

Bob turned to see the Cheese level his right arm as if lining up a target in his sights. With blurring speed Bob whipped a large packing case off the floor and held it in front of himself.

It sounded like a shower of hailstones was hitting the front of the improvised shield. Bob knew that the Cheese had fired his "D.A.G. Napper" device in an attempt to riddle him with tiny darts that would put him to sleep. For all he knew, the Cheese might have made the darts lethal this time.

"You fiend!" the Cheese cried, "What must I do to be rid of you?"

"That's just what I was going to say," said Bob.

With a bounce and a bound, Bob came face to face with his foe. The Cheese rained blow after blow on Bob with super human strength. But every punch that didn't miss Bob completely was absorbed. The energy of each walloping strike dissipated and disbursed to impotency, foiled by folds of fat.

As the two wrestled on the floor the Cheese was shouting, "I warn you, you are overlooking something!" Bob struggled to pin his enemy's arms back. He gasped, "Tell me, what am I overlooking?"

The Cheese responded in a hoarse croak, "When I told you that my hoards were all taken away from me...*I lied!*"

With those last two words the gang boss ignited his belt rockets which propelled him across the floor and away from Bob's grasp.

From every door and entry way an army of hundreds of gunmen streamed into the room like black ants at a picnic. There didn't seem space enough to hold them all, yet they kept coming.

The hoards of the Cheese had arrived and it was five minutes to midnight.

Chapter XX

Milking the Situation

Bob was in a fix. He saw fifty or sixty guns of every caliber all leveled at him. Five or six men were holding his arms and although that alone wouldn't be enough to stop him he was worried about those guns.

"I might take a bullet or two," he thought, "but this many is enough to kill me."

So Bob concentrated hard. The Cheese took one look at Bob's face and laughed his hideous laugh. The Cheese had jumped to a conclusion with booth feet.

"So the big, brave Blubber-Boy is too scared to move, eh? I told you I would have my revenge! I warned you!"

And while the Cheese ranted; Bob called out in the silence of his mind, "Psyche! Now's the time! Are you there? You better be there!"

"Yeah, Bob, we're coming! Hang on!"

Bob replied, "They're starting to swarm all over me, buddy! I think the time has come to call in some old favors. I made a lot of friends in the past few years and I'm planning on milking the situation for all it's worth."

The telepathic line was snapped. Psyche felt his marble go dead as he reached the warehouse and jumped in through the hole in the wall that Bob had put there.

He saw dozens of gunmen piled up in a heap, like a football pile up. They were trying to tackle or subdue something at the bottom. Every once in a while a crook would go flying out of the pile. However, for each one ejected, two more waited to take his place.

Then Psyche heard behind him a sound like trash cans rolling on the street. In raced Captain Speedball! Right behind him came the rest of the kids – the entire graduating class of 1960.

Psyche also saw something that escaped the senses of almost everyone there. Through a distorted mental image, Psyche perceived that the Absolute Locus had come back to join them.

He was speeding up his own personal time so that the bullets of the gunmen were practically standing still. As each weapon was fired, Locus made sure he got to the bullet before it traveled an inch. He deflected each projectile just enough to send it harmlessly into the wooden floor or ceiling.

Such was his speed (or rather, such was the slowing down of the local space-time) that he could go about his task in an almost leisurely way. Of course, nobody else could see him at all. All that sight could reveal was that guns – even machine guns – were being aimed and fired to no avail.

Some of the gangsters in their frustration tried spraying the room in an attempt to mow down friend and foe alike. But even at point blank range every shot missed.

The Green Blaster had made his way over by the big gun. He was trying to subdue its power build up by countering it with his own force beam.

Nova Rex had set up a blinding light display while Morpho and Purp rescued professor Wie. Bunny and Lib were untying him and leading him out of the building. They were almost stopped at the door when Bunny whispered something to the gunman guarding the exit. The crook actually bowed and held the door for them! Bunny flashed a smile and a thumbs-up sign to Bob.

As the crooks began to realize that they could shoot all they wanted, but they couldn't hit anything, they started to resort to fists.

But even as the fight was heating up; in came the parents. The Crunches were there in force. Even Patty was using her jumper-jets to good advantage.

Mrs. Kite and Wendy (mothers of the Wisp and Goldie respectively) were flying around and bopping bad guys. Wendy's husband (known only as "Billy" – he used to be a sidekick until he retired) Billy was tumbling and somersaulting with Willow–wand. Her method of combat would be to literally run up the legs of her opponents, do a flip and kick them in the jaw-bone on the way down.

Lil' Socko was punching out kneecaps two at a time. The Cosmic Duchess was waving her wand around and Judo Girl was leaping and kicking with Purp. Zorrina (mother of Swashbuckle) and Lib were using their whips to herd the crooks into confinement. (They were using the freight elevator as a temporary jail. Every time someone opened the door all the kids had to stop their ears so they wouldn't hear the atrocious language the Thug was using).

Master Cloak, Point Zero, Elemento, Omni-vac, all joined the fray. Dr. Jolt, Wondera, Inferno and Mentalus were also in the thick of it. Bob was startled to see Red Ranger on a very large horse jump through the hole in the wall. It looked like the good guys were winning when sheer bedlam

crashed through one of the walls. Robots from the future, automaton warriors without pain, fear or mercy advanced in wave after wave to push back the super heroes.

But with an explosive heave the opposite wall buckled inward. A flying saucer landed, its leading edge taking out half the building. Out of the space ship came the agents of the Cosmic Patrol! They were led by Moe's dad, and his two brothers were there too. Waves and torrents of combatants crested, broke and receded. In the center of the floor, where the fighting was thickest stood the True Believer. No shadow was able to touch him and it seemed to Bob that a light, born of no science and beyond the ken of humanity, surrounded his peaceful, uplifted visage.

Slowly the Believer raised both arms, palms outward, above his head. There sounded a tremendous crash, louder than anything preceding it. The entire warehouse jumped and rocked. The earthquake, for such it was, took down another whole section of the building as bodies continued to fly from every door, window and opening. And in one corner of what remained of the warehouse, the Big Cheese and Cheese Louise, working as one, finally plunged home the switch that activated the big gun.

"BOLOGNA!" shouted Blubber-Boy, and with that battle cry he threw himself into the breach of the gun like a cork in a bottle.

The base of the gun shone cherry red and all activity seemed to freeze. There was a ripping blast from the back and iridescent bubbles of force spilled from vents in its side. Like soap suds the globules floated and foamed. The bubbles didn't appear to be quite tangible. They drifted through walls and ceiling. One of these surrounded the Cheese and his partner. They were lifted up off the floor. There was a loud pop of displaced air and the bubble and its contents were gone.

The Big Cheese and Cheese Louise were now the problem of some other dimension.

"Get him down from there!"

"Is he breathing?"

"Bobby, can you hear me?"

Bob blinked his eyes and looked around. "We won, didn't we?"

"Yeah, the Cheese and his cheesy girlfriend got zapped to another universe or something."

"Are you hurt? You took the full force of that reducing ray!

"I know," Bob said, "It was supposed to be powerful enough to shrink a whole city and I believe it was. I must have lost twenty pounds!"

It only took about ten minutes for the Patrol to mop up the remaining criminals and robots. Without their bosses to give them orders they were too bewildered to carry on the fight. The Patrol's Anachronistic Displacement Medium (or flying saucer, if you insist) departed just in time. Fire and police vehicles were arriving. The local branch of the F.B.I. set up a cordon around the warehouse and provided a bus to take the super heroes back to the school. As the bus departed the kids all marveled at what had occurred.

"Cheese Louise may have been the brains behind the Big Cheese," said the Green Blaster, "But I have a feeling he was the more dangerous of the two."

"He was certainly the craziest!" Kid Psyche responded.

"Well, he's gone for good!" said Bunny.

"I can't believe we really got him," said Nova Rex.

"We did," said Mrs. White, "and we did it as a team!"

"I am so proud of each of you!" said professor Wie, "Tonight I saw my dream of a super team come true."

"Yes," agreed Dr. Unknown, "we ended an era today."

"It's a new day!" cried the Blaster.

"You know," said Captain Eugene, "we didn't really graduate until this night."

Goldie added, "That's true! With this little midnight confrontation behind us, we will be starting a whole new chapter in our lives."

Psyche looked at his pocket watch. "Yep," he said, "We started a new chapter nineteen minutes ago.

Chapter XXI

Quite a Bit at Stake

"**S**uper heroes must remain the stuff of comic books," Bob told Psyche, "After all, there's quite a bit at stake." They had been walking for the last twenty minutes and Psyche didn't need to listen to Bob's nervous chatter to know that his friend was upset.

Psyche could feel tangible waves of fear radiating from Bob. He thought, "Here's the guy who won the Valor award from the Patrol and beat the Big Cheese; and he'd rather do almost anything than face what's behind that door."

"We're here," Bob announced unnecessarily. "Look," he said, "You really don't have to come in with me."

"That's your opinion. We've gone all over this before. You need a friend with you today, and I happen to be it."

Bob took a swipe at his cowlick and Psyche adjusted his tie. The boys were wearing their best Sunday suits. They knocked on the door together.

A plain looking woman in her early thirties opened to the extent of the chain and peered through the crack.

"So you came. So come inside."

The boys entered a seedy looking apartment and sat in chairs that matched the overall look of the place.

Psyche spoke with obvious discomfort, "My name is Psyche, Mrs. Blob."

"There is no Mrs. Blob," the woman replied bitterly, "Julio left me and you can just call me Tiffany." She lit a cigarette. "Maybe it's better if you let me do the talking. I give you credit." She was talking to Bob.

"You got a diploma and you didn't come crying to me for money. That nutty school didn't even send me a bill. When I got your letter I thought about what I would say to you. Sometimes things don't work out in life.

"They sure didn't work out for your poppa and me. We weren't ready to be parents, let alone responsible parents. He's out of my life for good. Left me a lot of bills to pay and said I'd never see him again. Well, good.

"I'm making a go of it selling real estate. Without Julio I just might make something out of my life. You didn't get a fair shake from us and I'm sorry. We just didn't know what to do with a super kid.

"Anyway, I'm glad that we found that school. You did pretty good there, huh? You look good. In four years away you did okay." She snuffed out her cigarette and ground it into the ash tray as if crushing out an unpleasant thought. "I think it's better all around if we go our own ways."

Bob and Psyche walked back to the Crunch's house where friends would be waiting to welcome them home. They said no words. No words were needed.

•   •   •

And so, Dear Diary, today I bring my journal to a close. There are just one or two things to record in this last entry before I begin a new book: the chronicles of my official super hero adventures.

I'm staying at the Crunch's for the next two weeks until I can get my own place finished. It's just a small house that I'm leasing in a quiet residential neighborhood. But almost a mile underneath my new house I'm building the Fat Cave. I wanted to dig deeper but it can get pretty hot the lower you go.

Moe arranged to loan me a machine designed to disintegrate dirt and rock. The setup is pretty much like the Crunch's secret hideout only a lot bigger underground. I have a lot of hidden entrances. Mr. Crunch lets me have all the M46 I can use. Derick and Psyche are helping me.

Moe is going for his final Space Cadet training and then it's off to the stars for awhile. Thank goodness for our Reflection Marbles!

Elf is starting some new kooky quest. I promised to pay him a visit next year.

Now that he has graduated, Derick is going to team up with Speedball for awhile. They make a good team and he has wanted to do that since forever.

Yesterday Patty Crunch had a date with Spell-boy. I got to talking with him while Patty was "putting on her face". He wants to ask her to get married but he's scared she won't like his secret identity. Get this: his real name is Sylvester Kaykes. He's afraid she won't want to become Mrs. Patty Kaykes!

I told him that's not as bad as my friend Psyche. He went out with a girl named Kay Sarah Syrah! I think he thought I was making that up to make him feel better. Oh well, Mrs. White always said names were important.

Now, Dear Diary, I must record that I too went out on a sort of date yesterday. I met up with the Pink Liberator and we went out for a soda. She told me something I was wondering about for four years. I couldn't ever figure out why she never showed up for any of our Marksmanship classes back at school.

Turns out she's from a whole family of pacifists who don't believe in violence. I shared with her how much fear I had of hurting the bad guys and I told her how relieved I was to learn that I wasn't the only non-violent super hero out there. She only looked at me funny and said "you'd be surprised who's out there." Then she changed the subject.

Makes a fellow wonder.

I got to finally see Psyche's Mom for that fortune telling reading she promised me last summer. No wonder they call her the Eerie Cassandra. I think she has a no-fooling window to the future. She even hinted that she was watching over us kids with her psychic powers.

She said that I should remember that I had a lot of help for all my accomplishments. As she said this I couldn't help thinking about that time my Reflection Marble went off by itself. All it said was the word "Don't!" I wish I would have listened. I wouldn't have gotten into so much trouble.

It's funny the way things work out. I guess no one is ever really successful completely on his own. When I told her this she said, "...and I thought I was the mind-reader!"

Well, Dear Diary, that brings us up to today. As I was walking back to the Crunch's I saw two little kids playing catch. Suddenly this crazy driver zooms around the corner. Without even thinking I bounced over and grabbed the kid with the ball. The car just missed and kept on going. I was so mad!

The two little kids were a bit shook up. I told them my name was Bob and that I would walk home with them if they wanted. So, the one with the ball said to me, "That's okay! We live right on the corner. But gee thanks, Mr. He almost got me!"

And then the little kid said, "Yeah! He's my big brother and you protected him!" I bent down on one knee to hear what she had to say and she whispered in my ear, "You're my hero Mr. Bob!"

And you know, as I walked away smiling and waving at them, it was the first time I could say I really felt the part.